T0369606

Vātsyāyana's *Commentary* on the *Nyāya-sūtra*

OXFORD GUIDES TO PHILOSOPHY

Series Editors

Rebecca Copenhaver, Washington University, St. Louis
Christopher Shields, University of Notre Dame
Mark Timmons, University of Arizona

Advisory Board

Michael Beaney, Ursula Coope, Karen Detlefsen, Lisa Downing, Tom Hurka, Pauline Kleingeld, Robert Pasnau, Dominik Perler, Houston Smit, Allen Wood

Oxford Guides to Philosophy presents concise introductions to the most important primary texts in the history of philosophy. Written by top scholars, the volumes in the series are designed to present up-to-date scholarship in an accessible manner, in order to guide readers through these challenging texts.

Anscombe's Intention: A Guide
John Schwenkler

Kant's Doctrine of Virtue: A Guide
Mark C. Timmons

Sidgwick's The Methods of Ethics: A Guide
David Phillips

Spinoza's Ethics: A Guide
Michael LeBuffe

Bentham's Introduction to the Principles of Morals and Legislation: A Guide
Steven Sverdlik

Mary Shepherd: A Guide
Deborah Boyle

Candrakīrti's Introduction to the Middle Way: *A Guide*
Jan Westerhoff

Vātsyāyana's Commentary *on the* Nyāya-sūtra: *A Guide*
Matthew R. Dasti

Vātsyāyana's *Commentary* on the *Nyāya-sūtra*

A Guide

MATTHEW R. DASTI

OXFORD
UNIVERSITY PRESS

OXFORD
UNIVERSITY PRESS

Oxford University Press is a department of the University of Oxford. It furthers the University's objective of excellence in research, scholarship, and education by publishing worldwide. Oxford is a registered trade mark of Oxford University Press in the UK and certain other countries.

Published in the United States of America by Oxford University Press
198 Madison Avenue, New York, NY 10016, United States of America.

CIP data is on file at the Library of Congress

ISBN 978–0–19–762593–4 (pbk.)
ISBN 978–0–19–762592–7 (hbk.)

DOI: 10.1093/oso/9780197625927.001.0001

Paperback printed by Marquis Book Printing, Canada
Hardback printed by Bridgeport National Bindery, Inc., United States of America

Contents

Preface

This is a guide to Pakṣilasvāmin Vātsyāyana's *Commentary* on the *Nyāya-sūtra* (hereafter *Commentary*). For those wishing to "travel" to the thought community of classical India to engage with one of its most important philosophical works, this book will serve as something akin to a guidebook, map, and interpreter.

Treated as a single hybrid text, the *Nyāya-sūtra* with Vātsyāyana's *Commentary* (abbreviated as *NySBh*, the *Nyāya-sūtra-bhāṣya*) is a major part of what we could loosely speak of as the *Organon* of classical India: a collection of works on epistemology, logic, and dialectics by Brahmanical, Buddhist, and Jain thinkers that governed intellectual inquiry in the subcontinent for more than a millennium. Vātsyāyana's *Commentary* also provides groundbreaking arguments for distinct positions in metaphysics, epistemology, philosophy of language, and value theory that stand among the best contributions to world philosophy.

There are several ways to use a travel guidebook. Ideally, someone relies on one throughout their trip, so they may more easily recognize the contours of the land, navigate important landmarks, and understand the historical and social background that informs the areas to be visited. Even those familiar with a certain locale may consult an expert guide to discover or reconsider points of interest. A guide could be used to develop familiarity with an area that someone considers visiting, helping them gain a sense of the region that will inform their decision. In yet another use—less ideal but certainly plausible—one reads a guide without any intention of visiting directly. A desire to gain greater cultural literacy leads one to use a guide as a cursory but economical substitute for the real thing.

This philosophical guide may be used in similar ways. Someone could consult it to expand, challenge, or consolidate the understanding they glean from the text as they read it for the first time. Those who have already read the text may turn to the guide to refresh or expand their sense of the conceptual terrain. Others may use it to get a panoptic sense of the original material as they consider a deeper dive. Finally, some may use the guide as a substitute for reading the original. From my perspective, this last use is not ideal, as part of the pleasure and insight brought by reading the *Commentary* is learning to internalize its dialectical rhythms, being drawn into the argumentative back-and-forth that animates its pages. I hope the seeds will be planted for a future, if long-postponed, visit to the original sources.

My goal is to help the reader enter more fully into the *Commentary* by providing historical and conceptual background information, by clarifying and framing philosophical issues and arguments, by tracing internal connections and points of coherence, and by offering curated references and translations of other ancient works and relevant secondary materials. While the *Nyāyasūtra* and the *Commentary* are both structured in a straightforward way, examining each of the major topics of Nyāya in turn, Vātsyāyana often develops arguments about a philosophical issue in the context of what might seem to be tangential questions. For instance, he reflects on the metaphysics of individuals and universals while discussing the philosophy of language under *NyS* 2.2.58–69. I will try to unpack and make explicit the connective tissue between these sorts of apparently separate discussions, as well as that which tethers them to the broader discourse community of ancient Indian philosophy. Ultimately, my expectation is that this volume will not only facilitate a deeper understanding of the *NySBh* but will also illustrate the way it can serve as a lens through which the philosophical world of ancient India may be observed.

To move from the metaphorical to the practical, let me suggest how this book may be best used in tandem with existing translations. For those wishing to understand the *NySBh* in sequential order, I've arranged the contents of this book to match the order and structure of the original, following the flow of the sūtras and the *Commentary* section by section. In effect, it is a commentary on the *Commentary*. For those interested in a targeted study of specific issues or topics, I offer Appendix A, which has suggested reading plans.

For the last century, the most commonly used English translation of the *Nyāya-sūtra* with Vātsyāyana's *Commentary* has been Ganganatha Jha's *The Nyāyasūtras of Gautama with the Bhāṣya of Vātsyāyana and the Vārttika of Uddyotakara*. While textual and philosophical scholarship has advanced significantly since its publication, it still allows one to follow the main contours of the philosophical arguments in the text. Readers focusing on Vātsyāyana should note that Jha also embeds the subcommentary of Uddyotakara in his translation. They should make sure to distinguish between the two as they read.[1] Jha includes a number of helpful notes that summarize comments by later commentators on specific issues. His translation does not engage with contemporary philosophy or the history of philosophy outside of classical India. It is also occasionally cumbersome for the purely philosophical reader. It is available in print and online, at sites including archive.org.

The currently out-of-print *Nyāya-sūtra with Vātsyāyana's Commentary* by Mrinalkanti Gangopadhyaya is less cumbersome than Jha's translation and improves upon it in several ways. Still, it is also divorced from contemporary or global philosophy and has a significant amount of untranslated Sanskrit terms. It is available online, at sites including archive.org.

[1] In 1939, an edition of this volume was published by Oriental Book Agency with only Vātsyāyana's commentary. It is not easily available in print, but a digital copy is available at archive.org.

Satis Chandra Vidyabhusana's *The Nyāya Sūtras of Gotama* (revised by N. Sinha) translates the *Nyāya-sūtra* while adding a sparse commentary by the translator himself and a separate paraphrase of Vātsyāyana's *Bhāṣya* as an appendix. It is available both in print and online, at sites including archive.org.

Dasti and Phillips's recent *The Nyāya-sūtra: Selections with Early Commentaries* is the most accessible current translation and contains multiple apparatuses to assist readers. It is written to be easily integrated into the modern philosophy classroom. Most of the translation consists of the sūtras and Vātsyāyana's *Commentary*, with occasional supporting passages from the subcommentators Uddyotakara and Vācaspati Miśra. It is select and arranged according to major philosophical topics. Many of its chapters closely match the thematic readings listed in Appendix A of this volume. It is available in print.

I will cite and refer to passages of the *NySBh* according to the traditional ordering chapter.part.sūtra as opposed to page numbers of any particular volumes. For example, in the statement "This is illustrated by Vātsyāyana's response to the skeptical dilemma under 2.1.17–20," the reader is directed to the *Commentary* on *Nyāya-sūtra*, Chapter 2, Part 1, sūtras 17 through 20. Any mention of such numbered passages without title or abbreviation (e.g., 1.1.10) will refer to the *NySBh*. On occasion, the major translations have slight divergences in sūtra numbering, but these are generally easy to notice. I here follow the numbering of the Sanskrit edition of the text edited by Anantalal Thakur (1997).

Acknowledgments

Thanks to my family, Nandanie, Ana, and Leela, who have provided a peaceful and loving home life, supporting my work even in the times when it diverts me from more local obligations and concerns.

I continue to benefit from being situated in that rarest of academic departments where the faculty members are all genuine friends. My colleagues in the Bridgewater State University Department of Philosophy consistently make unheralded sacrifices that allow for an atmosphere of collegiality and kindness, and my work would be much diminished without it. I especially would like to acknowledge the support of our beloved late colleague and friend Laura McAlinden.

I would like to thank BSU's Center for the Advancement of Research and Scholarship for a course release grant that supported my work on Chapter 3 of this book.

One good thing to come out of the quarantine of 2020 was a decision that Malcolm Keating and I made to read Sanskrit texts together, including the *Nyāya-sūtra*. This practice has continued long after the quarantine ended. I thank him for countless discussions which have improved this project from the very beginning.

Of the scholarly resources that have benefited this project, three have been particularly helpful for tracking down references and ancillary materials: the richly annotated French translation of the *Commentary* by Michel Angot; the resources subsumed under the "Metaphysics and Epistemology of the Nyāya Tradition" project at the Department of South Asian, Tibetan, and Buddhist Studies at the University of Vienna; and the collection of digitized texts in the Göttingen Register of Electronic Texts in Indian Languages.

I would like to thank Stephen Phillips for a careful reading of the entire text while offering multiple corrections and helpful suggestions. Malcolm Keating and Edwin Bryant have also generously shared feedback on portions of the manuscript. It has been greatly improved by their comments. Thanks to Anand Vaidya, as well, for offering helpful feedback on Appendix C.

Thanks to my friend Michael Bühler-Rose for his clever suggestion for the cover image.

Finally, my thanks to Peter Ohlin as well as the series editors for Oxford Guides to Philosophy. They have been consistently helpful and gracious throughout this project. It is encouraging that Peter and the series editors recognize the importance of the *Nyāya-sūtra* and the *Commentary* in an initiative of this sort. Thanks also to Jan Westerhoff for his influence in this regard.

I dedicate this book to Stephen H. Phillips, Professor Emeritus of Philosophy at the University of Texas, Austin, and *nyāyācārya* in his own right. Stephen is a model scholar of Indian philosophy; a debate partner with the virtues of perspicuity, goodwill, and desire for truth; and a genuine friend and confidant. तस्मै श्रीगुरवे नमः

Abbreviations

ADhKBh	*Abhidharmakośa-bhāṣya* of Vasubandhu
AŚ	*Arthaśāstra* of Kauṭilya
BPER	*Buddhist Philosophy: Essential Readings* (Edelglass and Garfield 2009)
CS	*Caraka-saṃhitā*
EIPNV	*Encyclopedia of Indian Philosophies*, Vol. 2: *Nyāya-Vaiśeṣika* (Potter 1977)
MMK	*Mūlamadhyamaka-kārikā* of Nāgārjuna
MS	*Mīmāṃsā-sūtra* of Jaimini
MSŚBh	*Mīmāṃsā-sūtra* with the *Bhāṣya* of Śabara
NyS	*Nyāya-sūtra* of Gautama
NySBh	*Nyāya-sūtra* with the *Bhāṣya* of Vātsyāyana
NyV	*Nyāya-vārttika* of Uddyotakara
NyVT	*Nyāya-vārttika-tātparya-ṭīkā* of Vācaspati Miśra
NyVTP	*Nyāya-vārttika-tātparya-ṭīkā-pariśuddhi* of Udayana
PS	*Pramāṇa-samuccaya* of Dignāga
QKM	*The Questions of King Milinda* (*Milinda Pañha*)
SK	*Sāṃkhya-kārikā of* Iśvarakṛṣṇa
VS	*Vaiśeṣika-sūtra* of Kaṇāda
VV	*Vigraha-vyāvartanī* of Nāgārjuna
YS	*Yoga-sūtra* of Patañjali

Introduction: The *Nyāya-sūtra* and the *Commentary*

One of the notable features of scholarly literature in classical India is the use of concise, aphoristic sūtras (literally "threads"). As ancient traditions and attitudes coalesced into distinct philosophical schools during the early centuries of the Common Era, their core holdings and arguments would commonly be summarized within sūtra texts. Presumably, the purpose for this was mnemonic, allowing a student to hold the framework of an entire system within the mind. Sūtra works typically serve as root texts for Brahmanical scholastics during the classical period of Indian philosophy (for our purposes, roughly 200–1000 CE, when the major systems arose and were consolidated).[1] Sūtra texts are also found in other fields, including the study of grammar, religious ritual, ethics, and even the arts of pleasure and romance.

The *Nyāya-sūtra*, attributed to the sage Akṣapāda Gautama, was compiled and redacted during the early centuries of the Common Era, taking its final form by the end of the fourth

[1] I use "Brahmanical" here for those thinkers and traditions that see ancient Vedas and allied texts as authoritative in a broad sense. Scholars often use the Vedas as a line of demarcation for classical Indian philosophers. Whatever their philosophical differences, and however they might have been influenced by non-Vedic and extra-Vedic schools of thought, Nyāya, Vaiśeṣika, Mīmāṃsā, Sāṃkhya, Yoga, Vedānta, and allied classical systems all paid homage to the Vedas and the ancient cultural norms and traditions we might broadly speak of as "Vedic culture." This distinguishes them from Buddhists, Jains, and materialists, all of whom reject the Vedas. I will also use the terms "Hindu" and "Vedic" to make a similar demarcation. See Halbfass 1991, chaps. 1 and 2, for examinations of the relationship between the Vedas, "Hinduism," and classical Indian philosophy.

Vātsyāyana's Commentary *on the* Nyāya-sūtra. Matthew R. Dasti, Oxford University Press.
 DOI: 10.1093/oso/9780197625927.001.0001

century. *Nyāya* means "rule" and, by extension, "right reasoning" and even "logic." The work could thus be called *Sūtras on Reasoning*. Pioneering textual scholars have proposed that the most ancient core of the *Nyāya-sūtra* consists of the treatises on debate and reasoning (*vāda-śāstra*) housed in the first and fifth chapters, distinguishing them from the robust arguments on sundry topics found in Chapters 2 through 4.[2] They suggest that by the time Vātsyāyana (c. 425 CE) completed the *Commentary*, this core had been expanded or grafted to other preexisting materials to form the text.[3]

We will likely never have enough evidence to give a detailed account of the textual history of the sūtras before Vātsyāyana. In any case, the five-chapter *Nyāya-sūtra* as commented on by him is the canonical version as understood by the ensuing tradition. Combining a manual in logic and debate with arguments for specific positions on just about every major philosophical issue of the day, it stands as the root text for the school simply called Nyāya. Preisendanz (2005, 56) offers a concise summary of the school's influence:

> Inasmuch as the art of debate and reasoned argumentation is of relevance to all philosophical and scholarly endeavors, it is not surprising that the Nyāya tradition from early on occupied a central position in South Asian intellectual history, which is reflected in its strong influence on other philosophical traditions and Sanskritic sciences in general, from a doctrinal as well as a formal point of view.

[2] Cf. Tucci 1929, xxx. Important sūtras from Chapters 2 and 3, focusing on epistemology and metaphysics, had already been alluded to or cited by Buddhist authors who precede Vātsyāyana.

[3] The details of this account are debated. Bronkhorst (1985) has argued persuasively that much of the five-chapter *Nyāya-sūtra* commented upon by Vātsyāyana was already known to the great Buddhist dialectician Nāgārjuna (c. 200). He conjectures that the *NyS* began as a work by a Vaiśeṣika philosopher on rules of debate but became the foundation of a different, though closely aligned, school.

Epistemologically, the *Nyāya-sūtra* may be said to articulate an early form of reliabilism and—arguably—disjunctivism, while offering a number of anti-skeptical arguments. It also supports metaphysical positions that include external-world realism; a conception of the self as an enduring, substantial locus of mental states; and a categorial system adapted from Vaiśeṣika (sometimes called the sister school to Nyāya). Furthermore, it defends the dharma-oriented culture associated with Vedic tradition and the centrality of yogic contemplation to a virtuous life.

Sūtras are concise and sometimes ambiguous, practically demanding explanation. The first explanations of sūtra texts were likely oral, learned in the presence of living preceptors. In time, adherents would write lasting commentaries and cascading subcommentaries. Through generations of exegesis, defense, and creative interpretation of earlier teachings in light of the philosophical issues and rivals of the day, such authors expanded and consolidated specific systems of thought.

Among commentaries, one that stands as the first level of direct engagement with a root text is called a *bhāṣya*. *Bhāṣya*s help unpack and organize the teachings of a sūtra text while identifying and responding to possible challenges. They make interpretative choices on key passages that determine a school's positions on system-defining issues. Ensuing thinkers do not comment merely on the root text but also on the *bhāṣya*s which initiate systematic reflection upon them. Given this, *bhāṣya*s can approach a level of canonicity that approximates that of the sūtras themselves. This certainly holds for Vātsyāyana's *Commentary*, the earliest extant *bhāṣya* upon the *Nyāya-sūtra*. Udayana, arguably the greatest logician of early Nyāya and the pivotal figure who set the framework for the "New Nyāya" of the Middle Ages, thus says:

> The *Commentary* reveals the *Nyāya-sūtra*. It is not something additional since it is the very body of the system.[4]

[4] *NyVTP* 1.1.1. At the same time, it would be a mistake to think that subcommentators treat *bhāṣya*s with uncritical acceptance. In the case of the *Nyāya-bhāṣya*, see the introduction to Sen 2003 for examples of criticism by later subcommentators.

It is likely that there were other Naiyāyikas (Nyāya philosophers) active at the time of Vātsyāyana; he mentions competing interpretations of specific *Nyāya-sūtras*. Still, Nyāya tradition enshrines him as the first of the commentaries that make up the early school. The major early subcommentators, to be mentioned throughout this study, are Uddyotakara (c. 550), Vācaspati Miśra (fl. 960), and Udayana (c. 1000).[5]

A further element of the *Commentary*'s intimacy with the original sūtras is textual. As Bronkhorst (1985, 120) reminds us, "the author of a Bhāṣya . . . is more than anyone before or after him in a position to determine the final shape of a sūtra text." *Bhāṣya* authors determine the status of borderline sūtras, and their choices shape the canonical form of the root text. In a pioneering work, Randle (1930, 23) offers a speculative account of Vātsyāyana's influence as commentator and redactor: "He had to deal with a mass of material which formed the tradition of the school and which existed largely in sūtra form . . . there were also differences of opinion as to the interpretation of some of these traditional formulae. . . . Vātsyāyana's work presents itself as the first standard redaction and interpretation and there is nothing to show that anything except a relatively fluid tradition preceded him."

The oldest version of the *Nyāya-sūtra* available to us is embedded within manuscripts of the *Commentary*. But even for classical and medieval Nyāya philosophers, the *Nyāya-sūtra* was already mediated by its embeddedness within the *Commentary* on the palm-leaf manuscripts that preserved the text. Owing to inconsistent use of scribal indicators for transitions between root text and commentary, as well as Vātsyāyana's own style, which often integrates the sūtras into his own dialectical prose, classical

[5] While these four works have come to be seen as the major sources for early Nyāya, there were other important Nyāya philosophers active in the early period. Most of their works, however, are lost to us, only preserved in fragments, including what are likely multiple direct subcommentaries on Vātsyāyana's *Commentary*. Prets 2012 surveys the current scholarship on these lost works.

attempts to demarcate the sūtras from the *Commentary* were not always a straightforward affair.[6] For the purposes of this volume, such issues are not centrally important. Nor, for that matter, is the textual history of the *Nyāya-sūtra* before Vātsyāyana. My concern is to understand the philosophical richness of the *Nyāya-sūtra-bhāṣya* as understood by Vātysāyana's followers and critics on the classical scene. On occasions when philological or textual disputes are relevant to this endeavor, I will mention them. Otherwise, this guide will simply follow the masterful Sanskrit edition of Anantalal Thakur (*Gautamīyanyāyadarśana with Bhāṣya of Vātsyāyana*, 1997a), which—though not technically a critical edition—reflects painstaking examination of several manuscripts and notes on variant readings.[7]

But *who* and *when* was Vātsyāyana, and *how* did he become significant within the discourse community of systematic Indian philosophy? The question of who he is may be dispensed with quickly, simply because we have practically no information about him as an individual. Scholastic Sanskrit tends to focus on arguments and ideas and hardly at all on individual persons, their thought processes, or their biographies. One learns as much about them as one learns about a contemporary analytic philosopher by reading a scholarly paper on the logic of conditionals. The subcommentator Vācaspati Miśra refers to him as "Pakṣilasvāmin," informing us that it is his given name (*NyVT* 1.1.1). We also have some hints that he may have come from south India.[8] There is little else.

The question of his dates allows us a little more confidence. It is true that scholastic Sanskrit literature does not usually provide many references to historical events. But it is possible to

[6] See Muroya 2006; Preisendanz 2018, 182–185; Sen 2003, xlvi–liv.

[7] A research project at the University of Vienna is collecting, collating, and analyzing extant manuscripts of the *Commentary* in pursuance of a comprehensive critical edition. At the time of this writing, the project is at an early stage, having examined only the *Commentary* on the first three sūtras. See https://backend.univie.ac.at/index.php?id=10572&L=0.

[8] Vidyabhusana 1920, 117.

triangulate a range of dates for Vātsyāyana by considering the works he references or even alludes to and those that reference him. By this method, he may be placed in the first half of the fifth century CE.[9] At that time, the Gupta empire was still ascendant. Though the Gupta kings patronized Brahmanical traditions, Buddhism was flourishing in India as well, indicated by the construction of the celebrated monastery and university complex at Nalanda. This leads us to the question of *how* Vātsyāyana became canonical within the rich network of individuals, schools, and traditions of thought that constitute Indian philosophy around the middle of the first millennium CE.

The centuries that bracketed the turn of the Common Era were exciting times in Indian philosophy. Several distinct schools of thought were developing out of precursor views and traditions inherited from antiquity. Among these diverse thinkers and schools, we find a commitment to effectively navigate the intersections between intellectual analysis and ways of life directed to what is ultimately good. A remarkable assortment of scholarly treatises (tantras, śāstras) were written on topics including linguistics, medicine, law, statecraft, and religious practice. These treatises collectively gestured toward objective, shared methods of rational or "scientific" investigation. In works that predate Vātsyāyana, these practices are collectively called *tantra-yukti*s, "scholarly methodologies," and he appeals to one such methodology under *NyS* 1.1.4.

Inseparable from these developments was a culture of public debate. Debates and argumentative discourses of various sorts have deep roots in Indian antiquity. In ancient times, ritual experts on the Vedas debated the application of sacrificial rites, while the sages depicted in the Upaniṣads engaged in public disputations over metaphysical riddles and paradoxes. During the intellectual and

[9] For a summary of the relevant considerations, see Preisendanz 2018, 183n112.

cultural revolutions associated with the *śramaṇa* ascetic movements (c. 700–300 BCE), great teachers such as the Buddha rose to prominence through public lectures and debates with rival thinkers. In the centuries that ensued, debate was seen not merely as a tool for rhetorical victory but—for the open-minded—as a pathway to knowledge. The medical text *Caraka-saṃhitā* (c. 50 CE) advises physicians to engage in debate (*saṃbhāṣā*) with each other, as it "leads one to discover something they hadn't learnt before."[10] Manuals on debate and the rudiments of logical theory (*vāda-śāstra*) began to proliferate, penned by authors of all stripes: Buddhist, Brahmanical, and Jain. Despite the doctrinal and methodological diversity of these works, the development of shared scholarly apparatus such as the *tantra-yukti*s and objective standards of debate within the *vāda* manuals suggests an "empirical" drift and reliance upon modes of reasoning and observation.[11]

The *Nyāya-sūtra* marks a decisive step forward. Building on these earlier starts, it unites dialectics, epistemology, and tools for critical thinking in a more coherent way than predecessor works to which it is indebted, such as the *Caraka-saṃhitā* and the *Vaiśeṣika-sūtra* (c. 100 CE).[12] Consequently, as Solomon (1976, 29) notes, it "overshadowed other works that might have existed before it by its systematic formulation and treatment of dialectic and philosophical topics and problems."

Vātsyāyana's *Commentary*, then, marks a further and definitive step for the *Nyāya-sūtra* and for Nyāya as a distinct school of thought. Vātsyāyana was active in the period when Indian philosophical schools were increasingly self-conscious about

[10] *CS*, Vimānasthāna 8.16.

[11] Oberhammer 1967–1968, 603–605, illustrates that some of the *Nyāya-sūtras* on dialectics and logic reflect the convergence of debate theory with *tantra-yukti*s.

[12] For Nyāya's indebtedness to *Caraka-saṃhitā*, see Balcerowicz 2012, 207–211. The *Vaiśeṣika-sūtras* significantly influence the *Nyāya-sūtras* and the *Commentary*, as will be evinced throughout this study. Randle 1930, 7n1, identifies a number of direct correlations between *Nyāya-sūtras* and *Vaiśeṣika-sūtras*. Thakur 1963 identifies a number of *Vaiśeṣika-sūtras* quoted indirectly by Vātsyāyana.

systematically cataloging, understanding, and responding to positions of other camps. An early catalyst for this was the Buddhist skeptic Nāgārjuna (c. 200 CE), whose destructive dialectic targeted Buddhist system builders as well as early Nyāya. Careful, critical attention directed to the holdings of other schools eventually became commonplace, as epitomized in works such as the *Pramāṇa-samuccaya* (*Compendium on the Means of Knowing*) by the revolutionary Buddhist logician Dignāga (480–540 CE). Vātsyāyana was active a generation or two before Dignāga, and he defends the settled views of the *Nyāya-sūtra* against various competing camps. Typically, his targets are general positions held by Buddhists ("Those who profess there is no self" in 1.1.10) or by Vedic systems—especially Sāṃkhya and Mīmāṃsā.

In light of this complex interschool debate, Vātsyāyana seeks to provide an overarching, coherent articulation of Nyāya as a distinct and fundamentally important tradition of inquiry centered on "critical reasoning" (*ānvīkṣikī*). He subsumes several earlier scholarly practices advanced in other treatises into Nyāya's core methodology. He makes interpretive choices on various sūtras that set Nyāya's positions on issues such as the nature of selfhood, God, epistemological justification, and philosophy of language. These have stood for its entire history. He also advances positive arguments in support of Nyāya positions and against competing schools, Buddhist and Brahmanical, that would determine the battle lines for many of the most important debates within the whole of classical Indian philosophy. The *Commentary* thus helps bring Nyāya into philosophical maturity—and solidifies its standing as one of the most important participants within the tapestry of thinkers, systems, and traditions that make up classical Indian philosophy. Vātsyāyana is thus second only to the *Nyāya-sūtra*—and possibly tied for first—in constructing the self-conception of Nyāya as tradition of thought.[13]

[13] For further discussion of Vātsyāyana's role in the creation of Nyāya's self-conception, see Oberhammer 1964; Ganeri 2001a, 15; and the references collected in Preisendanz 2000, 222–223.

Principles of Selection, Organization, and Translation

Guides take different forms according to the primary materials to which they are devoted. Here the original text is expansive and hails from a language and culture historically remote from our own. While I address every section of the *NySBh* in order, of necessity I select certain sections for extended scrutiny, historical framing, and philosophical reconstruction as determined by what I consider most relevant to the philosophically interested reader. At the same time, passages that are purely proto-scientific or significantly engage with Vedic cultural assumptions will not be ignored. Indeed, they often require the most bridge-building for the nonspecialist reader. Minimally, I will identify and, as needed, clarify the major arguments of any particular section, and when possible, suggest the historical schools or figures with which they engage.

At times, I will intersperse translations as focal points for this study. Technical terms will often be italicized, as will transliterated Sanskrit. In modern English translations of classical Indian philosophy, there has been a tendency to stay as close to the original Sanskrit syntax as possible, where any element not found directly in the source material is bracketed. Such practices have served the scholarly community well, but here I minimize them. I focus on readability, without, I hope, forsaking relevant nuance. When appropriate I also avail myself of relevant analogues within academic philosophical vocabulary for core concepts in Nyāya. In cases where I use contemporary terms of art to translate near—but imperfect—analogues, I will provide nuance in my own commentary.

Relatedly, I use the terms "knowledge," "cognition," and "awareness" as near synonyms. Modern scholarship on Indian philosophy has spent much time debating the proper translations of the Sanskrit terms *jñāna*, *buddhi*, *upalabdhi*, *anubhava*, and other words for presentational mental states. I agree with those who prefer "cognition" to "knowledge" in general, for several reasons, including revulsion toward translations such as "false knowledge" that have been put forth for *mithyā-jñāna*. There are also some ways in which "cognition" falls short, especially with respect to special states of non-conceptual awareness championed by Buddhists and others. Still, I resist overly technical translations or hyphenated compounds that would border on pedantry in a volume of this sort. When using the plural of Sanskrit words, I add "s" but keep the "s" unitalicized. Thus, "parts," the plural of "part" (*avayava*) would be expressed as "*avayava*s" as opposed to the Sanskrit plural "*avayavāḥ*."

Finally, when I use the term "Nyāya" by itself to make claims about the core holdings of the school, I mean the school of thought embodied by the *Nyāya-sūtra* and Vātsyāyana's *Commentary*, not necessarily the tradition as developed for more than a millennium after Vātsyāyana.

Outline of the Text

There are five chapters of the *Nyāya-sūtra*, and each has two parts, traditionally called "daily lessons." In a practice dating back to Vācaspati Miśra (fl. 960 CE), editors of the *Nyāya-sūtra* have traditionally grouped individual sūtras into sections according to topic. In this outline, I generally follow the divisions and titles given in Sanskrit in the edition of Anantalal Thakur, with some adjustments.

Chapter 1: The Central Topics of Nyāya

Part 1 (1.1.1–41)

1.1.1–2: The core topics of Nyāya and the purpose of study
1.1.3–8: Knowledge sources
1.1.9–22: The objects of knowledge
1.1.23–41: Elements of formal investigation
  1.1.23–25: Preliminaries to inquiry
  1.1.26–31: Settled theses
  1.1.32–39: Parts of a proof
  1.1.40–41: Supplements to inquiry

Part 2 (1.2.1–20)

1.2.1–3: Types of debate
1.2.4–9: Counterfeit reasons
1.2.10–17: Equivocation
1.2.18–20: Dialectical rejoinders and defeat conditions

Chapter 2: Epistemology and Philosophy of Language

Part 1 (2.1.1–68)

Part 2 (2.2.1–69)

Chapter 3: Objects of Knowledge

Part 1 (3.1.1–72)

Part 2 (3.2.1–72)

Chapter 4: Objects of Knowledge and the Insight That Leads to the Supreme Good

Part 1 (4.1.1–68)

1

The Central Topics of Nyāya

Part 1 (1.1.1–41)

1.1.1–2: The core topics of Nyāya and the purpose of study

Vātsyāyana opens with the following statement:

> When cognition is generated by a knowledge source, it leads to successful action. Therefore, a knowledge source is effective [*arthavat*].

With the ensuing passage, he argues for the importance of cognitive success for success in life. Proper apprehension of objects is necessary for successful action, and a knowledge source is necessary to apprehend objects. Action depends upon cognition in two ways: motivation and guidance. As will be elaborated in 1.1.10, cognition of an object *x*, along with the standing memory "objects of *x*'s type are desirable," motivates purposive action to achieve *x*. A similar story applies for things deemed unpleasant and attempts to avoid them. Cognition further provides guidance throughout the process of acting, allowing one to navigate the world effectively.

That knowledge sources are fundamental to pursuing the goods of life is a consistent theme throughout the *Commentary*.

Vātsyāyana's Commentary *on the* Nyāya-sūtra. Matthew R. Dasti, Oxford University Press.
 DOI: 10.1093/oso/9780197625927.003.0001

> For all sciences, all purposive actions, and indeed all living beings, ordinary conduct relies on the settled output of knowledge sources. (4.2.29)

> For one who is motivated to achieve virtue, wealth, pleasure, and liberation [the "four goals of life" according to classical Hinduism], while avoiding things opposed to them, ordinary conduct is possible by knowing the sources of knowledge and their proper objects. (2.1.20)

The Sanskrit term translated as "effective" in the opening statement is *arthavat* (*artha* + the suffix *vat*), a word rich with resonances that cannot be captured by a single English analogue.[1] The semantic range of *artha* includes "object," "utility," "purpose," and "meaning." The -*vat* affix indicates possession. Here, in the opening line of the *Commentary*, *arthavat* means something like "object-possessing," as the context suggests that knowledge sources must have this property for action to succeed. The subcommentator Vācaspati Miśra notes that by describing them as "object-possessing," Vātsyāyana makes clear that *pramāṇa*-generated cognition properly scopes its target; it is veridical by definition. On this reading, *pramāṇas* are governed by a success grammar akin to the word "see" in English.[2] *To see* means to successfully see. If we are wrong about our perceptual experience, we typically say something like "I *thought* I saw Leela, but I didn't." The inerrancy that is internal to the definition of *pramāṇas* will be discussed further under 1.1.4.

A broader sense of *arthavat* as "useful" or "fruitful" is also evident when Vātsyāyana claims that a knowledge source's being *arthavat* leads the cognitive agent, the object of knowledge, and the state of knowing to all become *arthavat* themselves. These four

[1] Jha (1919, 1) translates it as "rightly effective," Gangopadhyaya (1982, 1) as "invariably connected with the object," Perry (1995, 183) as "valid," Dasti and Phillips (2017, 15) as "useful."

[2] See Dasti and Phillips 2010 for a concise study of *pramāṇas* as factive.

things—the knower, the instruments of knowing, the thing known, and the state of knowing—come together in the right sort of way and all become "fruitful." They jointly converge upon truth, "reality as ascribed to the real and unreality as ascribed to the unreal." On this basis, an individual can effectively pursue the goals of life.[3]

Vātsyāyana's opening line serves another purpose, as a preemptive strike against skeptical challenges to the entire *pramāṇa* project. Without mentioning him by name, Vātsyāyana is acutely aware of the attacks on Nyāya's *pramāṇa* methodology by the Buddhist skeptic Nāgārjuna (c. 150).[4]

> If for you, objects are established by knowledge sources, then tell us what establishes the knowledge sources? (*VV* 31)

This question is part of a skeptical quadrilemma advanced by Nāgārjuna that is addressed by Vātsyāyana under 2.1.17–20. Here he does not delve into the details but merely clarifies that the veracity of a *pramāṇa* can be established empirically. If cognition produced by *p* leads to successful action, then *p* is accurate. This analogue of reliabilist "track record" arguments has a rich history in Nyāya. Later in the *Commentary*, Vātsyāyana offers a medical example.

> In what lies the authoritativeness of expert medical testimony? When someone carries out its teachings—"Doing *this* helps you gain what is desired (health) and avoiding *that* helps you escape what is undesired (sickness)"—things happen accordingly. What it says is true, not false. (2.1.68)

[3] An interesting parallel use of *arthavat* may be seen in *Mīmāṃsā-sūtra* 6.2.18, which claims that Vedic scripture is useful or authoritative (*arthavat*) specifically with respect to things that are imperceptible to the senses. That is, such things are the distinct province of the Veda's epistemic authority.

[4] The use of "skeptic" for Nāgārjuna has a long history but is somewhat controversial. Mark Siderits and others have argued against it by rightly pointing out that at core, he is an anti-realist or anti-foundationalist. In Dasti 2018, 158n19, I argue that this finding is consistent with use of the label "skeptic."

With his opening preamble, we find in seed form the confluence of several philosophical commitments fundamental to Vātsyāyana and, by his influence, the entire Nyāya tradition. First, a conception of cognition as a relationship between a knower and an object, underwritten by identifiable knowledge sources. Second, a fundamental concern with successful action, which is held to be the pragmatic goal of cognition and an indicator of proper cognitive functioning. Third, a broad realism, which holds that success in action is determined by our ability to enter into right relations with the network of objects that constitutes our environment. These all point to the importance of knowledge sources and, by extension, the epistemological refinement advanced by Nyāya. We might even go so far as to say that *pramāṇa*s are thus *arthavat* in the sense of "important" or "significant," worthy topics of sustained inquiry.

Vātsyāyana then transitions to *Nyāya-sūtra* 1.1.1. The first two sūtras of the *Nyāya-sūtra* explain three things that bind the work together: the primary subject matter of the text, the good that comes from studying it, and how the two are related. The primary subject matter consists of sixteen topics listed under 1.1.1. The fruit of study promised by sūtra 1.1.1 is nothing less than the "highest good." The Sanskrit term *niḥśreyasa*, as explained by Vātsyāyana, is something of a placeholder, loosely akin to the Greek and Hellenistic use of "eudaimonia" as a general term for what is ultimately good.

> Attainment of the highest good [*niḥśreyasa*] should be understood according to the discipline where it is discussed. Here . . . it means ultimate liberation.[5]

[5] Filling this out, the subcommentator Uddyotakara provides examples from other major Vedic sciences: for study of Vedic ritual, the highest good is attainment of celestial realms; for agricultural science, it is a good harvest; and for statecraft, it is gaining territory. Perry (1995, 32n14) provides helpful citations from Sanskrit literature predating Vātsyāyana, making clear that the term is used as a sort of general placeholder.

Such a claim may seem like a mere honorific. Indeed, the scholar and philosopher Daya Krishna (1991, 30) expresses bafflement at the idea that things such as epistemology and dialectics would have any bearing on soteriology. Arguing that the promise of 1.1.1 likely stems from cultural pressure to pay homage to the religious goals of the day, he concludes that Nyāya has "nothing to do with *mokṣa* (liberation)." Students of Plato or Stoicism might already recognize that a connection between dialectics, clear reasoning, and the supreme good is not so far-fetched. But we need only look at Vātsyāyana's own explanation to address Daya Krishna's doubt. Vātsyāyana tells us specifically that proper understanding of "objects of knowledge" such as the deep self leads to the highest good. Nyāya's other topics of study serve this purpose by providing tools for epistemological clarity, robust understanding, and the capacity to defend one's beliefs within adversarial debate. We could schematize Nyāya's concerns as a hierarchy of practices which come together to serve this end, as in Figure 1.

Making clear the therapeutic orientation of Nyāya, Vātsyāyana says that supreme good requires knowing:

1. that which is to be removed (suffering)
2. that which perpetuates it (existential ignorance)
3. that which removes it completely (true knowledge of the self, etc.)
4. the means to prosecute such removal (philosophy as advanced within Nyāya)

This fourfold medical metaphor probably started with the historical Buddha and was soon employed by a number of the soteriological traditions of ancient India.[6] Vātsyāyana includes Nyāya within such traditions by calling it an *ādhyātmika* school of thought. Loosely translated as "pertaining to the self," this term

[6] See Wezler 1984.

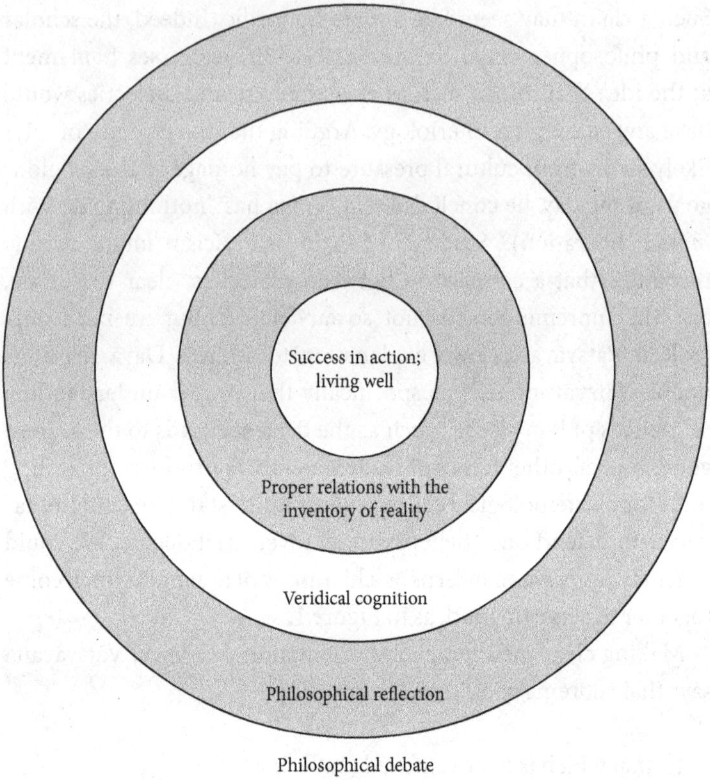

Figure 1. Vātsyāyana's vision of philosophy within a hierarchy of goods.

is used for disciplines focused on transformative self-knowledge and liberating insight. He further notes that what distinguishes the *Nyāya-sūtra* from paradigmatic *ādhyātmika* texts such as the Upaniṣads is a sustained concern with epistemology, philosophical methodology, and dialectics. It is for this reason, he tells us, that such topics are identified as distinct system-defining subjects in the initial sūtra, despite the fact that they could be subsumed within the broader categories "knowledge sources" or "objects of knowledge." As conceived by Vātsyāyana, Nyāya is, therefore, a unique discipline that combines objective, rigorous logical analysis and contemplative praxis.[7]

In the rest of his expansive comments on 1.1.1, Vātsyāyana provides concise descriptions and discussion of each of the sixteen major topics, explaining why each is singled out in the sūtras. He consolidates the notion of Nyāya both as a method of reasoning and as the school of thought named after such reasoning. Considering the fourth topic, motive, Vātsyāyana defines *nyāya* as reasoning: "It is the investigation of something by means of knowledge sources; the use of inference that is grounded in perception and authoritative testimony." This method of reasoning will be enshrined within a five-part "syllogism" that will be discussed under 1.1.32–39. As Nyāya is the school of thought devoted to perfecting such reasoning, Vātsyāyana says that it engages in "the re-examination of cognition that has been produced by perception and testimony." Nyāya is, therefore, fundamentally identical with "critical reasoning" (*ānvīkṣikī*), one of the four major sciences mentioned in earlier Brahmanical literature such as the *Arthaśāstra* (c. 100 BCE), a classical text on statecraft.

While on the topic of motive, Vātsyāyana also fires a shot across the bow of the skeptics, here framed as those who exclusively practice "destructive debate." Topics ten, eleven, and twelve of the *Nyāya-sūtra* are truth-directed debate, disputation, and destructive debate. Truth-directed debate is the paradigm of philosophical inquiry, where opposing theses are argued for in good faith and, since the goal is knowledge, all parties are willing to change their views in accord with the arguments. Disputation is more ethically dubious as the goal is victory, even by use of fallacies and tricks. Both kinds of debate have a clear objective. But what about destructive debate? Here one seeks to demolish an opponent's view but advances no positive thesis of one's own. Famously, the Buddhist Nāgārjuna claimed, "I advance no thesis," in the course of his own

[7] The connections between these two are the focus of 4.2.1–3 and 4.2.38–49.

skeptical dialectics.[8] In all likelihood, Vātsyāyana has Nāgārjuna in mind when he asks whether this position could be consistently maintained.

> One who only practices destructive debate is a skeptic [*vaitaṇḍika*]. When asked whether he has an objective, if he answers in the affirmative, then he does have a view or thesis. He thus abandons his skepticism. But if he does not answer in the affirmative, then he is neither a lay investigator nor a scholar (i.e., he is not a participant in inquiry at all).
>
> If, alternatively, he says that his objective is merely to prove that another's view is wrong, the same reasoning applies. If he admits that there is someone who proves something, another who understands it, reasoning which supports a proof, and something which is proven, then he abandons his skepticism. If he does not admit these, then the claim that he merely establishes the faults in another's view is meaningless.

Vātsyāyana wraps up his comments on sūtra 1.1.1 by citing a verse found in the *Arthaśāstra* (slightly modified):

> Critical reasoning is the light of all sciences, the means to accomplish all actions, the support of all morality [*dharma*]. (*AŚ* 1.2.12)

With this, he argues that Nyāya is far more than just one school among others. As it embodies critical reasoning par excellence, its teachings are fundamental to any systematic inquiry. It supports every intellectual discipline. Not only is the school firmly situated within Vedic orthodoxy, but it is also *the* tradition that offers rational reflection upon and defense of the teachings of the Vedas (sacred testimony) and allied works.[9] In the centuries before

[8] *VV* 29.

[9] Perry 1997 explores the tensions over orthodoxy that motivate Vātsyāyana and other early Nyāya thinkers.

Vātsyāyana, Brahmanical texts considered widely were ambivalent regarding the status of critical reasoning. In its most basic sense, *ānvīkṣikī* was seen as a methodology that critically examined various claims, practices, and outlooks through objective reasoning. By enshrining it as one of the four major "sciences," the *Arthaśāstra* celebrates its role within what we might call Hindu orthodoxy. But it was also a topic of concern and anxiety in texts that saw exclusive reliance upon reasoning as something dangerous that could erode confidence in Vedic cultural norms. The *Law Code of Manu* (2.11) states that "If, by resorting to logic, a Brahmin disparages the two roots of morality (the Vedas and tradition), he should be shunned by good people as a faithless blasphemer of the Vedas." The *Mahābhārata*, a massive, heterogeneous epic poem, gives voice to both perspectives.[10] By framing Nyāya as an authentically Vedic school of thought, Vātsyāyana stresses that the critical reasoning central to Nyāya need not be seen as the exclusive province of skeptics, deniers, and philosophical upstarts who are hostile to received cultural norms.

But how could this sort of critical investigation remove suffering? Vātsyāyana tells us that what is needed is not simply theoretical knowledge. He then transitions to sūtra 1.1.2, which presents a causal chain.

> *misunderstanding → vice → karmic entanglement → rebirth → suffering*

Existential misunderstanding leads to affective states that perpetuate karmic entanglement and the miseries of embodied life. Understanding this allows us to locate the way out. By addressing

[10] See Thakur 1974. Vidyabhusana (1919, xii–xv) tries to make sense of the mixed reception within Brahmanical literature by suggesting a developmental story: starting as tradition outside of Brahmanical orthodoxy, Nyāya was first an object of fear and derision for the Brahmin gatekeepers of orthodoxy but was ultimately accepted into the Vedic fold and extolled as a system of learning.

each link, starting with misunderstanding, freedom from suffering is possible.

As explained by Vātsyāyana, misunderstanding concerns the "objects of knowledge," the second of Nyāya's sixteen major topics. Among these objects, misunderstanding fundamentally concerns the self: thinking that there is no deep self or that the self is nothing more than the body, that unhealthy fixations actually benefit oneself, and so on. But it also involves mistakes about each link in the chain of suffering: thinking that vices do not lead to karmic entanglement, that such entanglement does not lead to entrapment in the cycle of birth and death, or that rebirth cannot be stopped through liberation. Even liberation can be an object of misunderstanding: enmeshed in worldliness, people see it as fearful, as losing out on all that is good in life.

Misunderstandings lead to vice:

> From misunderstandings like these, desire arises toward objects thought to be favorable, and aversion toward those thought unfavorable. Under the spell of desire and aversion, vices arise, including dishonesty, jealousy, resentment, pride, and greed. (*Commentary* 1.1.2)

Vices lead to immoral action, karmic demerit, and degradation.

Proper understanding is filled out by contrast: there is a deep self that contains within it the possibility of true, enduring liberation. Pleasures that debase us are contemptible. Vices do entangle us, and such entanglement perpetuates rebirth. The cycle of rebirth can be stopped, amounting to liberation, the most desirable thing, a state of perpetual freedom from suffering. Governed by such understanding, one pursues virtue and acts of duty and charity, the groundwork for the pursuit of liberation. As discussed further in 4.2.46–49, liberating knowledge requires mature internalization of the truth: "the removal of doubts, awareness of things previously unknown, and the reflective acceptance of something previously grasped." These are the product of philosophical investigation, coupled with meditational practice and rational discourse—including debate—with others bent on achieving life's ultimate good.

Thus, even in its most abstract and technical aspects, Nyāya's pursuit of proper understanding is ideally meant to serve the cause of moral improvement and ultimate freedom. As Halbfass (1997, 159) explains, for Nyāya, "addiction to enjoyment and the acquisition of its means is a symptom of a fundamental cognitive disease." The remedy to this disease begins with proper understanding of what is ultimately real and ultimately valuable.

1.1.3–8: Knowledge sources

Vātsyāyana begins his comments on this section by clarifying the purposes of a treatise (*śāstra*) such as the *Nyāya-sūtra*: to *identify* major topics, to provide *definitions* of each topic, and to engage in philosophical *investigation*, ensuring that the given definitions are apt while responding to special objections and problems. Sūtra 1.1.1 identified the major topics, and 1.1.2 described the fruit of understanding them. The rest of Chapter 1 consists of definitions and categorizations of each topic, while later chapters investigate special problems or questions, roughly in sequential order. Thus, for example, while perception is discussed at some length under sūtra 1.1.4, special problems and challenges with respect to perception are taken up later, under 2.1.21–36. (See Tables 1 and 2.)

Preliminaries finished, the sūtras now discuss their first major topic, the celebrated knowledge sources (*pramāṇas*). In a broad sense, *pramāṇa* commonly refers to instruments or agents of authoritative measurement or judgment. The *Bhagavad-gītā* thus tells us, "The standard [*pramāṇa*] set by a great person is followed by common folks" (3.21). As used in the great schools of philosophy such as Nyāya, *pramāṇa* typically means an irreducible cause

Table 1. The contents of the *Nyāya-sūtra* as expanded from sūtra 1.1.1.

Topic	Definition and initial analysis	Further investigation
[epistemology]		
1. knowledge sources	1.1.3–8	2.1.8–2.2.69
[metaphysics and value theory]		
2. objects of knowledge	1.1.9–22	3.1.1–4.1.68
[elements of formal investigation]		
3. doubt	1.1.23	2.1.1–7
4. motive	1.1.24	
5. example	1.1.25	
6. settled theses	1.1.26–31	
7. parts of a proof	1.1.32–39	
8. suppositional reasoning	1.1.40	
9. certainty	1.1.41	
[dialectics]		
10. truth-directed debate	1.2.1	4.2.48–49
11. disputation	1.2.2	4.2.50–51
12. destructive debate	1.2.3	4.2.50-51
13. counterfeit reasons	1.2.4–9	
14. equivocation	1.2.10–17	
15. dialectical rejoinders	1.2.18, 1.2.20	5.1.1–43
16. defeat conditions	1.2.19–20	5.2.1–24
liberating knowledge of the truth	1.1.1–2	4.2.1–47

Table 2. Detailed listing of knowledge sources and the objects of knowledge.

Topic	Definition and initial analysis	Further investigation
knowledge sources in general	1.1.3	2.1.8–20, 2.2.1–12
perception	1.1.4	2.1.21–32, 2.1.33–36*
inference	1.1.5	2.1.37–43
comparison	1.1.6	2.1.44–48
testimony	1.1.7–8	2.1.49–68; 2.2.13–61**
objects of knowledge in general	1.1.9	
self	1.1.10	3.1.1–26
body	1.1.11	3.1.27–31, 3.2.60–72***
senses	1.1.12–13	3.1.32–60
sense objects	1.1.14	3.1.61–72
cognition	1.1.15	3.2.1–55
mind (*manas*)	1.1.16	3.2.56–59
purposive action	1.1.17	4.1.1–9
vice	1.1.18	4.1.1–9
rebirth	1.1.19	4.1.10–13, 4.1.14–43*
results of action	1.1.20	4.1.44–54
suffering	1.1.21	4.1.55–58
liberation	1.1.22	4.1.59–68

* This passage is a tangential digression.

** This section is largely concerned with the metaphysics of sound and philosophy of language.

*** This section is focused on karmic merit but in relation to the body and embodiment.

or source of knowledge, for example, perception or inference.[11] Epistemological debate in India was typically about the proper analysis of specific *pramāṇa* types and whether certain candidate sources could be reduced to subtypes of others or even denied the status of a true source. Sūtra 1.1.3 offers Nyāya's list, and Vātsyāyana provides simple, provisional definitions of each:

> *Perception* is the functioning of the senses upon their proper objects.
> *Inference* generates "subsequent cognition," knowledge of something that follows from something else.
> *Comparison* generates knowledge of similarity.
> *Testimony* generates knowledge by understanding the meanings of words.

What they have in common is that each is an instrumental cause of knowledge. To be a *pramāṇa* is to be "that by which something is known." While Vātsyāyana does not discuss individuation criteria explicitly here, the major distinction of each type seems to be its function or process. Throughout the second chapter's investigations into separate knowledge sources (2.1.21–56, 2.2.1–12), each is held to function according to a unique type of causal process. Here he speaks of perception as a *vṛtti*, function. At times, Vātsyāyana also considers the way different sources generate different types of cognitive output (2.1.50, 2.1.52).

Accurate individuation is crucial because the epistemic status of cognition flows from the causal efficacy of the process that generates it. To put it simply, knowledge comes from a knowledge source, not a misfire. Certification of knowledge often consists in

[11] Buddhist Epistemologists such as Dignāga would demur, claiming rather that the output cognition itself is the *pramāṇa* and not the *process* that gives rise to it. Vātsyāyana does recognize such usage, noting that a word like "perception" can be used for output cognition itself (e.g., "My perception of Ana in the distance"). This usage is secondary for Nyāya in the context of the major knowledge sources.

tracing its causal ancestry to a genuine knowledge source. Proper analysis and individuation of the *pramāṇa*s are thus essential to make sure that the basic causal story is accurate.[12]

How do these sources interrelate? Are they restricted to their own distinct objects, or do they converge? True to his methodology throughout the text, Vātsyāyana appeals to common experience, noting that sometimes there are objects unique to a certain knowledge source, and sometimes there are objects on which multiple sources converge. An example of the former is learning about the heavenly rewards of sacrifice by means of sacred testimony. No other source can target such otherworldly content. An example of the latter involves learning there is a fire from another's testimony, then moving closer and seeing smoke over the site, which allows for an inference to fire, and finally walking right up to the fire and seeing it directly.

This "convergence of knowledge sources" certainly tracks ordinary experience, but it is also an important part of Nyāya's metaphysics. That an individual's distinct modalities of knowing can converge on a single object will be the central argument in support of an irreducible, nonphysical self in sūtras 3.1.1–3. "Convergence of knowledge sources" is, furthermore, a central plank of Nyāya's external-world realism insofar as both intersubjective agreement

[12] As a point of comparison, concerns over individuation arise for *pramāṇa* theory's modern analogue, process reliabilism. The issue is sharpened by Conee and Feldman (1998), who argue that a candidate process type may be individuated in a variety of ways and accordingly may be attributed various degrees of reliability, undercutting the reliabilist project. Nyāya avoids such indeterminacy by conceiving of knowledge sources as natural cognitive functions, processes that move from cognitive inputs to outputs. Therefore, the relevant process is identified according to the observable or introspectable features of the process itself. In this, Nyāya anticipates Alston (1995, 15): "By virtue of being a *functional* mapping of input features onto output content, [a reliable process] has a *built in* generality that is provided by the function . . . [and] is the one defined by the function, which is in turn defined by a certain way of going from input features to output features." From the perspective of Nyāya, when we are reflecting on the reliability of a doctor's expert testimony, we do not become confused by the fact that it belongs to the kind "sound vibration" or "emanation from a human" as well as the kind "reliable testimony."

and "inter-*pramāṇic* agreement" testify to the reality of objects external to consciousness.

Vātsyāyana also uses the fire example to underscore the primacy of perception:

> If one wants to know something and learns about it through testimony, she may still wish to understand it through inference. And after understanding it through inference, she may still wish to see it directly. But after seeing it, her desire to know ceases. (*Commentary* 1.1.3)

The centrality of perception for Nyāya is a dominant theme in that it provides the raw ingredients for the other knowledge sources to function. But here Vātsyāyana's point is about its phenomenological force.

Moving on to sūtra 1.1.4, which defines perception (*pratyakṣa*), we find four criteria that mark any particular cognition as perceptual. It must be (i) produced by the connection between a sense faculty and an object, (ii) not dependent on words, (iii) inerrant, and (iv) definitive. Criterion (i) is straightforward, as long as we allow for Nyāya's premodern account of the biology and physics involved.[13] What is central is simply that in perception, content is gleaned directly from the object of the cognition in ways that differ from the other knowledge sources, which are indirect.

Criterion (ii), not being dependent on words, establishes that perceptual cognition is causally independent of and prior to any verbalization of its content. Philosophers in India were acutely aware of and concerned with the relationship between experience, conceptual content, and language. Around the time of Vātsyāyana, we find a spectrum of views on this relationship. On one end, are Buddhist "idealists" such as Dignāga (c. 480 CE), who defines genuine perception as *kalpanā-apoha*, "free from conceptualization"

[13] See *NySBh* 3.1.34.

(*PS* 1.3). For him, any visual content involving names and repeatable properties is not the product of perception, strictly speaking, but rather inferences that depart from (and obscure) the pure content of perception. On the other end of the spectrum are thinkers such as Bhartṛhari, the Grammarian (c. fifth century CE), for whom all cognition is linguistic in form. It is not that we use language to understand perceptual experience, but rather, language is required in order to have any experience at all. The interlocutor whom Vātsyāyana brings forth is likely a member of this camp.[14] The following argument is given on his behalf:

> There are as many names as there are objects, and we comprehend things by means of names. Everyday practices rely on such comprehension. Here, cognition of an object arising from the connection between the object and a sense faculty has content like color or taste. Denotative terms "color" and "taste" are names for such content. Through them, cognition may be articulated: "She experiences color," "She experiences taste." As it is articulated through such names, perceptual cognition is fundamentally linguistic in nature. (*Commentary* 1.1.4)

A realist school like Nyāya is at the middle of the spectrum. Like the Buddhist idealists, Nyāya is empiricist in that it recognizes that all knowledge sources depend upon contents drawn from perception. But unlike them, it also holds that perception has the power to directly take robust content from the world. Perception directly apprehends not only shapes and colors but also macrosubstances,[15] properties as inhering in property bearers,[16] and even

[14] While unpacking Vātsyāyana's comments, Vācaspati Miśra directly cites Bhartṛhari's *Vākyapadīya* (1.123): "There is no cognition that is not connected to words. All cognition is comprehended in this way, as bound up with words." This does not constitute decisive historical evidence, as Vācaspati was prone to anachronistic readings. But it does suggest that for the early Nyāya school, Vātsyāyana's interlocutor is taken to be Bhartṛhari.

[15] 2.1.33–36.

[16] 2.2.67.

universals.[17] For this reason, Nyāya's empiricism does not collapse into idealism or phenomenalism as have so many other iterations (including the Buddhists just mentioned).

Vātsyāyana reads "not dependent on words" as expressing this power. We are capable of perceptually grasping objects without knowledge of their names. Even when names are known, deployment of language is downstream from perceptual experience. He identifies two levels of awareness. First is perceptual cognition of some object, where names are irrelevant. This is causally prior to and independent of the second level, reflection upon and communication of the content of experience. Here, by adding the Sanskrit term *iti* to the object's name (roughly akin to use of quotation marks in English), meta-cognitive discussion is possible. Only at this second level do names become centrally important.

Criteria (iii), being inerrant, makes clear that the *Nyāya-sūtra* is defining perception insofar as it is a knowledge source and not merely in terms of descriptive psychology. In his gloss, Vātsyāyana explains that the inerrancy requirement removes illusions and the like from the ranks of perceptual cognition: "Error is to cognize something as other than it is. Perception is inerrant, cognizing something as it is." To say that perception is inerrant is not to deny the fact of visual illusions or hallucinations. But here (and in most of the *NySBh*), "perception" is being spoken of as a knowledge source. By definition, it hits the mark. This is in accord with the way we use "know" in English. To know is to get something right. When we realize that we were wrong about something, we do not say, "I knew that, but I was wrong." Rather, we say, "I thought I knew that, but I was wrong." Similarly, perceptual errors are not the deliverances of perception, strictly speaking, but misleading imitators. Vātsyāyana applies a disjunctive analysis, where illusions and hallucinations are instances of "counterfeit *pramāṇas*" or "imitators," mere likenesses to the real thing. As such, our goal as knowers is to distinguish not

[17] 5.1.14–15.

between true and false perceptions but rather genuine perception versus faulty imitators. He applies this disjunctive analysis to other knowledge sources, where the true thing just is the successful case and mistakes are an entirely different kind.[18]

Just as criterion (iii) removes errors from the ranks of perceptual cognition, criterion (iv), being definitive, is meant to remove doubtful, unclear presentations. "Looking at something from a distance, one is unable to determine whether it is smoke or a cloud of dust." While this is not a case of error, it is doubtful and as such does not generate knowledge. Such presentations are not *perceptual* in the relevant sense.

Before Vātsyāyana concludes his discussion of perception, he entertains an objection that alleges a compositional defect in the sūtra. It concerns the mental faculty of attention, the *manas*, arguing that it should have been mentioned explicitly as the inner sense faculty that directly apprehends mental states. In response, Vātsyāyana appeals to one of the ancient scholarly methodologies (*tantra-yukti*s), namely, that views of other systems that do not oppose one's own may be tacitly accepted.

Next is sūtra 1.1.5, on inference (*anumāna*). Let me start by admitting that the translation "inference" sacrifices perfect accuracy to avoid cumbersome technical phrasing. There are many forms of reasoning that are not *anumāna*, including suppositional reasoning (*tarka*, discussed below under 1.1.40). The knowledge source discussed here is fundamentally the way we discover truths

[18] Under 1.1.1, Vātsyāyana speaks of reasoning that contradicts perception and authoritative testimony as *nyāya-ābhāsa*, "pseudo-reasoning" or "counterfeit reasoning." Throughout the sūtras and *Commentary* (esp. 1.2.4–9), certain argumentative fallacies are called *hetv-ābhāsa*, "pseudo-reasons." Under 1.1.37, he says that "pseudo reasons are not reasons at all, as they lack the proper relationship with what is to be proven." Under 2.1.38, "It is not that inference deviates (from its target). Rather, this (mistaken) case is a mistaken notion of an inference where there is none. . . . The fault is with the person who is inferring, not inference as such." A similar argument is offered in 2.2.4, regarding postulation, which Nyāya reduces to inference. He goes so far as to call a bad example a "non-example" under 3.1.23. For further analysis of this issue, see Dasti and Phillips 2010; Dasti 2012.

by mentally traversing the connection between certain inputs and what they entail. Such traversing is, in short, inferring. As noted above, Vātsyāyana frames inference as an epistemic process that begins with an indicator (*liṅga*) and terminates with an output target fact, something "indicated" (*liṅgin*). He glosses the sūtras' claim that inference depends upon perception in two ways. First, through experience, we discover the general tie between an indicator and target fact (e.g., between smoke and fire). Second, inferences are paradigmatically triggered when one sees an indicator. Seeing smoke in the distance, one's standing memory of the tie between smoke and fire is triggered, allowing for an inference to fire.

The sūtra offers three subtypes of inference: *pūrvavat*, "as before"; *śeṣavat*, "as after"; and *sāmānyato-dṛṣṭa*, "from the experience of commonality." While glossing these terms, Vātsyāyana offers two separate readings of each, without adjudicating the case. (See Table 3.)

This has vexed scholars and engendered multiple explanations. One suggestion is that the exact meaning of the sūtras was receding into the hazy past, and Vātsyāyana could at best offer speculative forensics. Another is that the first reading is according to Nyāya while the second is according to Vaiśeṣika.

The three subtypes are mentioned in a handful of extant sources earlier than or contemporary with Vātsyāyana, including the influential Buddhist debate manual *Upāya-hṛdaya*. There are some instances of agreement with Vātsyāyana's interpretation of *pūrvavat* and *śeṣavat* but enough divergence among all the sources to suggest that the terms were not consistently applied.[19] *Sāmānyato-dṛṣṭa* is also interpreted in multiple ways, but it has a more consistent sense as something that involves analogical or extrapolative reasoning that goes beyond ordinary experience. In both Śabara's

[19] Tucci (1929, xvii–xviii) offers a table comparing early treatments of the three subtypes.

Table 3. Vātsyāyana's interpretation of the three subtypes of inference in *NyS* 1.1.5.

Type	Gloss	Example
First interpretation:		
pūrvavat	from cause to effect	inferring that it will rain from overhead nimbus clouds
śeṣavat	from effect to cause	inferring that rain occurred upstream due to a swelling, rapidly flowing river
sāmānyato-dṛṣṭa	(no general gloss of this type of inference is offered)	inferring the sun's movement from its change of location
Second interpretation:		
pūrvavat	from prior observation	inferring fire from smoke
śeṣavat	argument from elimination	inferring that sound must be a property, since it cannot be a substance or an action
sāmānyato-dṛṣṭa	one infers something unseen through similarity with something experienced	inferring that the self is a psychological substance, since it bears psychological properties

commentary on the *Mīmāṃsā-sūtra* (under *MS* 1.1.5) and in the *Vaiśeṣika-sūtra*, it is contrasted with *dṛṣṭa* (literally, "seen") inferences.[20] *Dṛṣṭa* inferences rely on direct observation of the indicator. Exactly what must be *seen* to count as this inference varies among different thinkers. Some sources suggest that it is the indicator itself, others that the relationship between the indicator and target, and others that the target must be in principle perceptible. In any case, we may note that in the standard example of smoke and fire, both are visible in principle, and their connection is something that is directly observed. We might say that these sorts of inferences stay within the world of observed and observable things. By contrast, *sāmānyato-dṛṣṭa* inferences rely on connections extrapolated from or analogized from experience. Owing to this difference, they have the capacity to discover imperceptible truths but also have distinct limitations or challenges. The *Vaiśeṣika-sūtra* remarks that the target fact of a *sāmānyato-dṛṣṭa* inference cannot be known in its specificity (*VS* 2.1.16, 3.2.6–7).[21] In a paradigmatic use, the *Sāṃkhya-kārikā* (c. fifth century CE) relies on *sāmānyato-dṛṣṭa* inference to establish that there is a primordial matter, an original "unmanifest" reality anterior to any particular material thing (*SK* 6).

Ultimately, this threefold classification belongs to an older typology that would be superseded by the logical innovations that arise in the generations after Vātsyāyana. From that point on (that is, after Dignāga), subcommentators such as Uddyotakara would anachronistically interpret the claim that inference is "threefold" as expressing rigorous logical distinctions unknown to the author(s) of the *Nyāya-sūtra*.[22]

[20] A robust analysis of *sāmānyato-dṛṣṭa* inference is also found in the Sāṃkhya text *Ṣaṣṭitantra*, by Vārṣagaṇya (c. 300 CE), now only available in a reconstructed form. Schuster (1972, 358–363) argues that Vātsyāyana's interpretation of the three subtypes is especially indebted to the *Ṣaṣṭitantra*.

[21] When citing the *Vaiśeṣika-sūtra*, I will follow the numbering conventions in the GRETIL edition entered by Nozawa Masanobu.

[22] See Dasti and Phillips 2017, 32–34.

A final note made by Vātsyāyana is that unlike perception, inference can apprehend both existing and non-existing things. It can range beyond the present moment to target things that exist in the past and those that will exist in the future. The relationship between inference and "the three times" will be taken up again in the special investigation of inference under 2.1.39–43.[23]

The next sūtra is 1.1.6, on comparison (*upamāna*). As described in the sūtra, and according to Vātsyāyana's laconic remarks under 1.1.3, this knowledge source functions through similarity. But, as explained by Vātsyāyana here (and accepted by later tradition), it has a more precise and restricted role, as a way we learn how to refer to formerly unknown objects. Learning through testimony that "a water buffalo is like a cow" and later seeing a water buffalo, one realizes what it is through comparison: "*that* is a water buffalo." Interpreted by Vātsyāyana, it is a very limited *pramāṇa*, and he often ignores it when he collectively speaks of knowledge sources. If we take it merely to be a method of understanding the correct use of naming terms through similarity, I am sympathetic with those who think it could be excised from the list and reduced to other knowledge sources.[24] If we take it in a broader sense to be a process by which we learn and extrapolate from individual cases, as argued by Tuske (2008), it would seem much more significant. That Vātsyāyana later appeals to comparison to explain how we discover genuine entailment relations versus mere resemblance indicates that Tuske's suggestion might have a foothold within the *Commentary* itself.[25]

Sūtras 1.1.7–8 discuss the final *pramāṇa*: *śabda*, testimony (literally, "word" or "sound"). *Śabda* is a fundamental and distinct source

[23] Joshi (1981) appeals to this issue of temporal divisions to argue that the original meaning of sūtras is misunderstood here by Vātsyāyana and that *pūrvavat* is an inference to something in the past, *śeṣavat* to something in the future, and *sāmānyato-dṛṣṭa* to something in the present moment.

[24] I argue this in Dasti 2013, 622–623.

[25] *NySBh* 5.1.5.

of knowledge. In opposition to Buddhist Epistemologists and Vaiśeṣika (and, for that matter, European thinkers such as David Hume), Nyāya argues that testimony cannot be reduced to a subspecies of inference (2.1.52, 2.1.55). The account offered here sees testimony as an act of sharing. Someone attains knowledge through some *pramāṇa*(s), and, in a properly functioning testimonial exchange, she then passes it on to a listener. This would be an instance of what Lackey (1999, 471) calls the "transmission" account of testimony, which presupposes that one must have knowledge to share it.

As testimony is the "assertion of an authority," Vātsyāyana defines an authority (*āpta*): "a speaker who has direct knowledge about something and who wants to effectively communicate what they know." Later, under 2.1.68, he adds compassion to the criteria. I use "one who has direct knowledge" to translate *sākṣāt-kṛta-dharman*, a somewhat challenging term. Some have highlighted the use of the word *dharma* here to suggest that authority requires at least a partial connection to knowledge of morality or proper behavior.[26] The challenge for this thesis is that Vātsyāyana is very clear throughout the *Commentary* that testimonial authority functions the same way whether it involves deep spiritual teachings or completely mundane instructions by completely mundane people. Commenting on this very sūtra, he says that "the character of authority is the same for sages, proper followers of the Vedas, or those outside of Vedic culture." Certainly, he would not hold that the latter group has direct insight into *dharma*. Besides, the paradigm testimonial authority discussed under 2.1.68, Vātsyāyana's most thorough discussion, is a competent medical practitioner. Therefore, I rather read *dharma* here with the sense of "feature" or "character," and a reliable speaker *has the character of* direct knowledge (*sākṣāt-kṛta*).

This leads us to the other challenging aspect of this term. The word *sākṣāt* is an indeclinable adverb meaning "immediate" or "direct." It is often used to express the immediacy of experience.

[26] See Chemparathy 1987 for a nuanced argument to this end.

Indeed, *sa* + *akṣa* means "with the eyes," and *sākṣāt* + *kṛ* often conveys what contemporary philosophers might speak of as the phenomenal force of perception. Read strictly in this way, this qualification would require that only those persons whose knowledge of something is perceptual could be legitimate testifiers. But Vātsyāyana denies this explicitly under 1.1.8:

> One should not think that the assertion of an authority is a *pramāṇa* about perceptible things alone, on the grounds that such objects can be definitively ascertained. Their assertions are *pramāṇa* for imperceptible objects too, as such objects may be inferred.

The paradigm of testimonial authority, a medical practitioner, uses all of the knowledge sources—including reasoning and the testimony of other physicians—to make discoveries which they explain to their patients. I thus soften the term a bit to underscore that the knowledge of a testifier is secure and strong but not necessarily that it must be derived from a testifier's own perceptual experience.[27]

Sūtra 1.1.8 tells us that sacred testimony functions the same way as the ordinary sort; the only difference is that it communicates otherworldly facts.[28] This is a significant part of Nyāya's epistemology of religious belief in that it suggests that, at least in principle, there are criteria to test for the authority of scripture (a claim made explicitly in 2.1.68). We have already seen Vātsyāyana argue that Nyāya is the shelter of other intellectual disciplines, including Vedic study (1.1.1). While Nyāya remains a faithful defender of Vedic revelation and is scripturally "conservative," the seeds planted by Vātsyāyana

[27] Mohanty (1994, 30–33) has suggested that for Nyāya, a testifier "must be known to be competent" in advance. But this requirement is too strong and not representative of Vātsyāyana or of Nyāya in general. As evidence for this, we may note that *NyS* 2.2.2, reduces tradition, "an assertion that is passed down in the form 'they say . . .' but for which the original speaker cannot be identified," to a subspecies of testimony.

[28] See also 2.1.58 and 2.1.61.

are developed by Uddyotakara and Vācaspati Miśra into what could *almost* be a Lockean position about reasoning and scripture. As Perry (1995, 155) puts it, "The possibility of validating otherworldly testimony depends . . . on inference alone . . . [and] since inference, which Nyāya uniquely teaches, must be employed to validate the apprehension of many non-perceptual apprehensions, Nyāya's supremacy over all sciences is complete." We can compare John Locke's (1975, 695) dictum, "Whatever GOD hath revealed is certainly true; no Doubt can be made of it. . . . But whether it be a divine revelation or not, *Reason* must judge."

Before we conclude the topic of testimony, a short digression on the subject may be forgiven. When engaged in historiography, a scholar of premodern philosophy—and especially premodern, *non-Western* philosophy—eventually discovers that what counts as "philosophy" is significantly influenced by the interests and prejudices of the day.[29] In this regard, many pioneering scholars of Indian philosophy were engaged in a struggle to disentangle it from religion in the eyes of their peers. This struggle, along with the residual effects of the Enlightenment bias toward epistemic individualism, led some of them to be embarrassed by the importance of testimony in classical India. Strikingly, in his landmark *History of Indian Philosophy*, Surendranath Dasgupta (1922, 394) thus professes:

> Śabda or word [testimony] is regarded as separate means of proof by most of the recognized Indian systems of thought excepting the Jain, Buddhist, Cārvāka and Vaiśeṣika. *A discussion of this topic however has but little philosophical value and I have therefore omitted to give any attention to it in connection with the Nyāya, and the Sāṁkhya-Yoga systems.* . . . Evidently a discussion of these matters has but little value with us, though it was a very favorite theme of debate in the old days of India. (emphasis added)

[29] Halbfass 1988 richly illustrates this point.

Happily, the disciplinary bias against testimony has waned in the last few decades, and work on the subject has exploded. Perhaps not coincidentally, one of the first major analytic works on the epistemology of testimony was carried out by two professional philosophers who were also Sanskritists and scholars of Nyāya.[30] Here the academy is catching up to the ancients.

1.1.9–22: The objects of knowledge

This section lists and describes the objects of knowledge (*prameya*). *Prameya* means "knowable," "that which is to be known," or even "that which should be known." It is a correlate term with *pramāṇa*, "means of knowing." As the second of Nyāya's sixteen topics, it roughly corresponds to metaphysics and value theory. Sūtras 1.1.9–22 list and subdivide the twelve primary objects of knowledge. From the outset, the list seems idiosyncratic, cutting across various categories.

physics/metaphysics: self, body, sense faculties, sense objects
psychology: cognition, *manas* (faculty of selective attention), suffering
ethics/action theory: intentional action, vice, karmic result, rebirth, liberation

Seemingly acknowledging this, Vātsyāyana recognizes a different schematization of *prameya*s, as a metaphysics of categories:

> There is another way to articulate the objects of knowledge: substance, quality, action, universal, differentiator, and inherence. (*Commentary* 1.1.9)

[30] Matilal and Chakrabarti 1994.

These are the famous categories championed by Nyāya's sister school, Vaiśeṣika. Though not separately defined in the sūtras, these categories are presupposed throughout the *NySBh*.[31] Reaffirming the *ādhyātmika* orientation of Nyāya, Vātsyāyana suggests the *Nyāya-sūtra* offers the list it does because "understanding these things leads to liberation, and misunderstanding of them perpetuates the cycle of birth and death." Thus, we could say that the *Nyāya-sūtra*'s selection of special knowables does stress the injunctive force of *prameya* as "that which *should* be known" and is not to be taken as an exhaustive list of fundamental reals.

The centerpiece of this section is 1.1.10, an argument for the self (*ātman*). Nyāya is a "Vedic" philosophical tradition that inherits the insights and speculations of the Upaniṣads.[32] For such traditions, not only is the self a real part of the inventory of reality, but understanding the deep nature of the self is the very key to liberation. In this, they are diametrically opposed to Buddhist scholastics, who deployed various arguments meant to undermine the commonsense idea of the self as a unified psychological substance. Some of these arguments are radically empiricist and reductionist, anticipating those for which David Hume would become famous a millennium later: when we attend carefully to the contents of experience, we only find bundles of momentary psychological events. "Self" is a false projection of psychological stability on what is merely a stream of ephemeral psychological events.

Sūtra 1.1.10 lists six indicators for a self. "Indicator" (*liṅga*) is a term used within inferential contexts for something that generates knowledge of a target fact; smoke is an indicator of fire. Read straightforwardly, the sūtra argues that "desire, aversion, effort, pleasure, pain, and cognition are indicators of a self" in that they are present only when there is a self. By contrast, the rocking chair

[31] He mentions this list again, under 2.1.34, as constituting "everything." Also see 4.1.38.

[32] Under 4.1.60–62, Vātsyāyana cites a number of Upaniṣads directly.

in my office lacks a self. There is nobody home, no locus of cognitive or affective states. None of these indicators is present. In living beings, however, these indicators are present because there is somebody home, a self, which is a unique substance serving as the locus of psychological properties. Structurally, Vātsyāyana has already noted that this argument falls under the *sāmānyato-dṛṣṭa* type.

> "From something commonly observed" is when there is an unobserved relationship between an indicator and a target fact. One infers an unobserved target owing to similarity between the indicator and something else. For example, inferring the self because of qualities like desire. Desire and other psychological states are qualities, and qualities are located in substances. And the substance which serves as their location is a self. (*Commentary* 1.1.5)

In this argument, ordinary qualities such as "round" or "red" are the *something else* that is similar to the indicators. Properties of this sort must be instantiated in property bearers, things that are round or red. Insofar as desire and the rest are also qualities or properties, they, too, must be instantiated in a relevant sort of substance. "Self" here almost functions as a placeholder for whatever that substance must be. There is an implicit eliminative premise: no other type of substance could fulfill this role.[33] This seems to be the straightforward reading of the sūtra's argument, supported by the fact that the earlier *Vaiśeṣika-sūtra* offers a similar argument to this end, including phenomena such as the blinking of eyes as further indicators of a self (*VS* 3.2.4).

This might work well enough for those interested in distinguishing between brute matter and living, "ensouled" bodies. But in light of Buddhist arguments, it is arguably question-begging. Buddhists typically embrace trope metaphysics. There are only

[33] A significant amount of *NyS* Chapter 3 serves to carry out this argument from elimination.

properties, with no need for property bearers. Against this background, we can see Vātsyāyana's creative innovation within the *Commentary*. He offers a more sophisticated gloss of the sūtra, centered on the notion of synthetic cognition or recognition (*pratisaṃdhāna*), serving to counter Buddhist reductionism.

Vātsyāyana argues that each of the psychological states listed in the sūtra "is generated by a cognition that unifies the experiences of a single perceiver of multiple objects." *Desire* is generated when one sees an object and remembers that it is of a type that brought pleasure in the past. Likewise for *aversion* and painful things. Recollection of pleasure and pain are conjoined with current cognition as individuals engage in *effort*, performing various goal-directed activities. With respect to *cognition*, someone who comes to know something through deliberation engages with a question for a period of time, finally achieving knowledge as the result of various inputs and reflections strung together over time. As the self is an enduring substance that locates cognitive states, it makes possible synthetic cognition of this kind. Vātsyāyana argues that "This could not occur if a person were nothing more than a series of distinct cognitions, each restricted to its own objects, like different embodied beings."

A feature of Nyāya arguments that has been an object of curiosity for Western scholars is the requirement of an example of inductive support (discussed at length under 1.1.32–29).[34] As seen here, the example *different embodied beings* serves as a non-question-begging instance that the interlocutor, "one who denies the self," would accept. To argue that "selves co-locate diverse experiences, so there must be a self" is obviously circular reasoning. But it is uncontroversial that different people—that is, different embodied individuals—do not have synthetic cognition of others' experiences. Vātsyāyana leverages this to make his point:

[34] Chakrabarti (1999, xii–xv, 8–12) speaks of this principle as the "general acceptability of inductive examples" and offers various illustrations of its use.

> Those who deny the self do accept that for different embodied beings, distinct cognitions—each restricted to their own contents—would not be recollected. But (on their account), the same should hold for distinct cognitions belonging to a single embodied being. There is no relevant distinction between the two cases. It is a commonplace that someone recollects something that she saw originally . . . and, for multiple beings, one person does not recollect what was seen by another. Someone who denies the self has no resources to account for either of these cases.[35]

Everyone agrees that one person does not recollect another's experiences. For a Buddhist flux theorist, this amounts to the notion that no fleeting cognition from person-stream A engages in recollection of content from person-stream B. Vātsyāyana argues that a flux theorist has no account for why the same should not hold with respect to a single stream. On the no-self theory, there is nothing more than individual momentary cognitive events, each restricted to its own content. In a single stream, that c_2 could incorporate the content of c_1, and so on, would require something that bridges the two together, permitting diachronic synthesis. Vātsyāyana's argument also puts pressure on Buddhist philosophers to address what we could call the issue of demarcation, noting that an enduring substantial self not only accounts for synthetic cognition but also provides a metaphysical basis for the boundaries between knowers, such that person A does not recollect B's experiences. Individuals engage in complicated causal interactions with other individuals. And yet the metaphysical boundaries between them remain fixed. Vātsyāyana here plants the seeds for later Nyāya criticisms that causal continuities between time slices are not enough to preserve personal identity.[36]

[35] The two cases being that an individual (i) only recollects what they have formerly experienced and (ii) never recollects another's experiences.

[36] Buddhist philosophers offer various responses that try to account for the phenomena without conceding a self. The core of their case is that causal connections between cognitive events are enough to bridge the mnemonic gap between them.

The conclusion of Vātsyāyana's augmented reading of sūtra 1.1.10 is that a substratum of psychological properties is ineliminable in light of synthetic cognition. And Nyāya's self is, therefore, an enduring nonphysical psychological substance that is the locus of cognitive and affective states, allowing them to be synthesized. On what we could call a surface level, the self and its countless, interconnected psychological properties constitute the empirical person. On a deeper level, by unearthing and identifying with the deep self alone, one may achieve the highest good (1.1.22). Nyāya's metaphysics of self is thus dualist. The self is irreducibly psychological and nonmaterial. But it is an interactionist dualism, where the self is necessary but insufficient for personhood in a robust sense. A self must be conjoined with a complex of body/senses/*manas* to undergo experience and engage in the activities that constitute personhood. These other faculties are defined immediately below.

The analysis of body (1.1.11) hints at the complexity of Nyāya's dualism. While the self is ultimately the true agent of actions and experiencer of pleasure, pain, and the rest, the body is the "shelter" or "seat" (*āśraya*) of pleasure, pain, and bodily movements. And, as will be discussed under 1.1.22, without being tethered to a body/*manas* complex, a self cannot do anything at all.

Following sūtra 1.1.12, Vātsyāyana argues that the senses are "elemental," constructed out of the basic elements earth, water, fire, air, and ether. This, he argues, is why they are each restricted to distinct contents, in accord with a widely held ancient notion that "like apprehends like."[37]

"Personhood" is then reduced to a particular stream of momentary cognitive events that have an intimate causal connection with each other. In response, Naiyāyikas will argue that the proposed solutions are either too weak to account for the phenomena ("If a causal connection is all that is necessary, why doesn't a baby remember its mother's memories?") or so strong that they effectively concede there is a self by another name. These dialectics culminate in Udayana's monograph *Determining the Nature of the Self* (c. 1000 CE).

[37] See 3.1.61–72.

Sūtra 1.1.15 does not directly define *buddhi* ("cognition") but claims that the term is equivalent to the terms *upalabdhi* and *jñāna*. The background here is a dispute with Sāṃkhya, a fellow Vedic school (rather, a family of schools) typically seen as a sister tradition to Yoga. Sāṃkhya is well known for an account of the manifest world as a transformation of primordial matter. When fully articulated, such matter unfolds into a discrete number of identifiable reals. Identifying and analyzing these reals is the metaphysical project of Sāṃkhya. But Sāṃkhya is also famous for its psychology, arguing that a self is enshrouded by an "inner organ" consisting of *manas* (also accepted by Nyāya, as seen in 1.1.16), "ego" (*ahaṃkāra*), a sort of ontic glue that binds a self to the inner organ; and *buddhi*, an insentient psychological instrument that, in effect, takes on many of the capacities that Nyāya assigns to the self. The true self, according to Sāṃkhya, is a pellucid locus of pure consciousness and nothing more.

Sāṃkhya's dualism is radical and uncompromising. Change of any kind belongs to "matter." Any propositional awareness, affective state, or other sorts of changing properties that seem to belong to the self actually belong to a faculty such as *manas* or *buddhi*, subtle forms of matter, which somehow "reflect" the self's pure consciousness. This final point is the disagreement that animates Vātsyāyana's comments on this sūtra. While accepting the *manas*, Nyāya rejects that there are separate faculties of *buddhi* and *ahaṃkāra*. Nyāya's self is a locus of various properties, as illustrated under 1.1.10. The proper meaning of the word *buddhi* as seen here is just "cognition" and nothing more. It is a property belonging directly to a self. And *ahaṃkāra* simply means a special sort of error, one that involves one's own self-conception (4.2.1). Anticipating arguments developed in much more detail under 3.2.1–9, Vātsyāyana contends that the Sāṃkhya notion of *buddhi* is untenable: it is impossible to bifurcate consciousness and cognition. By assigning propositional awareness to *buddhi*, an insentient instrument, Sāṃkhya would require something insentient to be sentient—an absurdity.

Sūtra 1.1.16 addresses the *manas* directly and makes clear that it is fundamentally a faculty of selective attention. While we are awake, the senses are constantly open to experience. Not only that, but the contents of our memory remain, waiting to be accessed. Despite all of these available data, propositionally structured cognition strikes the mind sequentially. Therefore, there must be a gatekeeper faculty that selects inputs for attention, something besides the senses and the knowing self. Vātsyāyana offers a long list of other phenomena that serve as indicators for the *manas*, including mnemonic retrieval and introspection. Already under 1.1.4, he has argued that insofar as introspection is a special kind of perception, the operative "sense faculty" is the *manas*. Through it, the self perceives its own mental content, just as it sees external content through the five senses. *Manas* is radically different from the other senses, however, in that it is non-elemental and is unrestricted in its content. Later, Vātsyāyana will argue that "there must be an inner sense, an instrument of thinking, capable of targeting any content" (*Commentary* 3.1.16).[38]

Sūtras 1.1.17–21 define purposeful action, vice, rebirth, karmic results, and suffering. These topics concern worldly entanglement, setting the backdrop for liberation, an issue to which Vātsyāyana devotes much attention. Vices such as attachment are "impellers," dispositions that give rise to purposive actions (1.1.18). Such actions generate karmic results, positive and negative, which lead to pleasure and pain, respectively.[39] In either case, however, they tether one to embodiment and rebirth. One continues to pursue pleasurable results while avoiding painful ones, birth after birth (1.1.20). A fundamental change in direction requires an ideational

[38] It is not uncommon for translators to use the English "mind" for *manas*. While I myself have done so on occasion, the rendering is unsatisfactory, since in English, "mind" connotes many features of "self." Given Nyāya's complete distinction between the self (*ātman*) and the *manas*, with the latter being an insentient instrument, I will usually leave *manas* untranslated in this study.

[39] Under 3.1.38, Vātsyāyana glosses *karma* in this sense: "karma, in the form of merit and demerit, serves the purpose of generating experiences for the conscious self."

shift, one that is pessimistic toward the prospect of satisfaction in ordinary, embodied life (1.1.21). Such pessimism is common in the soteriological systems of classical India, as is the notion that philosophical and contemplative therapy can help one overcome suffering.[40] Taken plainly, however, the claim that *everything* is suffering is obviously false. Vātsyāyana will nuance this later in the commentary, arguing that while embodied life certainly offers both pleasure and pain, the two are so intertwined that suffering is unavoidable.[41] A simile is repeated: just as one would entirely reject delicious food mixed with poison, one should turn away from worldly life, which is mixed with suffering.

The highest good, then, is "the complete liberation from suffering." Under 1.1.2, Vātsyāyana told us how liberation takes place in the Nyāya system:

> Knowing the truth removes misunderstandings. Upon their removal, vices depart. When vices depart, then karmic entanglement ceases. When karmic entanglement ceases, rebirth comes to an end. And then, suffering is finished. The complete cessation of suffering is liberation, the highest good.

Though Vātsyāyana identifies liberation with the *Brahman* celebrated in the Upaniṣads, valorizing it as a state "without fear, old age, and death," he devotes much effort to arguing that it is not a positive state of spiritual bliss but rather the permanent absence of pain.[42] Contrasted with the robust view of liberation championed by schools such as Vedānta, and even by the maverick Nyāya philosopher Bhāsarvajñā (c. 950), Vātsyāyana's account is threadbare.

[40] A stark expression of this sentiment is seen in the *Yoga-sūtra*: "For one who can discriminate properly, everything is suffering" (*YS* 2.15). Likewise, the Buddha's first noble truth is that ordinary life is innately a form of suffering.

[41] 4.1.55–57; 4.2.1; 4.2.3.

[42] Under 4.1.63, he compares it to a state of deep sleep insofar as both provide freedom from pleasure and pain.

Indeed, the subcommentator Udayana (c. 1000) mentions a maxim chiding Nyāya, which claims that Gautama (the author of the sūtras) would "rather be born a jackal in the sacred Vṛndā forest" than achieve liberation as described by Nyāya and Vaiśeṣika.

The argument may be schematized as having four major elements (see Figure 2).

Chakrabarti (1983, 169) divides the argument into two portions, *speculative* and *practical.* As I frame them here, arguments A and B are likewise concerned with metaphysics, while C and D are concerned with practical reason. It seems to me that Vātsyāyana's metaphysical arguments are motivated by a sense of philosophical consistency. If a connection with a body/*manas* complex is ordinarily a necessary condition for undergoing experience, the suggestion that a self could undergo experience post-liberation seems like a pious hope. If one is going to go "beyond observed experience" by positing that the liberated state may be pleasurable, the door is open to posit all sorts of things, including the notion that a liberated person has a body and *manas*. To Vātsyāyana, these are patent absurdities.

The arguments about practical reason center on the notion that attachment (*rāga*) generates worldly entanglement and that the object of attachment is immaterial. The immediately preceding sūtras have discussed the way vices lead to purposive action, and they perpetuate karmic entanglement and the cycle of rebirth. Vātsyāyana's position is that the belief that liberation promises eternal joy would engender attachment to such joy, thus perpetuating the very conditions that obstruct liberation. Being attached to a future state of blessedness would thus undercut the very prospect of attaining such a state. We may compare Joseph Butler's famous paradox that being fixated on "self-love," our own happiness, precludes us from acting in ways that are constitutive of happiness. Acts of love and charity make us happy, but if we are motivated to do them in order to become happy, we fail to truly love and hence lose out on such happiness. There seems to be a similar paradox at play here.

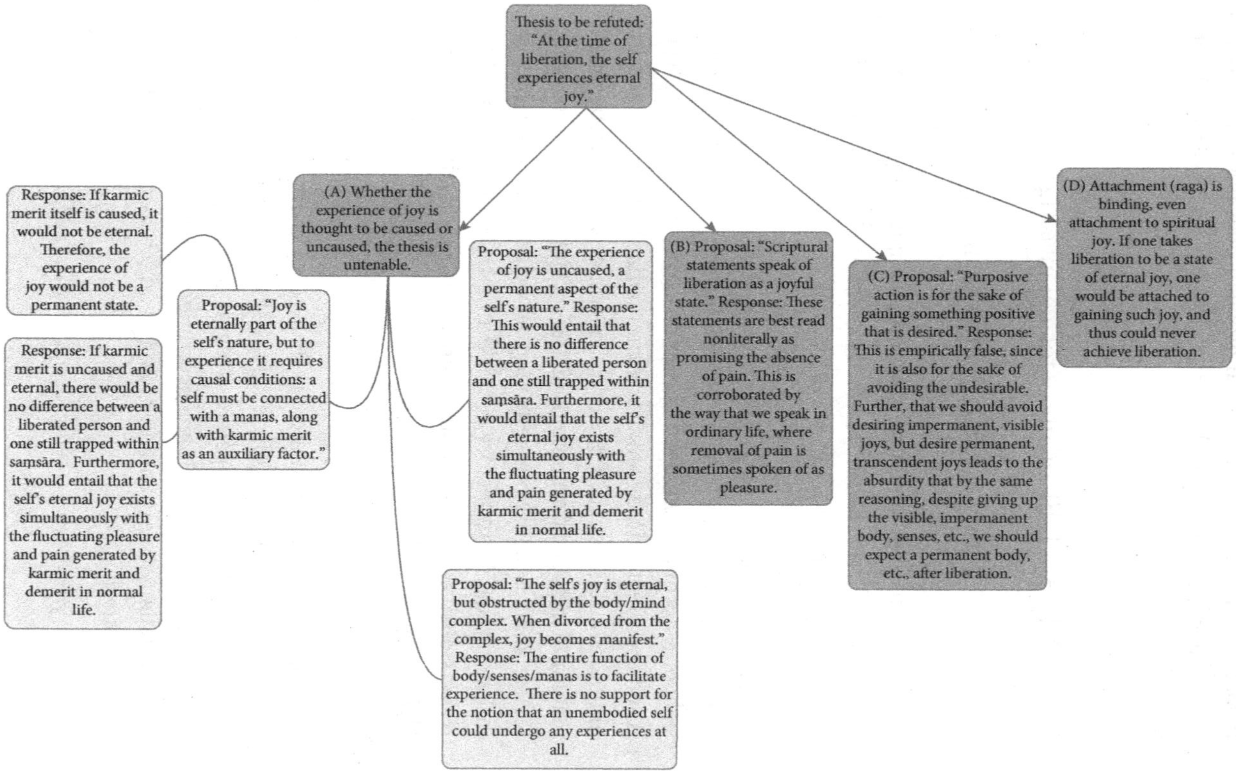

Figure 2. A map of Vātsyāyana's argument about liberation under 1.1.22.

If so, recognizing the motivational problem does not require one to concede the corresponding metaphysical conclusions about liberation.[43]

1.1.23–41: Elements of formal investigation

1.1.23–25: Preliminaries to inquiry

Topics three to five—doubt, motive, and example—are grouped together as preliminaries to inquiry (1.1.23–25), followed by settled theses (1.1.26–31) and, the centerpiece of Nyāya's argumentative machinery, the parts of a proof (1.1.32–39).

Doubt is a catalyst for cognitive review. As a rule, the proper functioning of a knowledge source, without any conscious oversight or reflection, is enough to generate knowledge (1.1.3; 1.1.41). And the correct attitude toward cognition may be called "innocent until reasonable doubt," a position that will be supported by pragmatic and theoretical arguments (2.1.20). Doubt, however, triggers review and self-conscious reflection on evidence. As mentioned in Vātsyāyana's introductory remarks to 1.1.1, doubt is central to Nyāya's distinctness as a system, since it is the starting point for Nyāya's logical and dialectical procedures.

Sūtra 1.1.23 offers five qualifiers for doubt:

> Doubt is a wavering awareness in need of clarification. It is produced (i) from the experience of a shared property, (ii) from the experience of a property belonging to distinct things, (iii) from disagreement, (iv) from uncertainty with respect to positive presentations, and (v) from uncertainty with respect to negative presentations.

[43] See Chakrabarti 1983, 179–181.

Vātsyāyana reads these as five distinct doubt triggers. To waver is to oscillate between options, or at least to recognize multiple, incompatible properties that could apply to a single object or topic. That doubt may arise *from the experience of a shared property* is straightforward, as is the stock example of seeing a something in the distance and being uncertain whether it is a post or a person.

The examples used to illustrate the trigger called *the experience of a property belonging to distinct things* invoke Vaiśeṣika metaphysical categories. For Vaiśeṣika, each element is associated with a distinct type of sense experience (1.1.14): earth with scent, water with taste, fire with visible form, air with touch, and ether with sound. The fact that earth is the locus of scent distinguishes it from other elements but also from other kinds of things, such as actions. The doubtful case that Vātsyāyana cites is that of sound. A distinct feature of sound is that can be produced by disjunction (e.g., breaking a piece of bamboo). But this alone is not enough to tell us the metaphysical category to which sound belongs: substance, property, or action? Until this is resolved, doubt remains, triggered by a property belonging to distinct things. Elsewhere, I offered an archaeological example to explain this doubt trigger.

> An archaeologist could discover a stone tablet with a unique type of script. The script, let us say, distinguishes the makers of the tablet from people in other ancient cultures, but given the uniqueness, doubt would remain about its larger cultural milieu and indeed how to read it. (Dasti and Phillips 2017, 42)

The most important doubt trigger for philosophy is that arising from *disagreement*, "incompatible views" on the same subject. The recent explosion of contemporary work on the epistemology of peer disagreement provides yet another avenue to connect Nyāya to recent developments in analytic epistemology. Vātsyāyana leaves it to later commentators to reflect on what counts as an "epistemic peer," but his example is telling for his philosophical sensibilities:

> One view is "the self exists." Another is "the self does not exist." And it is not possible for genuine existence and nonexistence to hold simultaneously with respect to a single thing.

In this case, the disagreeing parties are clearly philosophically informed, reflecting Nyāya and Buddhist positions on an important issue. Disagreement as such need not be a perpetual cause of doubt; if it were, very few things of importance would ever be believed. But when someone is aware of the disagreement, held by putatively reasonable and informed individuals, doubt, "the non-determination of what is true," remains until they discover a decisive reason that settles the case for them.

Vātsyāyana takes the final two qualifiers in the sūtra as referring to separate triggers for doubt. *Uncertainty with respect to positive presentations* occurs because some positive experiences are known to mislead: "Real water is truly apprehended within things like ponds, and falsely apprehended in mirages." Similarly, in *uncertainty with respect to negative presentations*, the experience of an absence does not always correspond to an absence in reality: "Though real, things like roots, spikes, and water are not experienced (when they are underground). Things that are not real—owing to never occurring or having been—are also not experienced."[44]

[44] We might note that in his subcommentary, Uddyotakara disagrees with this analysis. He argues that the best reading of the sūtra is that the first three qualifications are doubt triggers, while the latter two are tacit conditions that qualify each of them. That is, when any of the first three grounds for doubt are in place and there is uncertainty with respect to positive and negative presentations (which would have immediately settled the issue), doubt arises. He argues that if the fact that positive and negative presentations sometimes mislead us were held to be independent grounds for doubt, then radical skepticism would be inescapable. Although unintended by Vātsyāyana, this does seem to be a consequence of his interpretation. Beyond this, the fourth and fifth triggers already overlap with the first in that they all hinge on shared properties that are not resolved. All of this leads me to favor Uddyotakara's reading.

At first glance, motive (1.1.24) seems oddly placed among the elements of formal investigation. Vātsyāyana explains that motive is something that initiates intentional action, a goal determined to be worth pursuing or avoiding. As such, it might be better situated among the other objects of knowledge that involve action, motivation, and entanglement. Vātsyāyana does not address this question, but his commentary shows again the pragmatic element of Nyāya's epistemological program. I would suggest that motive is placed among the machinery of formal investigation simply because doubt is not always worth following up on. That is, doubt need not trigger cognitive review if the stakes are too low, the issue unimportant. This will be amplified when Vātsyāyana discusses curiosity.

> Why would want to inquire about something that is not properly known? Because he thinks, "I will avoid, pursue, or remain indifferent toward an object known as it is." And thus, the point of knowing something in truth is to avoid, pursue, or be indifferent to it. (*Commentary* 1.1.32)

Indeed, we see that Vātsyāyana paraphrases the sūtra on motive later in the *Commentary*, when explaining why an issue is taken up for investigation.

> Having taken up a certain object, one proceeds. That object is one's motive. (*NyS* 1.1.24)

> Here, the motive is to understand what is apprehended through words. And, having taken up nouns in particular, we investigate them. (*Commentary* 2.2.58)

The next topic is example, "a case about which laypersons and investigators are in agreement" (1.1.25). While they have a special role within the *illustration*, a distinct part of a proof (1.1.36–37), examples generally serve the role that *endoxa* do for Aristotle, as points of consensus that allow disputants enough shared ground to make their arguments.[45] It would be a mistake to think that a layperson's disagreement would necessarily undermine an example accepted by experts. The core point, however, is that there must be significant agreement, enough for disputants to come to consensus about what counts as evidence. We have already seen a telling instance of this under 1.1.10. While Buddhists and Nyāya philosophers tend to approach the world through very different metaphysical orientations, Vātsyāyana takes it as indisputable that one embodied individual cannot recollect events experienced by a separate embodied individual. This is the example that he leverages to argue against the Buddhists.

1.1.26–31: Settled theses

Settled theses (*siddhānta*) are the sixth topic of the sūtras. Paradigmatically, these are the outputs of investigation that serve as major tent poles for a school and provide the backdrop for its response to an issue. To appeal to *siddhānta* is normally to insist on a claim and focus, in accord with a network of interlocking positions that form a system. To the extent that coherence is a normatively binding consideration, we might think of settled theses as gravity wells of coherence, governing legitimate moves within investigation and debate. Sūtra 1.2.1 tells us that truth-oriented debate, the paradigm of philosophical discourse, is conducted in agreement with settled theses. And a reason put forth that contradicts one's own *siddhānta* is considered a fallacy (1.2.6). Finally, it is a recognized defeat condition in adversarial debate to violate the *siddhānta*s one has already accepted (5.2.23).

Without further qualifier, the term *siddhānta* typically means a system-defining position, what is spoken of here as a

[45] *Topics* 1.1.

pratitantra-siddhānta, one set down within a particular system. Vātsyāyana defines a "system" (*tantra*) as "an organized body of knowledge; mutually connected teachings about a collection of topics" (1.1.26). His examples are apt, contrasting the major views of Sāṃkhya (one of the rare instances where he explicitly identifies a specific school of thought by name and not epithet) with those of a group he calls "the Yogas" (1.1.29).

The views attributed to Sāṃkhya neatly match the classical school of the same name, which holds that primordial stuff is never destroyed or created, only transformed, and that individual selves are pellucid, qualitatively identical motes of consciousness. However, the contrasting views being attributed to the "Yogas" are not those held by the classical Yoga school. As a discrete school of thought, "Yoga" typically refers to the ideas associated with the *Yoga-sūtra* of Patañjali (c. 200–400 CE) and its commentaries. The core holdings of the Yoga school are nearly identical to Sāṃkhya's; they are merely two shadings of the same tradition. But the views mentioned by Vātsyāyana as belonging to "Yoga" are mainstream Nyāya-Vaiśeṣika positions in direct opposition to Sāṃkhya, as is illustrated throughout the third chapter of the *NySBh*. It is highly improbable that Vātsyāyana is making a mistake; he is clearly familiar with the Yoga school, quoting Vyāsa's commentary on *Yoga-sūtra* 3.13 in his remarks on *NyS* 1.2.6.[46] There is precedent, however, for the term "Yogas" to refer to Nyāya and Vaiśeṣika philosophers. Discussing those who practice critical reasoning, *ānvīkṣikī*, the *Arthaśāstra* uses the term "Yogas" to refer to Nyāya-Vaiśeṣika philosophers of some sort. Within Jain sources, too, Nyāya-Vaiśeṣika thinkers are also spoken of as "Yogas." In their subcommentaries on this sūtra, classical and medieval Nyāya philosophers therefore consistently interpret Vātsyāyana as speaking of Nyāya or Nyāya-Vaiśeṣika, in

[46] Arguably, Vātsyāyana's notion of God is also influenced by the *Yoga-sūtra*. Compare *NySBh* 4.1.21 with *YS* 1.24–26 with Vyāsa's commentary.

some cases, arguing that *yoga* is derived from *yukti*, "reasoning," a cognate term.[47]

The last two types of settled theses also govern investigation and disputes. But unlike the first two, they center on tracing the entailment relations between claims. A "settled thesis from a primary claim" (1.1.30) is derived from other established views. "When *x* is established, *y* is entailed. It is not possible to establish *x* without *y*. Since *y* serves as *x*'s basis, *y* is a settled thesis from a primary claim." Clearly, this sort of *siddhānta* is akin to a necessary condition. A "settled thesis from a supposition" is exploratory, a hypothesis posited as true for the sake of investigating what follows (1.1.31). Thus, it is related to suppositional reasoning (*tarka*), the eighth topic of the *NySBh*, as will be seen under 1.1.40.

The importance of settled theses illustrates the conservatism of Nyāya and other schools. It is commonly suggested—not without reason—that the classical Indian schools of thought have a built-in conservatism in that each generation of philosophers saw themselves unpacking and defending the core holdings given voice by the wise, sometimes enlightened sages, who composed the sūtra texts. We might consider the place of innovation within this picture. Put otherwise, could *siddhānta*s be revised?

As a historical fact, there are many instances of subcommentators critiquing the work of their predecessors. Already, we have noted Uddyotakara's disagreement with Vātsyāyana about the sūtra on doubt (1.1.23). This is not an isolated instance. When it comes to more fundamental holdings, there are some revolutionaries who remain adherents to the school. Famously, Bhāsarvajñā rejects comparison as a separate knowledge source, in contradiction to the *Nyāya-sūtra* itself, while remaining a Naiyāyika. He also disagrees with Vātsyāyana on the nature of liberation. We also find instances where Vātsyāyana reinterprets sūtras with new meanings that were likely unknown to the author(s) of the *Nyāya-sūtra*, including

[47] See Balcerowicz 2012; Halbfass 1988, 288; Bhattacharya 1974, 42–43.

2.1.19, which sets the agenda for the entirety of later Nyāya epistemology. Here creative interpretation gives voice to new ideas while anachronistically reading them into the older texts.

Beyond all of this, we might think of the most important settled theses as benchmarks for participation in a school. It would be hard to conceive of a Nyāya school that does not defend external-world realism or a nonmaterial, substantival self, but someone who finds themselves in disagreement with these views would likely realize that Nyāya is not a fitting philosophical home.

1.1.32–39: Parts of a proof

The seventh topic of the *Nyāya-sūtra* is the parts of a proof (*avayavas*). This is the same word for *part* used mereologically in relation to the *whole* (*avayavin*) (2.1.33–34). Here it means five distinct parts of a demonstration, concise statements that—when properly linked together—establish a conclusion. This five-part "syllogism" is methodologically the centerpiece of Nyāya, from which the school derives its name (introduction to 1.1.1). While Dignāga is famous for popularizing the notion that there are inferences "for oneself" and "for another," the latter consisting in verbalized arguments, we see a similar distinction in the much earlier *Nyāya-sūtra*. Under 1.1.5, inference is discussed as a cognitive process that generates knowledge for an individual. In this section, inference is set within an argument (*vākya*, *nyāya*), where each part plays a role in leading another person through a process of reasoning terminating in a conclusion.

Vātsyāyana notes that "certain Naiyāyikas" identify ten parts of a proof, including curiosity, doubt, ascertainment of capacity, motive, and removal of doubt as well as the five parts discussed here. Whom exactly he is speaking of is unclear. In Indian philosophy broadly, *naiyāyika* typically refers to a member of the Nyāya school. But in Vātyāyana's backward-looking usage, it likely means "logician" in a general sense, consistent with a number of possibilities, including Jain or Sāṃkhya philosophers.[48] We have already noted that the *Nyāya-sūtra* marks a step forward from the somewhat heterogeneous lists of logical and dialectical categories found in earlier works. With respect to the five extra parts considered here, Vātsyāyana agrees that they are connected to investigation and debate. Indeed, doubt and motive are categories three and four within Nyāya's list of sixteen and are grouped among the "preliminaries to investigation" already laid out. But since they are not directly involved in proving something, he remarks that they are accessories or background factors.

Throughout his analysis, Vātsyāyana employs an example argument about the metaphysics of sound. This was one of a number of stock examples found in ancient debate manuals.[49] The nature of a repeatable sound or word like "cow" was a point of contention between Nyāya-Vaiśeṣika and Mīmāṃsā. Nyāya-Vaiśeṣika holds that words like "cow" are ephemeral utterances, conventionally bound to certain meanings. Mīmāṃsā holds that words are *nitya*, "constant" or "fixed." Multiple utterances are not so much new instances of the term but are manifestations of something that is singular and repeatable, invariably tied to a certain meaning.[50]

Because the reason or "prover" can function in two ways, through similarity or dissimilarity, Vātsyāyana offers two formulations of a standard proof. (See Table 4.)

Vātsyāyana remarks that the parts of an argument function interdependently in a proof, and each subsumes a specific knowledge source (1.1.39; 1.1.1). The proposition subsumes testimony,

[48] Dasgupta (1922, 280) suggests that Vātsyāyana is referring to Jain ten-part arguments as found in Bhadrabāhu's *Daśavaikālika-niryukti* (c. fourth century BCE). Ram (1958, 16) rejects Dasgupta's suggestion, as the components of the ten-part arguments mentioned by Bhadrabāhu differ from the those given by Vātsyāyana here. Ram suggests that it is rather a Sāṃkhya account, as preserved in the *Yuktidīpikā* commentary on the *Sāṃkhya-kārikā*, which is indeed a closer fit.

[49] It is thus also found in the *NyS* discussion of dialectical rejoinders in the Fifth Chapter.

[50] See 2.2.13–39.

Table 4. The parts of an argument.

Part	Argument by similarity	Argument by dissimilarity
proposition:	sound is impermanent	sound is impermanent
reason:	since it is produced	since it is produced
illustration: (implicit entailment relation)	an earthenware pot (*if produced, then impermanent*)	a self (*if unproduced, then permanent*)
application:	sound is like that	sound is unlike that
conclusion:	sound is impermanent	sound is impermanent

the reason subsumes inference, the illustration subsumes perception, and the application subsumes comparison. The conclusion illustrates how they all effectively come together to prove something. This one-to-one correspondence between sources and parts is a bit overstated, perhaps a case of Vātsyāyana's being attracted to a certain symmetry. The proposition is not, for example, a true instance of testimony; if it were, then the case would be settled upon hearing it. Conceding this, he suggests that the proposition differs from ordinary testimony by being a statement of plausibility. This is something other than the knowledge source testimony as described earlier.

As a declarative sentence with a particular content, there is little difference between the proposition and the conclusion. Contextually, though, the proposition sets an agenda by identifying what is to be proven, in the form of a *property that qualifies a property bearer* ("the impermanence of sound") or *a property bearer as qualified by a property* ("sound is impermanent"), while the conclusion restates this as warranted by a legitimate reason and thus proven. The central thread of a proof is the relationship between the reason, illustration, and target fact expressed in the conclusion. Under 1.1.25, it was shown that an example allows disputants to ground their arguments in widely held points of commonality. The relationship between the reason and the illustration is a more precise and developed form of this idea. Here, *being produced* will work only if it is an invariant prover of *impermanence*, the target fact. The illustration provides a noncontroversial example of the co-presence of the reason and the target property. An earthenware pot is both produced and impermanent. Conversely, it provides a noncontroversial example of the co-presence of the absence of the *reason* and the absence of the target property. A self, as understood by Nyāya and the unnamed—likely Mīmāṃsaka—interlocutors in this passage, is unproduced and eternal.

Ganeri (2003) points out that before the *Nyāya-sūtra*, Indian logic was largely a form of case-based reasoning. In Chapter 5, the *Nyāya-sūtra* itself moves away from merely analogical reasoning, but it is Vātsyāyana who consolidates this shift and makes it decisive.[51] In case-based reasoning, to say that the reason functions through similarity or dissimilarity with the example (1.1.34–35), would then call attention to the way in which one leverages the data from a paradigm case to come to judgment about the issue in question. This makes great sense in the context of medical texts such as *Caraka-saṃhitā*, whose portions on methodology and dialectics anticipate the *Nyāya-sūtra*. But Vātsyāyana offers a deeper account of the relationship between the reason and the illustration: a reason is similar to an example *in that the two share a distinct property that reliably indicates the target property.*

> The purpose of the illustration is to make clear the entailment relation between two properties that are co-located. (*Commentary* 1.1.39)

[51] *NyS* 5.1.3 claims that entailment must rest on an objective, universal property.

The entailment relation is what is fundamental; the example simply helps us to acknowledge it in a noncontroversial case. Vātsyāyana explicitly denies that similarity or dissimilarity as such is adequate (1.1.39).[52] He is here a transitional figure, as Ganeri (2003, 37) notes, "largely responsible for shaping the direction Indian logic was later to take," from case-based reasoning to a "rule-governed account," and setting the stage for the logical revolutions of Dignāga.

In the current example, the entailment relation is between *being produced* and *being impermanent*. An earthenware pot is impermanent precisely because it is produced. Built up through the contingent conjunctions of smaller parts, it is subject to the eventual disunion of those parts in due course. A reason that functions through dissimilarity trades on the absence of the reason correlating with the absence of the target property.[53] Selves are eternal precisely because they not produced. They are metaphysically simple and cannot be broken apart. Unlike later thinkers, Vātsyāyana does not use the term *vyāpti* ("pervasion") for the entailment relation.[54] He uses the general phrase *sādhya-sādhana-bhāva*, "relationship of prover and proved."

Vātsyāyana seems to have a pet project of cleaning up the practice of appealing to examples without proper supporting argumentation. Throughout the *Commentary*, he chides those

[52] Vātsyāyana's focus on an entailment relation as opposed to mere resemblance or analogical thinking is diffused throughout several discussions in the *Commentary*. Besides this current section, see 1.2.5–6; 2.2.2–4; 5.1.2–5.

[53] When contrasting "similarity" and "dissimilarity," Vātsyāyana does not employ contraposition (as becomes standard after Dignāga). As noted by Gillon (2010), he rather employs obversion. *Everything produced is impermanent* would be obverted as *everything that is not produced is permanent*. This led Matilal (1977, 81) to claim that Vātsyāyana "mis-states the contrapositive of the inferential relation." While Vātsyāyana is operating in an early stage of logical analysis in India, prior to the revolutions of Dignāga and those who followed him, I think that what is happening here is more subtle than a mere logical mistake. I discuss this at length in Appendix C.

[54] If every instance of *H* is an instance of *S*, then *H-hood* would be "pervaded by" *S-hood*, making *H* a suitable reason or prover for *S*. While he does not use the term "pervasion" for an entailment relation, under 1.2.5, Vātsyāyana does invoke the notion while addressing fallacies.

thinkers who deploy examples carelessly by expecting them to be probative without properly tying them to decisive reasons.[55] "An example disconnected from a legitimate reason proves nothing" (2.2.43).

The final two parts of a proof—application and conclusion—restate the subject of the proof (sound) as invested with a legitimate reason (sound is *produced* which entails *impermanence*) and, thus, the target fact (sound is *impermanent*). From a logical perspective, the application and conclusion seem superfluous, vestiges of the period in Indian philosophy when logic and dialectics were not sufficiently distinguished. Many logicians contemporary with or after Vātsyāyana did argue for their irrelevance or simply ignored them, offering only the first three parts when making a demonstration.

Throughout its history, Western scholarship on Indian logic has applied different models to make sense of "the Indian syllogism." Early scholars attempted to frame it as akin to an Aristotelian categorical syllogism, while others, after the logical innovations of the early twentieth century, saw it as a straightforward proof employing rules like substitution.[56] Although contemporary scholars sometimes employ language from categorical logic (e.g., calling the *hetu* the "middle term") or use propositional logic to express some of its elements (e.g., glossing the entailment relation as a conditional "if *p*, then *q*"), the trend is to understand the five-step *nyāya* in its own terms. As a general principle, we may note that an important distinction between the five-step argument of the *NySBh* and logic as taught in a modern classroom is that the former does not make an absolute distinction between content and form. Put differently, Nyāya's is a material logic and not a formal logic.

[55] *NySBh* 2.1.19–20; 2.1.36; 2.1.41; 2.2.43; 3.1.19; 3.2.9; 3.2.17; 5.1.1–3.

[56] See Ganeri 2001b for several of the most influential scholarly interpretations of the five-step syllogism.

1.1.40–41: Supplements to inquiry

The final two topics taken up in *NySBh* Chapter 1, Part 1, are suppositional reasoning and certainty, the eighth and ninth of the list of sixteen. The term translated as "suppositional reasoning" is *tarka*, which often simply means "argument" or "debate" as far back as the *Kaṭha Upaniṣad*, where Naciketas is told that the mystery he wants to know "cannot be reached through argument [*tarka*]" (2.9). Here the word has a more restricted sense, a type of reasoning that assists the *pramāṇa*s by tracing out entailments of candidate beliefs and evaluating them on grounds of coherence. Those that fail the test fall prey to reductio ad absurdum, infinite regress, and other unacceptable consequences. *Tarka* does not generate knowledge directly but rather provides the grounds to approve or disapprove of putative deliverances of the *pramāṇa*s.

In sūtra 1.1.40, suppositional reasoning is cast as deliberation over competing, contradictory responses to a specific question. Vātsyāyana has already offered an example in his commentary on 1.1.1, regarding rebirth and whether it is due to external causes or has no cause. By suppositional reasoning, he concludes that the view that rebirth has no cause is untenable. Here, too, we find a metaphysically rich question, whether the individual self, the conscious knower, is created or uncreated. He applies suppositional reasoning as follows: If uncreated, then the self is eternal, both preceding and surviving its current state of embodiment. The self then endures the passage of time and preserves moral responsibility not only in this lifetime but in the karmic consequences that span multiple incarnations. Its endurance also makes sense of an individual's quest to achieve liberation by eliminating the various causes for its continued embodiments. On the other hand, if the self were created, then it would be ephemeral, dependent on the conditions that give rise to its current embodiment. As an ephemeral being, it would not inherit the moral weight of past choices, mediated by karma. It would not endure long enough to suffer the consequences of its own choices. Further, it could not be liberated, as it would not survive the dismantling of the material conditions upon which it depended. Given these considerations, the proposal that the self is created fails the test of coherence and is rejected through *tarka*.

Tarka is explained as careful, self-conscious deliberation, but this is not always the case. Vātsyāyana uses suppositional reasoning in his introduction to 1.1.1 while elucidating how we may know of absences. He offers a general perceptual explanation that when we fail to see something in clear light that should be visible, we know it is absent. An example might help. Looking into a small room, I do not see any horses. I have the background *tarka* in place: "If there were a horse here, I'd see it. But I do not." Thus, perception, aided by suppositional reasoning, informs me that there is no horse in the room.

The fact that *tarka* can deliver error-removing judgments and still does not count as a full-fledged knowledge source has more to do with what is expected from a *pramāṇa* than any deficiencies of suppositional reasoning. I would suggest that it is because it eliminates candidate beliefs through negative coherence that Vātsyāyana denies that it is a full-fledged knowledge source. Each of the four knowledge sources tells us something positive in the form of a property bearer qualified by a property. Perception informs us that a pot is brown. Or that *that* is a pot. Inference informs us that *that* hill has a fire on it, since it has billowing smoke above it. Comparison says that *that* animal, which is like a cow, is what "water buffalo" refers to. Testimony, in the form of my friend's knowledgeable statement, informs me that *that* person is the famous Devadatta, whom I've never seen before. But suppositional reasoning only tells us what is out of bounds, sifting out dubious proposals from the true deliverances of the *pramāṇa*s. Vātsyāyana therefore says "*tarka* does not settle an issue, nor give definite knowledge, nor certainty" of something's positive nature. From a historical vantage, *tarka* finds parallels with the Socratic *elenchus* in that it serves to discredit claims or views that fall prey to inconsistency and other flaws. While its outputs are "negative," it still supports positive views by clearing the road of obstructions.[57]

Tarka joins memory in playing a crucial role in our cognitive lives without technically being a *pramāṇa*, since it does not fulfill a technical requirement.[58]

Certainty (*nirṇaya*) is the final topic of this part of the *Nyāya-sūtra*. It is the culminating purpose of inquiry. Certainty is akin to what a contemporary philosopher would call high-grade positive epistemic status. Sūtra 1.1.41 says that certainty follows deliberation upon both sides of a disputed issue. The two sides spoken of here are a "thesis" and a "counterthesis." Vātsyāyana notes that this simply means that in the course of establishing their own view, someone will naturally rebut a relevant contrary position. If the latter were an open possibility, doubt would remain.

Vātsyāyana's remarks at the end of his commentary reinforce that Nyāya's epistemology is reliabilist in orientation. Although the sūtra suggests that *nirṇaya* follows from deliberation and the careful weighing of evidence associated with methodical investigation, Vātsyāyana notes that it could be produced simply by perceptual experience. This position makes explicit that the basic unreflective functioning of a *pramāṇa* is enough to generate high-grade positive epistemic status. It is also consistent with his earlier remark (under 1.1.7) that animals use *pramāṇa*s.

Coupled with the notion of doubt as a review trigger, this suggests a two-tiered epistemology for Vātsyāyana. On the ground level, it is akin to reliabilism. A *pramāṇa* generates knowledge simply by its proper functioning. When legitimate doubt arises and

[57] See *Gorgias* 527b, where Socrates appeals to the *elenchus* as supporting his core moral principles by illustrating that contrary positions consistently fall apart under scrutiny.

[58] Memory is left out because it is preservative, not generative; it keeps record of deliverances of the *pramāṇa*s (and other things such as imagination). Still, "For living beings, all conduct takes place under the guidance of memory" (*Commentary* 3.1.14).

the topic is important enough to generate requisite motive, an individual then shifts to self-conscious reasoning or dispute with an interlocutor. As already noted under suppositional reasoning and settled theses (and will be discussed further under 2.1.16–20), on this second level, centered on what we may call the certification of doubted cognition, coherence becomes a major criterion.[59]

Part 2 (1.2.1–20)

Each chapter of the *Nyāya-sūtra* is divided into two parts called "daily lessons." Here, in the second daily lesson, the definitions of the sixteen topics are completed, focusing on dialectics and debate theory.

1.2.1–3: Types of debate

Three types of debate are topics ten through twelve. The first type is truth-directed debate (*vāda*). In early literature, *vāda* or *saṃvāda* often just mean "debate," which is why a general word for debate manuals is *vāda-śāstra*. Here it is a distinct modality of debate.

We might distinguish truth-directed debate from the others in two ways, according to motivation and structure. With respect to motivation, the goal is truth. One debates with like-minded friends and teachers in a collaborative, constructive spirit and with a willingness to be corrected (4.2.47–49). It is therefore the paradigm of legitimate intellectual inquiry, "an ideal of fair-minded and respectful discourse."[60] Structurally, *vāda* incorporates the logical categories discussed in the first half of the chapter while disavowing

[59] See Phillips 2012, Chapter 2, for an exploration of this two-tiered epistemology of the *Nyāya-sūtra*.
[60] Ganeri 2003, 34.

equivocation and dialectical rejoinders, tricks, and fallacies employed for the sake of rhetorical victory. Furthermore, as truth is the goal, not victory, defeat conditions are largely irrelevant. Vātsyāyana does clarify that some defeat conditions involve use of fallacies or faulty structure within a demonstrative proof. These are still operative in the sense that use of the truth-obscuring practices they prohibit would still undermine one's case in truth-directed debate.

The second type of debate, disputation (*jalpa*), is also distinguished along similar lines. Motivationally, the goal is victory. Commenting on 4.2.51, Vātsyāyana notes that it "is motivated by a desire to win, not to know the truth." One seeks to win and leverage any resources available for that purpose. Therefore, structurally, it employs the truth-conducive resources found in *vāda* along with equivocation and dialectical rejoinders. And because of its competitive nature, it permits use of defeat conditions, which provide rules for what is ultimately a contest. Overall, the *Nyāya-sūtra* seems to have an ambivalent position on disputation. As defined, it lacks the integrity of truth-directed debate, but it is not entirely rejected. Even for truth seekers, it has a use: "defending the truth" against sophistical challengers or others who, for whatever reason, are not fit to be rebutted by truth-conducive methods alone (4.2.50). Perhaps loosely akin to Plato's grudging allowance for rhetoric in the service of philosophy, early Nyāya allows it a space within somewhat narrow boundaries.[61]

The third type of debate is destructive debate (*vitaṇḍā*). As sūtra 1.2.3 tells us, this is simply disputation without the debater advancing any positive thesis of their own. Structurally, its nature is therefore clear. When it comes to motivation, however, its status is a bit murky. We have already seen under 1.1.1 that Vātsyāyana takes the exclusively destructive debater to be akin to a doctrinal skeptic, worthy of contemptuous refutation. As interpreted by him,

[61] *Phaedrus*, 277a–279c.

such a debater seems to think that they can demand answers from others without sharing in the obligations expected for participants in truth-directed debate. The status of *vitaṇḍā* was indeed controversial among Indian thinkers. Those associated with skepticism in some form or another, Nāgārjuna (c. 150 CE) and the Prāsaṅgika Buddhists who follow him, as well as the materialist Jayarāśi (c. 800 CE) and the Vedāntin Śrīharṣa (c. 1150 CE), take it to be a philosophically respectable practice.

1.2.4–9: Counterfeit reasons

Vātsyāyana introduces this section by noting that there are "non-reasons" (*ahetavaḥ*) that misleadingly look like good reasons, things put forth as probative yet fail to establish their target fact. Commonly, these are spoken of as "fallacies" by scholars of Indian philosophy, for good reason. Not every single bad argument involves an identifiable fallacy; we reserve the term for those that are particularly misleading or commonplace. So, too, this section of the sūtras makes note of five specific bad arguments, all called *hetv-ābhāsa* ("semblance of a reason," translatable as "counterfeit reasons," "pseudo-provers," or "fallacious reasons").[62] These five are best seen as a starter pack.[63] Later Naiyāyikas will reinterpret them, replace some with others thought more important, and situate them within an increasingly precise logical vocabulary.[64] Vātsyāyana's project is not revisionist; he seeks merely to explain why each of these counterfeit reasons is fallacious.

The *deviant* (*savyabhicāra*) is in many ways the most fundamental of the counterfeit reasons (1.2.5). As seen above, a true

[62] I owe the phrase "counterfeit reason" to Malcolm Keating.

[63] The *Nyāya-sūtra* and the *Commentary* recognize other counterfeit reasons besides these five. *NyS* 2.2.35 mentions *anapadeśa*, "unfounded," a precursor to what will later be called *asiddha*, "unestablished." *Anapadeśa* is defined in *VS* 3.1.7.

[64] See Joshi 1965.

reason has an entailment relation with its target fact. A deviant reason, however, is "nonexclusive" in that it fails this test of invariance. Continuing the debate over the metaphysics of sound, Vātsyāyana remarks that *being intangible* fails to prove the eternality of sound, since we have counterexamples such as cognition, which is intangible yet impermanent.

The *contradictory* (*viruddha*) involves self-contradiction in a broad sense (1.2.6). That it is a counterfeit reason illustrates the connection between settled theses and argumentation. Narrow self-contradiction would be when a reason contradicts the very conclusion an arguer is trying to prove. Following the sūtra, Vātsyāyana understands the *contradictory* in a wider sense, as contradicting or undercutting the fundamental tenets that motivate the arguer's position. Like many fallacies recognized in contemporary discourse (e.g., circular reasoning), the fault here is not exactly logical as much as dialectical.

The examples Vātsyāyana cites are taken directly from Vyāsa's *Yoga-sūtra* commentary (c. fifth century CE).[65] The Sāṃkhya metaphysics presupposed by the *Yoga-sūtra* holds that material objects are not created or destroyed. They are rather eternal realities that exist inherently within eternal primordial matter and can be either "manifest" or "unmanifest." Any current manifestation is simply a *modification* of primordial mater. This approach is called *satkāryavāda*, the "doctrine of the preexistence of the effect."[66] Vātsyāyana and other Naiyāyikas who follow him reject this view and identify the notion of *manifestation* (*vyakti*) as a weak spot. The Sāṃkhya adherent argues here that any specific modification of primordial matter (for example, a clay pot that is currently manifest) eventually becomes unmanifest, "since its being eternal is denied." This, however, contradicts the core thesis that these objects

[65] *Yoga-sūtra-bhāṣya* 3.13. Vātsyāyana substitutes the term "modification" (*vikāra*) for "the three worlds" (*trailokya*) found in the *Yoga-sūtra-bhāṣya*.
[66] See 3.2.15–17 for further discussion of *satkāryavāda*.

exist, both pre- and post-manifestation, within the matrix of primordial matter: "'Existence' and 'going out of being' are contrary properties that cannot simultaneously obtain. Thus, the reason advanced, having come under the aegis of a settled thesis, contradicts that very thesis."

The counterfeit reason called the *inconclusive* (*prakaraṇasama*) is put forth to settle a case between *P* and not-*P* but fails adequately to address the issue, perpetuating the very doubt that motivates the discussion (1.2.7). While it may superficially seem akin to the deviant, Vātsyāyana makes clear that the fundamental difference is that while a deviant reason correlates both with instances of the target fact and instances of its absence, the inconclusive simply fails to adequately address the issue. It thus seems to be akin to the fallacy "irrelevant conclusion." Tellingly, Vātsyāyana's specific example, "Sound is impermanent, since we do not observe it to have the quality of permanence," would be categorized as an "appeal to ignorance" in contemporary dialectics. Appeals to ignorance are inconclusive with respect to what they purport to prove. "That we have not been explicitly contacted by an advanced alien civilization" may be true, but it is inconclusive with respect to the issue of whether such civilizations exist in the universe or not.

The *unproved* is literally *sādhyasama*, "equivalent to the conclusion," where a reason is as dubious as the target fact it is meant to establish (1.2.8). In Vātsyāyana's example, a debater is trying to prove that shadows are, metaphysically, substances. The reason put forth is that they are loci of action. In Nyāya-Vaiśeṣika metaphysics, being the locus of action is a characteristic of substances (*VS* 1.1.14). The problem here is that this reason is as dubious as the conclusion. "What remains to be proven is whether a shadow also moves in the manner of a human being, or rather that it is a continuous sequence of obstructed light." In modern discourse, a faulty reason of this sort is sometimes typed as a subspecies of begging the question. "Abortion is wrong because it is murder" is an example sometimes cited. To equate abortion to murder is to claim something that the opposite side does not accept, and as such, the premise is as dubious as the conclusion it is meant to prove.[67]

The *mistimed* (*kālātīta*) is a peculiar fallacy. The debater here wants to establish that while what we hear seems to be temporary, sound itself is eternal (1.2.9). It's just the *manifestation* of sound that comes and goes. The analogy to color underscores this: even when it is dark, the orange book on my desk is still orange; it just needs light to be manifest. So, too, it is argued with sound: sound is always there in a latent state but is manifest only under specific conditions. The problem with this argument is that sound travels more slowly than light travels from something nearby. As such, we know that one might hear the sound caused by an event that has passed. We don't have the same experience of delay with visible color. This fallacy seems frankly convoluted and restricted when construed in this way.

Nyāya philosophers after Vātsyāyana reinterpret and ultimately replace the mistimed with another counterfeit reason that is loosely related, *bādhita*, "defeated in advance." A reason that is defeated in advance is undermined from the outset by a knowledge source of greater strength. Should I argue that my brother must be in town, since I see his car parked on the street, such a reason would be defeated in advance if the person I am arguing with (on the phone) is standing next to my brother, and looking at him, in another city.

Vātsyāyana's final remarks under 1.2.9 push back against a reading of the mistimed as an improper ordering of the inferential parts. He reminds us that a good reason, even offered at the wrong time, is still a good reason! Beyond this, there is a defeat condition that speaks to the issue of improper ordering (5.2.11), which would make this fallacy redundant.[68]

[67] The sūtras themselves accuse interlocutors of committing this fallacy under 3.2.3 and 3.2.62.

[68] Putting aside Vātsyāyana's remarks here, Kang (2004, 103) speculates that the pre-*NyS* origin of this fallacy is likely that ancient Indian debate was a time-bound "game," where a failure to properly respond at the appropriate time renders a reason otiose.

1.2.10–17: Equivocation

Equivocation (*chala*) is the fourteenth topic of the sūtras. A *chala* is a response that distorts the original speaker's position to dismiss it.

> Equivocation opposes another's argument by misconstruing an alternative meaning. (*NyS* 1.1.10)

In informal logic, the term "equivocation" is not restricted to rebuttals. However, as a teacher of informal logic, I do find it noteworthy that it is not easy to conjure many quick examples of equivocation that seem plausible. Many textbook cases come off as jokes or puns, not something students would encounter in everyday life. Some of the best examples of equivocation in common discourse rather involve taking an opponent's statement out of context to interpret it as saying something foolish or offensive. This makes it easier to score points against them.

Framed as a response to an argument, *chala* thus seems to include elements of the straw man fallacy but hinging on ambiguity. The three types are equivocation "on an expression," "through generality," and "with respect to figurative meaning." For each, Vātsyāyana suggests a response. (See Table 5.)

The final sūtras in this section address the question of reduction. An interlocutor suggests that equivocation with respect to figurative meaning is nothing more than equivocation on an expression. Vātsyāyana concedes that there is some similarity between the two linguistic phenomena—after all, they are both instances of equivocation—but that in the former case, a literal meaning of the term is imputed by the equivocator, while in the latter, an entirely different meaning is construed. We might here suggest that the purpose of this section requires that types of equivocation are individuated for the sake of recognizing them within discourse. This is akin to the way fallacies in contemporary manuals are sorted as "fallacies of relevance," "fallacies of presumption," "logical

Table 5. The three types of equivocation (*chala*).

Type	Example	Suggested response
on an expression (*vāk*)	taking "the boy has a new [*nava*] blanket" to mean "the boy has nine [*nava*] blankets"	1. Demand an account for why the equivocator selected the meaning they allege. 2. Note that statements are rightly interpreted according to what is plausible given ordinary practice.
through generality (*sāmānya*)	exploiting the fact that the word "Brahmin," which suggests *one properly carrying out the duties of a priest*, can also generally mean *anyone born a Brahmin*	Clarify the context of what is being said. Here the context is praising someone by pointing out that their qualities are fitting for a *Brahmin*, not trying to allege that *being a Brahmin* is sufficient for *having good qualities*.
with respect to figurative meaning (*upacāra*)	treating "the stands are shouting" as a literal statement	Make clear the speaker's intention to use secondary meaning.

fallacies," and the like, yet there will always be fallacies that could fit into multiple categories.[69]

1.2.18–20: Dialectical rejoinders and defeat conditions

This section's treatment of dialectical rejoinders (*jāti*) and defeat conditions (*nigraha-sthāna*) is skeletal, to be filled out in *NyS* Chapter 5.

[69] Solomon (1976, 140–144) illustrates that the Nyāya commentarial tradition continued to wrestle with the classification question long after Vātsyāyana.

Dialectical rejoinders are responses by an interlocutor that leverage similarities.

> A *jāti* is a retort based on similarity and dissimilarity. (*NyS* 1.2.18)

In ancient texts on debate, *jāti*s are stock moves to controvert arguments. In the earliest pre-*NyS* strata, they seem to be neutral tools in a debater's arsenal.[70] Like equivocation and other truth-neutral dialectical tricks, these are looked at with increased suspicion and aversion by Nyāya thinkers. Scholarly translations of *jāti* as "misleading" or "futile" rejoinders stress this distrust, treating them as mere sophisms. A more subtle feature of the *NySBh* analysis of rejoinders is that it serves as a study of what does *not* constitute a true entailment relation. This will be discussed further in Chapter 5.

Despite the claim of *NyS* 2.1.18, the rejoinders listed in the fifth chapter do not all fit easily under the banner of similarity or dissimilarity. But they are highlighted likely because the paradigm arguments in sources that precede the *Nyāya-sūtra* function through analogy or case-based reasoning. The counterarguments subsumed under the heading of *jāti* were attempts to counter analogical reasoning, often by appeal to surface-level similarities or connections.[71]

Defeat conditions at core are instances of misunderstanding or failing to understand while debating an interlocutor. They are akin to rules in a sporting competition and do not have a major role to play in truth-directed debate.

[70] Prets 2001.
[71] See Kang 2009, 84–85.

2

Epistemology and Philosophy of Language

Part 1 (2.1.1–68)

Vātsyāyana's scholarly methodology involves three elements: identifying major topics (*uddeśa*), offering definitions or analyses (*lakṣaṇa*), and systematic investigation (*parīkṣā*). The first chapter of the *Nyāya-sūtra* provides a list and definitions of the sixteen major topics. Chapters 2–4 investigate them, defending the composition of the sūtras as well as the ideas contained therein from the attacks of varied challengers.

2.1.1–7: Doubt

This first section, 2.1.1–7, is a rare instance of departure from the order of the sixteen topics. Doubt is the third, after knowledge sources and objects of knowledge. It is, however, investigated first. Vātsyāyana justifies this deviation by noting that critical investigation, in both scholarly treatises like the *Nyāya-sūtra* and in public debates, presupposes doubt (2.1.1; 2.1.7). The objections in this section are little more than pedantic critiques of the phrasing of sūtra 1.1.23, which defines doubt. They have little philosophical value. It is noteworthy, however, that the opponent identifies "limitless doubt" as an undesirable outcome should the doubt triggers of 1.1.23 be defined too generously. Vātsyāyana shares this concern but argues that following the sūtra on doubt does not lead to

Vātsyāyana's Commentary *on the* Nyāya-sūtra. Matthew R. Dasti, Oxford University Press.
 DOI: 10.1093/oso/9780197625927.003.0002

such an outcome. Sūtra 2.1.7 is also noteworthy for underscoring that doubt removes default trust in apparently true cognition, demanding a more critical and reflective level of inquiry.

2.1.8–20 Skeptical challenges to *pramāṇa*-theoretic epistemology

This section of the sūtras gives voice to skeptics who pose multiple challenges to *pramāṇa* epistemology. We may divide it into two major subsections: the argument of the three times (2.1.8–16) and the problem of justificatory regress (2.1.17–20). These naturally flow together, and the division is rough.

The argument of the three times alleges that knowledge sources are not authoritative, since they are not properly grounded with respect to their objects in any of the three times, past, present, and future. The term for "authoritative" (*prāmāṇya*) is derived from the term *pramāṇa* itself. In some contexts, *prāmāṇya* can be translated as "justified," "warranted," or "entitled," as used in contemporary epistemology. Some scholars translate it as "valid" in a non-formal sense.

The crux of the argument is that knowledge sources are ineffective whether they are taken to be prior to, posterior to, or concurrent with their objects. The options are presented as exhaustive: if *pramāṇas* exist wholly before their objects, then there could be no perception (as it operates in the present moment only). If they exist wholly after, then it would not be possible for the *pramāṇa* to uniquely inform us of the object, which is already a given. If they exist wholly concurrently, then the content of knowledge sources would be discharged entirely in the present moment, and the typical succession of cognitive events we experience over time would not occur. This last charge is somewhat obscure. Departing from Vātsyāyana's explanation, my sense is that the way we might learn about an object over time would be impossible. A chain of cognitions such as "This flower is white," "It has a particular scent," and "It has a distinctly rough texture underneath each petal" would have to be discharged in the present moment, flooding our awareness with countless cognitions at once (2.1.11).

The interlocutor is not identified in the sūtras or in the *Commentary*. Interestingly, the argument pattern is identified within Chapter 5 as a stock dialectical rejoinder (5.1.18–20). As presented there, it is a topic-neutral sophism employed by a debater to undermine any sort of argument. Tucci (1929, xxvii) shows that this rejoinder, *being a non-reason (in the three times)*, was cataloged within ancient Buddhist debate manuals as a stratagem to controvert opposed views.[1] In his subcommentary on this section, Vācaspati suggests that the current interlocutor is a Madhyamaka Buddhist (*NyVT* 2.1.8). Without offering a name or label, Vātsyāyana does frame the criticisms as if they were coming from a Madhyamaka source, identifying uses of relational paradoxes and, arguably, equivocation that bring to mind Nāgārjuna's destructive dialectic. If we take the interlocutor of this entire section to represent a single school or position, the fact that the criticisms advanced in 2.1.17–19 are practically identical to those advanced by Nāgārjuna in the *Vigraha-vyāvartanī* strengthens the case.[2]

[1] Prets (2003, 277) speculates that in early texts, dialectical tropes of this sort were employed by Buddhists to undermine Brahmanical doctrines like that of the self.

[2] *VV* 31–51, translated in Westerhoff 2010, 30–35. (Similar arguments are also found in *Vaidalyaprakaraṇa*, an anti-Nyāya work sometimes attributed to Nāgārjuna.) The direction of influence is unclear, however, since both *NyS* 2.1.17–20 and passages in the *VV* seem to presuppose each other. Matilal (1977, 78), Bhattacharya (1977, 273), and others suggest mutual influence between the two texts. Given that various portions of the *Nyāya-sūtra* may have existed piecemeal before taking the form of the five-chapter volume commented upon by Vātsyāyana, there are various ways such mutual influence could have occurred. Bronkhorst (1985, 107–132) argues for an alternative thesis, that *Nyāya-sūtra* 2.1.8–11 was originally influenced by Sarvāstivāda Buddhism. He argues that the *Nyāya-sūtras* precede Nāgārjuna, were likely known to him in a form that is approximately similar to that known to us, and were the target of his refutations. He contends that much later, Vātsyāyana interprets these sūtras as being responses to Nāgārjuna's attacks and does so with such skill that it has convinced almost every classical and modern scholar. Bronkhorst's interpretation requires us to interpret "objects of knowledge" in 2.1.8–11 as referring only to mental states, however, a matter that could be disputed.

The argument of the three times provides a context for Vātsyāyana to make explicit his method of epistemological theorizing. Fundamentally, Vātsyāyana endorses something akin to Ernest Sosa's (1980, 4) notion of *particularism*: We do not start by venturing a priori determinations of the specific relationships between knowledge sources and their objects (e.g., that they are "prior to" their objects). Rather, we start by identifying instances of cognitive success and their causes, *pramāṇa* tokens, and then determine their nature by reflection upon experience. On this basis, theorists may further elaborate distinct analyses of knowledge sources, their objects, and how the two relate.

With this methodology in the background, Vātsyāyana diagnoses the argument of the three times as trading on the use of terms like *pramāṇa* in a general, uncontextualized manner. To motivate this point, he appeals to ordinary linguistic practice: naming terms are rightly applied when certain grounds or conditions hold. The basic meaning of the word *pramāṇa* is "cause of knowledge." We find that grounds for its application span the three times: "She knew," "She knows," "She will know." Likewise for *prameya*, "object of knowledge": "It was known," "It is known," "It will be known." The objection of the three times is, therefore, mere sophistry. It is akin to rebuking as absurd the phrase "Bring the cook, so he can make dinner," on the grounds that he cannot be a "cook" before he starts cooking.

The above is Vātsyāyana's own reasoning under 2.1.11. Between 2.1.12 and 2.1.15, the *Nyāya-sūtra*'s response is to charge the interlocutor with self-refutation and to cite counterexamples that illustrate the way knowledge bridges temporal divisions. As unpacked by Vātsyāyana, I count three major arguments.

1. The three times redirected (2.1.12): The dialectic of the three times could be employed with respect to "refutation" and "refuted," rendering any refutation impossible or otiose.[3]

[3] 5.1.18–20 offers a similar rebuttal.

2. Self-refutation (2.1.13–14): If the interlocutor takes themselves to be making an argument for their view, it would be based on the reason "since knowledge sources are unestablished in each of the three times." As discussed under 1.1.32–39, a well-formed argument must include an illustration. An illustration is an uncontroversial example, backed by common experience, showing that the reason is probative. If the "reason" here is taken to be effective, however, perception would be unauthoritative and the example unfounded. "Since knowledge sources are unestablished in each of the three times" would then be self-refuting, an instance of the counterfeit reason known as "the contradictory."
3. Appeal to counterexamples (2.1.15): it is uncontroversial that we can hear an instrument and afterward infer what it is. This is an instance of a "posterior" knowledge source, amplifying Vātsyāyana's comments on 2.1.11 above.

Under 2.1.16, Vātsyāyana develops the notion that the same thing may be a knowledge source and an object of knowledge. His deep point is that one should not place knowledge sources into one half of an artificial division between *source* and *object* of knowledge, such that they cannot be known or confirmed by other sources. To motivate the idea more fully, he appeals to the *kāraka* system developed by Sanskrit grammarians. *Kāraka*s are factors involved in the accomplishment of an action, "agent," "direct object," "indirect object," "locus of action," and the like.[4] The distinct *kāraka* terms serve as a conceptual toolkit to understand action, one that profoundly influences metaphysics and action theory throughout Indian philosophy. Vātsyāyana illustrates them with the example of a tree. In the sentence "The tree exists," the tree is the agent (*kartṛ*).

[4] The rules for application of *kāraka* names are found in Pāṇini's *Aṣṭādhyāyī* (c. fifth century BCE), from sūtras 1.4.23 to 1.4.54. Vātsyāyana cites some of these rules while alluding to others. See Cardona 1972 for a classic article-length study of the *kārakas*.

In "She sees the tree," it is the object (*karman*). In "You can locate the moon by using the tree (as a point of reference)," it is the instrument (*karaṇa*), and so on. Terms such as "agent" or "object" may be applied to the same thing according to context. The same tree is the agent of the act of standing but the object of someone's vision as she gazes at it.

Following the grammarians, Vātsyāyana notes that *kāraka* terms do not designate bare substances or bare actions. They designate specific factors that contribute to an act, factors with specific functions according to how they contribute. From here, Vātsyāyana returns to the question of *pramāṇa* and *prameya*. These appellations are also, he argues, *kāraka* terms of a sort. Accordingly, they may each refer to the same object according to context. Knowledge sources can thus be objects of knowledge. This is the import of sūtra 2.1.16, "Just as a scale which is a source of knowledge is also an object of knowledge."

This argument leads in turn to the famous skeptical attack portrayed in *Nyāya-sūtra* 2.1.17–18.[5] Importantly, this attack presupposes the "particularist" methodology just outlined. Vātsyāyana's preamble to 2.1.17 starts with a concession by the interlocutor.

> Sir, this is true. Different *kāraka* terms apply to the same object according to circumstance. It is also true that perception and the rest are sources of knowledge insofar as they are causes of cognition, but objects of knowledge insofar as they are the content of cognition. We reflectively identify them as such: "I know through perception," "I know through inference"... "My knowledge is perceptual," "My knowledge is inferential"... knowledge sources, which are distinctly known in this way, are understood according to definition.

[5] The following discussion is an expanded and revised version of Part 3 of Dasti 2017.

The skeptical challenge targets that specific cognition said to take perception or another knowledge source as its own object (e.g., "My cognition is perceptual"), to which we appeal when speaking of *common reflection* upon cognitive practice. The interlocutor asks, "Is this cognition, which takes perception and the rest as its object (i) itself established by another knowledge source, or (ii) posited without needing to be established?" Thus, a dilemma ensues:

> If the knowledge sources are established by another knowledge source, there is the unwanted consequence that yet another knowledge source is to be established. (*NyS* 2.1.17)

If, like any other object of knowledge, knowledge sources must be established by the deployment of knowledge sources, this would lead to an infinite regress, as we would need knowledge source$_3$ to support knowledge source$_2$ and so on.

The interlocutor next addresses a proposal to escape this problem.

> If no additional knowledge source is required to ground them, then let the objects of knowledge be established in the same way. (*NyS* 2.1.18)

If a knowledge source is simply posited to escape an infinite regress, one would abandon the very principle that motivates Nyāya epistemology: when things are known, there must be knowledge sources by which we cognize them. If this can be violated here, why not simply posit the things claimed to be objects of knowledge sources at the ground level? The parallels between this argument and Nāgārjuna's attack on *pramāṇa* epistemology in his *Vigraha-vyāvartinī* are striking:

> If you hold that the various objects are established by *pramāṇas*, then again, you must explain how it is that the *pramāṇas* are

themselves established. If the *pramāṇas* are established by other *pramāṇas*, then there would be an infinite regress. In that case, neither the beginning, middle, nor end would be established. But if you think that the *pramāṇas* are established without need for other *pramāṇas*, then your position [that claims about an object's existence or nature must be supported by appeal to *pramāṇas*] has been abandoned. There is inconsistency in this, and you must provide a specific reason for it. (*VV* 31–33)

Vātsyāyana's response starts from *NyS* 2.1.19:

No, the *pramāṇas* are established like the light of a lamp.

At first glance, this sūtra would appear to support foundationalist considerations: Light makes itself evident in the act of illuminating other things. It does not require yet another source of illumination. So, too, would *pramāṇas* generate knowledge of themselves as they generate knowledge of their objects. On this reading, the status of *pramāṇas* as knowledge sources is established without appeal to any other support. The justificational regress would end by appeal to knowledge sources that are known to be veridical by means of their own functioning.

This "foundationalist" solution avoids the perils of mere postulation mentioned above. That it is the original meaning of the sūtra is supported by two considerations. The *Nyāya-sūtra* itself deploys the lamp simile to illustrate regress-stopping "illumination" under 5.1.10. There Vātsyāyana notes that "in order to see a lamp, there is no need for another lamp." Moreover, Nāgārjuna (*VV* 34–39) takes up the metaphor of lamplight immediately after his attacks on the *pramāṇas* that match those identified under *NyS* 2.1.17–18. And he interprets it as an attempted rebuttal involving self-illumination.[6]

[6] Also see Bronkhorst 1993, 507–508, which catalogs instances of the lamplight metaphor in works roughly contemporaneous with the *NySBh*, each of which express notion of self-support.

Vātsyāyana mentions this "foundationalist" interpretation but explicitly rejects it. He takes the lamplight metaphor to reiterate the idea of mutual support among knowledge sources: as lamplight is a cause of perceptual cognition, it may be loosely spoken of as a *pramāṇa*. Yet it can be an object of knowledge as well:

> Lamplight is directly apprehended through connection with the visual faculty. It is also inferred to be a cause of perception, since the occurrence of perceptual experience correlates with the presence of light, and its absence correlates with the absence of light. It is furthermore known by the statements of an authority, as when an elder says "Carry a lamp to light your way in the dark." (*Commentary* 2.1.19)

In the same way, he argues, we grasp various features of knowledge sources through what we may call "inter-*pramāṇic* support." The skeptic has, therefore, offered a false dilemma between infinite regress and postulation. (See Table 6.)

Vātsyāyana's view that the very knowledge sources with which we are familiar provide mutual support for each other has some parallels with coherentist accounts of justification, as it recognizes that any attempt to assess our knowledge sources requires us to

Table 6. Nāgārjuna's four lemmas represented in the sūtras and *Commentary*.

infinite regress	*VV* 31–32	*NyS* 2.1.17
postulation	*VV* 33	*NyS* 2.1.18
self-support of each *pramāṇa*	*VV* 40–41	the "foundationalist" interpretation of *Nyāya-sūtra* 2.1.19, rejected by Vātsyāyana
inter-*pramāṇic* support	*VV* 42–50	the "coherentist" interpretation of *Nyāya-sūtra* 2.1.19, accepted by Vātsyāyana

avail ourselves of them. There is no way to step out of the web of putative *pramāṇa*-generated cognition to evaluate it from the outside. But Vātsyāyana's epistemology is *not* a wholesale coherentism. On the ground level, it is determined largely by externalist or reliabilist considerations, whether cognition is the product of a genuine knowledge source as opposed to a misfire. We look for inter-*pramāṇic* support primarily in cases of doubt or cognitive review. If anything, *negative* coherence plays an important role here, as apparent incoherence between cognitions triggers doubt and review.[7]

The skeptical interlocutor follows up, appropriately, with a charge analogous to circular reasoning. As construed, *pramāṇa* epistemology would allow "something to apprehend itself." This would violate the same intuition that motivates sūtra 2.1.18's concern about postulation.[8] Here the problem is not exactly postulation, though, but a very small (in fact, the smallest possible) justificational circle. For example:

1. Perception is accurate.

____

2. Perception is accurate.

Vātsyāyana resists the charge of circularity by making clear that inter-*pramāṇic* support occurs between *pramāṇa* tokens. The skeptical challenge seems persuasive if baldly stated in the following form: "Perception cannot ground perception," taking *pramāṇas* as types. But, again appealing to common epistemic practice, Vātsyāyana

[7] See *NySBh* 3.2.8 for an example of how an apparently reasonable inference is not only made doubtful but overridden by a stronger one.

[8] It would also violate an "anti-reflexivity" principle widely held among classical Indian thinkers, that an instrument specified to the appropriate level of detail cannot act upon itself. A knife cannot cut itself, and so on. The *Nyāya-sūtra* appeals to this principle elsewhere, noting that a sense faculty cannot perceive itself (3.1.70). Vātsyāyana rejects the imprecise application of the principle here. He remarks that the self, for example, can be both apprehender and apprehended.

points out that token knowledge sources are used to support other token knowledge sources of the same type as well as other types. Clearly, this tracks ordinary experience. If I'm dubious about something I thought I saw, I may go back to take another look, confirming the original experience. A perceptual token thus certifies another perceptual token. Or I may ask a friend if she saw the same thing, now supporting my perceptual token with a testimonial token. And so on. In each case, epistemic support takes place between token knowledge sources.

Even granting this, however, there remains the danger of infinite regress, as a skeptic could demand an account of which knowledge source $token_2$ supports knowledge source $token_1$ and so on. What blocks *this* regress? In his commentary on 2.1.20, the final sūtra of this section, Vātsyāyana responds to the challenge:

> Does cognition of perception and the rest by perception and the rest lead to an infinite regress? No, since we are fit to engage in the activities of life based simply on our understanding of the causes and objects of knowledge: "I know through perception," "I know through inference," "I know though comparison," "I know through testimony," "My knowledge is perceptual," "My knowledge is inferential," "My knowledge is analogical," "My knowledge is testimonial." One motivated to achieve virtue, wealth, pleasure, and spiritual felicity,[9] while avoiding things opposed to them, is able to conduct the activities of life [*vyavahāra*] by understanding the sources of knowledge and their proper objects. Such activities continue on this basis alone, and there is no other kind of activity that would necessitate an infinite regress. (*Commentary* 2.1.20)

Vātsyāyana does not seek to end the regress with cognition to which one is entitled because it is *epistemically* justified in the sense that it is the product of self-consciously attested *pramāṇa*s, as this expectation would just perpetuate the regress. Rather, the regress

[9] These are the four "goals of human life," famous in Hindu tradition.

ends with cognition to which we are indeed entitled but *pragmatically* so. As we have seen from the beginning of the *Commentary*, Vātsyāyana stresses that we are concerned with epistemic reflection because we want to live well. Successful action requires knowledge, and because of this, we are driven to resolve unclear or contradictory cognitions. But in the absence of legitimate doubt, epistemic overscrupulousness is not only unnecessary but stultifying, being at odds with the very motivation that leads us to be concerned with epistemology in the first place. Our default trust in putatively veridical cognition is thus justified on pragmatic grounds.[10]

In an allied line of reasoning, Vātsyāyana contends that we need not search for epistemic resources outside of the well-known knowledge sources to justify them prior to investing our confidence in them. Unless a genuine explanatory need were to arise, the knowledge sources with which we are familiar may be trusted. Just as it would be epistemic overscrupulousness to try to trace the chain of epistemic grounding as far back as possible, so, too, would it be to worry about lacunae in our knowledge sources in the absence of compelling reasons.

Dialectically, his use of pragmatic entitlement as a limit on skeptical challenge allows Vātsyāyana to frame purely hypothetical skepticism as something akin to mere contentiousness. If, having illustrated to a skeptic that all of the available *pramāṇa*s establish that a certain drink is safe, she still claims, "We aren't sure, since it is possible that we cannot detect the poison," Vātsyāyana could respond, "Okay, then, never ever take a drink." But of course, the skeptic eats and drinks like everyone else. In ordinary life, once we have apparently veridical deliverances of knowledge sources regarding something of practical import, we act with confidence, and "there is no other kind of *activity* that would necessitate an infinite regress" (emphasis added). The knowledge sources fundamentally

[10] Later anti-skeptical arguments under 4.3.26–37 will provide purely theoretical arguments involving the dependence of falsehood upon truth.

Table 7. Vātsyāyana's comprehensive epistemology.

Default status: An individual is entitled to prima facie trust in apparent deliverances of knowledge sources on largely pragmatic grounds, as well as inter-*pramāṇic* coherence (2.1.20). The ground-level epistemic status of cognition is determined through reliabilist considerations, that is, whether they are the products of genuine knowledge sources (1.1.3–8).
Review and certification: Under conditions of legitimate doubt, a putatively true cognition loses its default entitlement (1.1.23; 2.1.7). The agent may review dubious cognition by deploying other knowledge sources, including token instances of the source that generated the cognition in the first place. After review, the original cognition may be certified or rejected (2.1.19–20).
Identification of knowledge sources: Knowledge sources are identified by reflection upon successful epistemic practice, determining the irreducible types of cognitive processes that generate truth, leading to success in action (1.1.1; 1.1.3–8; 2.1.11; 2.1.20; 2.1.68).

guide action, and in this regard, no one, skeptic included, has the luxury of sitting on the sidelines.[11]

We might also note that this strategy is not to commit the postulation discussed in sūtra 2.1.18. The principle that knowledge sources must be cited to support truth claims is not violated here but rather circumscribed. When legitimate doubt arises, then one can reflect on which knowledge sources support the currently doubted cognition. In the absence of such doubt, however, we are entitled to take apparently veridical cognition at face value. (See Table 7.)

2.1.21–36: Perception

Having completed an investigation into *pramāṇa* epistemology in general, the sūtras now consider each *pramāṇa*

[11] For two accounts in recent literature that echo Vātsyāyana's pragmatic defense of prima facie trust in cognition, see Alston 1993, 124–138; Enoch and Schester 2008.

type. The investigation into perception has three major subsections: 2.1.21–30, which defends the definition given in sūtra 1.1.4; 2.1.31–2, which responds to a challenger who argues that perception is merely a form of inference; and 2.1.33–36, which defends composite wholes.

The criticism advanced under 2.1.21–23 is that the perception sūtra is incomplete, as it fails to mention the involvement of the *manas* (the "inner sense") and the self.[12] Vātsyāyana mentions this objection in his commentary on 1.1.4, but here he develops his answer in more depth. Nyāya, along with precursor traditions, does hold that perceptual cognition requires a fourfold connection: object—sense faculty—*manas*—self.[13] As the faculty of selective attention, the *manas* must be targeting, or "in contact with," the inputs of a particular sense modality for its information to be delivered over to the self.

The response of the sūtras and *Commentary* consists of four major arguments. First, the participation of *manas* and self are already implied in the sūtra, so there is no need to mention them specifically (2.1.24–25). Second, the *manas* and self participate in *every* type of cognition. Therefore, they are less important to the definition of perception than the connection between sense faculty and object (2.1.26). Third, sense/object connection is occasionally so powerful that it pulls someone who is inattentive or sleeping into perceptual cognition. Therefore, it is phenomenally prior to, and more powerful than, other contributing factors (2.1.27). Finally, ordinary linguistic practices refer to perceptual cognition by the operative senses and particular objects, underscoring the primacy of sense/object contact in perceptual cognition (2.1.28).

12 See 1.1.16 and 3.2.56–59 for further discussion of the *manas*.

13 *VS* 3.1.13 and 3.2.1 and *CS*, Sūtrasthāna 11.20. Franco and Preisandanz (1995) suggest that the interlocutor found in *Nyāya-sūtra* 1.1.4 may represent an idiosyncratic Mīmāṃsā view.

At the end of this discussion, Vātsyāyana reflects on the factors that influence the *manas* when cognition occurs without conscious focus, for people who are sleeping or inattentive:

> Volition, which arises from desire and impels the mind [*manas*] of the knower, is a quality of the self. Likewise, there is another quality of the self, generated by purposive actions and vices, which is a causal factor in anyone's being aware of anything. This quality impels the *manas* to come into contact with the senses (even without volition). For if the *manas* were not impelled by it, then in the absence of such connection, cognition would not arise, and one would cease to be aware of any objects.
>
> One must also appeal to this quality as a cause of substances, qualities, and actions, otherwise, the four kinds of subtle atoms and the *manas* would remain unconnected to any other cause for motion (at the beginning of creation), and there would be the unacceptable consequence that bodies, senses, and their objects would not arise. (*Commentary* 2.1.30)

Trying to make sense of what other factors could "move" the *manas* in the absence of volition, Vātsyāyana appeals here to a "quality of the self" other than volition. He effectively makes an appeal to the best explanation. There must be *some* causal factor operative when one's selective attention is made to focus without conscious direction. In early Vaiśeṣika metaphysics, the term *adṛṣṭa*, "unseen," is used as a catch-all for causal factors that are not observable, like the capacity of a magnet to attract metal shavings at a distance. In many instances, the term is also used as a near synonym for the soteriological sense of karma or *dharma*, a moral residue or momentum carried by an individual that influences their future embodiment and circumstances.[14] Vātsyāyana appeals to *adṛṣṭa* here. Instead

[14] *NyS* 3.2.60–72 elaborates at length on *adṛṣṭa*'s role in an individual's embodiment. In his comments on 3.1.4, 3.1.24, and 3.1.38, Vātsyāyana also explicitly accepts the moral weight of *adṛṣṭa* as informing rebirth.

of postulating multiple unseen forces, the property that causes the *manas* to significantly "move" in the absence of conscious oversight is the same as that which leads atoms to combine during times of cosmic re-creation.

Sūtras 2.1.31–32 are concerned with *pramāṇa* individuation. An interlocutor argues that perception is reducible to inference:

> Perception is merely inference, since perceptual cognition occurs though apprehending a part of something. (*NyS* 2.1.31)

As defined under 1.1.3, inference produces knowledge of something indicated via experience of an indicator. Seeing smoke triggers an inference to fire. The interlocutor argues that "seeing" a tree only involves seeing a specific part of the tree. We don't see its other side. Insofar as we think we are seeing a tree, the content of cognition ranges far beyond the portion we directly encounter visually. Therefore, what we normally call perception is really inference.

In the generations after Vātsyāyana, sophisticated arguments of this type were developed by Dignāga and his Buddhist followers. Vātsyāyana implies that this objection could have come from various camps, noting that the metaphysical presuppositions of the challenger need to be clarified. If they are a mereological nihilist, then the objection runs as follows. We visually encounter a portion of the aggregate that we call a tree and then infer the other portion(s) of the aggregate, generating the cognition "Tree." If, alternatively, the objector accepts the reality of composite wholes, then it runs as follows: we visually encounter a portion of the composite whole that we call a tree and then infer both the other portions and the composite whole itself.

Vātsyāyana's initial concern is not to argue for any metaphysical position as much as to refute the basic objection in both forms. Against the first interpretation, he argues that if the content of the inference is the unseen portion of the aggregate "tree," such does not constitute the entire tree. Therefore, there would be no cognition of a tree at all. Should the objector respond that we infer the other parts, and then put it all together as "tree" in an act of synthetic recollection, the cognition of a tree would not be inferential but rather a creative act of mental combination. Against the second interpretation, he argues that cognition of the tree as a composite whole cannot be inferential, because we would never have independent perceptual awareness of the composite whole as related to its constituent parts. That is, if the composite is not a direct object of perception, we could not have the inferentially necessary background experience of part and whole as consistently connected relata. The part could not therefore be a legitimate indicator of the whole. Should the objector respond that we can visually apprehend the whole, this concedes the point that we perceive wholes directly.

The sūtras themselves respond with the observation that even in the portrayal of the interlocutor, there is an irreducible place for perception. One must directly see the part, whatever else happens on the course of apprehending the totality (2.1.32). This is enough to refute the objector. Vātsyāyana expands upon this this by reminding us that inference is "preceded by perception" (1.1.5). One must experience the relationship between things like smoke and fire before one makes any inferences at all. Paradigmatically, one makes an inference after *seeing* an indicator, which triggers the inference to a target fact. While inference thus depends on sense inputs, Vātsyāyana offers a general principle to distinguish inference from perception: "Inference does not arise merely from the connection between a sense faculty and the thing to be inferred. This is the basic difference between it and perception."

At this point, the metaphysical question of holism comes entirely to the fore, setting the stage for the ensuing sūtras. The competing options mentioned so far have been taking, for example, a tree to be either a mere aggregate (*samudāya*) without deep metaphysical coherence or a whole (*avayavin*), a composite that has an irreducible reality of its own. In the Vaiśeṣika metaphysics presupposed by the sūtras and Vātsyāyana, wholes are a subspecies of *substance* (*dravya*). Some substances are non-composite, like atoms. Others are composite, like trees, chariots, and other sorts of medium-sized dry goods. What substances have in common is that they are loci of qualities (*guṇa*) and actions (*kriyā*) (*VS* 1.1.14). Vātsyāyana argues that since composite wholes are real, existing over and above their parts, we directly perceive things like trees. A composite whole is a singular reality that is apprehended even when we visually encounter fewer than all of its parts. The notion that we merely see parts is false:

> The whole exists: when certain of its parts are in contact with a sense faculty, it is visually apprehended along with them; when certain parts are obstructed, it fails to be apprehended through them. (*Commentary* 2.1.32)

Vātsyāyana argues that if one denies that wholes exist, then we should never have knowledge of things like trees. That is, we never apprehend all the parts in a cluster, nor do we apprehend every aspect of a distinct configuration of parts. However the reductionist account is unpacked, things like trees could never be apprehended in their unity and totality. Crucial here is to remember that up to this point, the discussion is about perception as a source of knowledge, and the conceit presupposed by both sides is that cognition of a tree is indeed knowledge, not error.

Sūtras 2.1.33–36 transition completely to the metaphysical issue of wholes, with the interlocutor effectively accusing the sūtras of deploying the counterfeit reason *the unproved*. Appealing to wholes to justify the status of perception fails as long as the status of wholes is disputed and, hence, dubious (2.1.33).

The interlocutor is commonly understood to evoke Buddhist reductionism. This was expressed centuries before Vātsyāyana with the example of a chariot in *The Questions of King Milinda* (c. 100 BCE). A Buddhist monk, Nāgasena, attempts to illustrate the unreality of composites to the Bactrian-Greek King Milinda:

NĀGASENA: If, you came in a chariot, Sire, explain to me what it is? Is it the pole that is the chariot?

MILINDA: I did not say that.

NĀGASENA: Is it the axle that is the chariot?

MILINDA: Certainly not.

NĀGASENA: Is it the wheels, or the framework, or the ropes, or the yoke, or the spokes of the wheels, or the goad that are the chariot?

MILINDA: No.

NĀGASENA: Then is it *all* these parts of it that are the chariot?

MILINDA: No, sir.

NĀGASENA: But is there anything outside of them that is the chariot?

MILINDA: Again, no.

NĀGASENA: Then, I can discover no chariot. "Chariot" is a mere empty sound. . . . There is no such thing as a chariot! (*QKM* 2.1.1)[15]

One interesting feature of Vātsyāyana's response is that it presupposes atomism. This does not necessarily mean that he is assuming Nyāya's metaphysical picture here, since some Buddhist reductionists—particularly Sautrāntikas and Vaibhāṣikas—are also atomists of a sort.[16] Some of the language of 2.1.35 suggests the possibility of the interlocutor's representing a Jain position. While the Jain view expressed in texts such as *Tattvārtha-sūtra* (c. second–fifth century CE) was not "reductionist" in a strong sense, it does hold that the clustering of atoms into macro-objects creates aggregates, not distinct composite wholes.

In response, two initial counterarguments are put forth. First, if wholes did not exist, we would not apprehend anything at all (2.1.34). If there were nothing but clouds of atoms, we would not see anything, since atoms are imperceptible. And since perception

[15] Adapted from translation in Rhys Davids 1890, 43–44.

[16] See Gangopadhyaya 1980, 10–17.

offers the raw ingredients for the other knowledge sources, we would not grasp anything at all.

Second, wholes can "act" in a unified way (2.1.35). In the simplest sense, entire wholes can be moved by only holding and pulling on one part. They have a principle of inner cohesion and integrity. Vātsyāyana leaves this second argument somewhat undeveloped, leaving his subcommentator, Uddyotakara, to develop these seeds into a full-blown argument from causal capacity: wholes have different causal powers from their parts, and as such, they are metaphysically distinct from them.[17]

I'd like to pause briefly to note a subtext of this debate, what we might call competing empiricisms. Buddhist schools lean in a direction that is reminiscent of early modern European empiricists. They are frankly dubious of "metaphysical" entities that seem to disappear when we look closely and carefully at experience itself. Nyāya, too, is empiricist, in that perception is the most fundamental of the knowledge sources, supplying other sources with the raw ingredients they need to function. But Nyāya takes perception to be much more powerful than its Buddhist counterparts. Perception has the capacity to directly apprehend certain universals and substances like composite wholes. It does not merely provide us with globs of color and shape.

Another subtext is alternative criteria for what makes something real. Buddhist Abhidharma philosophers argue that insofar as something can be broken down into smaller constituents, it depends upon them and is not fully real. For Nyāya, on the other hand, to be fully real does not mean something has to be independent of any causal (or conceptual) conditions but rather to possess certain features, properties, or capacities. While a whole depends upon its parts, it also has properties and capacities that the parts lack.[18]

[17] E.g., "Yarn is different from the cloth made from it, since the two have different causal capacities, like poison and antidotes" (Dasti and Phillips 2017, 107–108).

[18] This argument is developed under 4.1.37–40.

Vātsyāyana has the interlocutor push back in a somewhat obscure passage. Two counterexamples are offered.[19] Things like a pile of dust may have parts but are not subject to "holding and pulling." Other things, like a cluster of debris stuck together with glue, may be subject to "holding and pulling" without being a genuine unified whole. Part of the problem with these counterexamples is that typically, a pile of dust or sand would be an example of a heap (*rāśi*), which is just an aggregate, not a composite whole. To be generous, a cluster of wet sand or dirt may have some sort of distinctness such that it has "parts," despite its lack of deep cohesion. And we could suggest similar but better counterexamples to the same end, for example, a beach sculpture made out of damp sand. Instead of objecting to the examples, Vātsyāyana makes a more fundamental point by returning to the question of experience:

> The following should be answered: In the cognition expressed as "This is a single substance," what exactly is the content? That is, is the content "this is one thing" really about a multiplicity of objects, or rather an undivided object? If you accept the latter, then you concede our point that there is something over and above the parts, proving the whole. If you accept the former, then it would be untenable that experience of a unity could be directed to a multiplicity. (*Commentary* 2.1.35)

This leads to the famous objection in 2.1.36:

> This perceptual experience is like that of an army or a forest.

By claiming that our experience of composite wholes is akin to the way forests or armies falsely seem to be unified entities at a distance, the

[19] I follow the reading of Uddyotakara, who takes this portion to represent the challenger's view. As noted by Jha (1919, 761n), this passage has sparked significant reflection in the commentarial tradition. He offers a possible reading of the "dust and cluster" argument as representing Vātsyāyana's own position, as does Potter in *EIPNV*, 251.

interlocutor asserts that perceptual experiences of trees and the like are mental constructions, falsehoods. The unified content of such cognition is owing to mere projection, not any sort of metaphysical "glue" that is *out there*. In a lengthy response, Vātsyāyana offers two major arguments:

1. The analogy is inapt: The analogy fails because the "diverse objects" that make up armies or forests are themselves perceptible, whereas atoms are not. It would be impossible to misidentify a cluster of atoms as a unified thing.
2. Arguments from parasitism: The objector holds that the unified experience of objects is a mistake. But error is parasitical upon veridical cognition, and therefore, the objector must admit some instance of veridical cognition of a unified object.

This second argument requires the most unpacking. What I call *arguments from parasitism* are a fundamental plank of Vātsyāyana's realism.[20] The core of these arguments is that error/falsehood/illusion is not possible without true cognition/truth/veridical awareness. We might compare them to Gilbert Ryle's (1954, 94–95) observation that counterfeit coins are only possible if some coinage is legitimate. Vātsyāyana explains:

> If the apprehension "This is a single, undifferentiated thing" arises from a failure to notice differences within a variegated cluster of atoms, this would be a case of taking something that is not-*F* to be *F*, like seeing a post as a person.
>
> —What of it?
>
> Taking something not-*F* to be *F* depends upon a prototype for *F* and therefore establishes the prototype.
>
> —What is the prototype when a post is mistakenly seen as a person?

[20] They are found under 2.1.36, 2.1.42, and 4.2.33–37.

> The experience of a person as a person. With that as a background condition, there arises the mistaken notion of *person* directed toward something that is a *non-person*, because one apprehends some similar features. Likewise, seeing multiple things as a single thing, because one apprehends some similar features, requires a prototype. If we could not truly see anything, there would be no possibility of a prototype. Therefore, cognition of something as undivided, with the content "This is one thing," must be able to target a unified entity. (*Commentary* 2.1.36)

Vātsyāyana continues by arguing that a host of experiences would have no prototype if veridical cognition of composite wholes did not occur: (i) that something has a size, like "large," (ii) that something is conjoined to another, (iii) that something moves, (iv) that something belongs to a class or kind. These arguments follow the general formula described above.

2.1.37–43: Inference

The investigation into inference has two major subsections: 2.1.37–38, which defends inference as a legitimate knowledge source, and 2.1.39–43, which argues that the present time is real.

Unlike the critique of perception, the challenge of 2.1.37 is not a matter of reduction. The interlocutor argues that inference is unauthoritative (*apramāṇa*) because of "deviation." A concern with inferential deviation was expressed earlier, under the heading of counterfeit reasons, and specifically the deviant (1.2.5), which fails to reliably indicate the conclusion it purportedly establishes. The interlocutor here argues further that deviation is a fundamental defect of inferential reasoning in general. Inference itself fails to be reliable. There are three allegations put forth in 2.1.37 and unpacked further in 2.1.38. They do not track the three types of inference listed in 1.1.5, under either of Vātsyāyana's interpretations

Table 8. The three examples of inferential deviation under 2.1.37–38.

Deviation-inducing flaw	Explanation	Temporal division targeted
obstruction	*Swollen waters* fails to prove that it had rained upstream, because the water may have been obstructed by a dam.	past
destruction	*Ants are carrying their eggs* fails to prove that it will rain, because they may be fleeing an anthill that was destroyed.	future
similarity	*Cry that sounds like a peacock's* fails to prove that a peacock is nearby, because the cry may be mimicked by a skillful person.	present

of that sūtra. Only one example is carried over, the *śeṣavat* inference to rain upstream from the swelling of a river. The other two are new. Given the following section, Vātsyāyana reasonably interprets the three examples as referring to the divisions of past, future, and present time, respectively. (See Table 8.)

The identity of this interlocutor is not made clear, but criticism of inference as a genuine source of knowledge is associated with ancient materialists, called Cārvāka and Lokāyata. Only fragments remain of early works by materialists, typically preserved by unsympathetic opponents. In these, and in works that postdate Vātsyāyana, materialists are represented as world-affirming and anti-speculative thinkers. Their attacks on inference tend to be framed as attempts to undercut the planks used to support otherworldly metaphysical and religious views. We cannot be certain that the current opponents are materialists or proto-materialists, but it is not an unreasonable conjecture.[21]

[21] A leading scholar of Indian materialism chose to include this passage from the *Nyāya-sūtra* in an anthology of materialist thought. See Chattopadhyaya and Gangopadhyaya 1990.

Vātsyāyana offers a twofold response. First, he diagnoses the interlocutor's examples as, in effect, straw men: "Some vague object cannot serve as a legitimate indicator." The examples offered are not what Vātsyāyana takes to be legitimate reasons; therefore, they don't impugn inference at all. Mere swollen water is not enough to infer rain; the true sign of rain upstream is a river that is not only swollen but flowing rapidly and carrying telltale debris. Likewise, ants carrying eggs are a sign for future rain only when they are scattered everywhere on the ground. This could not be the result of a mere single anthill or two being destroyed. Finally, those people (or animals) who are skilled in discerning the cry of a peacock can distinguish the real thing from imitators. Therefore, something that vaguely sounds like a peacock is not a legitimate indicator. The mention of serpents here is inspired by a long-attested animosity between the two species. Since peacocks hunt and attack snakes, the latter are said to be expert at discerning true peacock cries.

Second, Vātsyāyana invokes the factive conception of *pramāṇa* discussed under 1.1.4. By definition, inference, like perception, produces knowledge. For any of the challenger's examples, Vātsyāyana remarks that "this is not an inference which deviates. Rather, this is the mistaken notion of an inference where there is none." The proper construal of the situation is not that inference sometimes deviates but rather that we are sometimes confused about the difference between a true inference and a faulty imitator. "The fault is with the person trying to infer, not with inference as such." This clears inference from the interlocutor's charges. Of course, the skeptic may argue that nevertheless, we individuals are lost at sea with respect to determining which reasons are legitimate and which are not. But as already illustrated elsewhere in the *Commentary*, Vātsyāyana has confidence that we can improve our ability to distinguish between legitimate and illegitimate reasons through training and experience. Neither the bare possibility of error nor the actual occurrence of occasional error undermines the working of our knowledge sources. That both the challenger and Vātsyāyana agree that the three cases here are *not* legitimate inferences is itself a cause for optimism.[22]

At 2.1.39, the sūtras pivot to the question of the present moment. We may recall that Vātsyāyana's initial comments on inference concluded with the following:

> While perception targets existing objects, inference targets both existing and non-existing things. Why? Because it apprehends things within the three times. Objects within the three phases of time are grasped by inference. *What will be* can be inferred, as well as *what is* and *what was*. (*Commentary* 1.1.5)

As inference can span temporal boundaries, the current discussion is triggered by concerns with the nature of time and especially the present moment. This concern mirrors a similar transition in the inquiry into perception, where the notion that perception targets composite wholes led to a separate discussion of wholes as real and metaphysically irreducible (2.1.33–36). Here the interlocutor argues that the present moment vanishes under scrutiny. "There is no present moment, since something falling is known either according to the time it has taken to fall or the time in which it will fall" (2.1.39). That is, when we consider something that is falling, we may think of it according to the distance traversed (the past) or that which it will traverse (the future) but there is no option corresponding to the present.

This paradoxical challenge raises several interrelated issues. As illustrated in the sūtra, time is often understood in relation to motion. Hours are measured by the movements of the sun, as are days, months by the cycle of the moon, and years by the annual patterns of the sun and other heavenly bodies. But motions consist

[22] Phillips (2017, 544–547) offers a creative account of Vātsyāyana's reasoning here that goes beyond the distinction between legitimate versus illegitimate reasons. He sees in each of them an illustration of Nyāya's default trust in cognition, followed by a state of doubt, and then reinstatement of cognition after sufficient review.

in a series of related events. At any given moment, a chain of events constituting motion is known largely in the form of former events that are held in the memory and future events that are expected. Thus, motion is known through synthetic recollection and inference, not perception.[23] If time is understood as a function of motion, the present disappears.

Who, if anyone, is being represented in this skeptical challenge? Cardona (1991) has shown that concern with the nature of the present moment has a robust history in grammatical works that predate Vātsyāyana and the *Nyāya-sūtra*. Among the grammarians, reflection on the present moment departs from a concern to correctly articulate the rules that govern the application of verb endings for the present tense. Distinctly metaphysical attacks on the present moment, involving paradoxes of time and action, are also cataloged by Patañjali (c. 150 BCE) in his *Great Commentary* (*Mahābhāṣya*) on Pāṇini's *Aṣṭādhyāyī* (*Eight-Chaptered Treatise on Grammar*). Patañjali quotes a few verses associated with "those who deny the present time." For example:

> A young man, wise and held in respect, considered himself one who pondered on matters, and questioned the crow: "Tell me crow, what it is that makes up your flight. You are not flying in the time that is yet to come or in the time that has passed; and if you are flying in the immediate moment, then this entire world is in flight. Even the Himālaya then is in motion." (*Great Commentary* II.124.1–5, on *Aṣṭādhyāyī* 3.2.123)[24]

It is not unlikely that ancient arguments of this sort were widely known and preserved here in *Nyāya-sūtra* 2.1.39. As Vātsyāyana unpacks and responds to the challenge, he frames

[23] An example of *sāmānyato-dṛṣṭa* inference under 1.1.5 is that sun has moved, owing to the observation that its location has changed.

[24] Translated by Cardona (1991, 452).

it such that it resembles the relational paradoxes of Nāgārjuna's *Mūlamadhyamaka-kārikā*, especially Chapter 2, "An Analysis of the Traversed."[25]

The response under 2.1.40–43 appeals to the fact that the past and the future depend upon the present. Vātsyāyana begins by claiming that time is manifest by action (*kriyā*), not by distance traversed (*adhvan*). The present time is when actions *are occurring*, as opposed to their *being completed* or *not yet initiated* (2.1.40; 2.1.42). In a series of actions like cooking that involve various coordinated sub-actions, or a sequential repetition, like cutting wood, the series itself is nothing more than a string of actions in the present moment that span into the past (sub-actions that are finished) and the future (sub-actions that must be accomplished to complete the task) (2.1.43).

Should the objector claim that the past and the future can be established simply in relation to each other, by analogy with other opposed binaries (e.g., long and short), this would amount to nothing more than an inapt comparison without solid argumentation (2.1.41).

The present is also presupposed in knowledge of things past or future in that it is the vantage point by which they are determined. To put it slightly differently, knowledge of the time already passed presupposes the present moment as its demarcation point (2.1.43). More fundamentally, knowledge of any kind presupposes the present moment, since perception functions only in the present, providing the raw materials for all the other knowledge sources (2.1.42). Here Vātsyāyana argues that besides being known through sequential actions, the present moment is also known through the current existence of objects, for example, "This substance exists."

[25] For an English translation of this chapter, see Siderits and Katsura 2013, 31–42. I would add that it is unlikely that the sūtras are themselves targeting a Madhyamaka position, since the challenger affirms the past and future as objectively real, which is not a Madhyamaka view.

Finally, Vātsyāyana appeals to ordinary linguistic usage, which richly evinces the reality of the present time (2.1.43).

2.1.44–48: Comparison

That comparison is a marginal *pramāṇa* has been noted. Often, as just above under 2.1.42, it is ignored by Vātsyāyana when he speaks of knowledge sources in general. This section is fittingly shorter than the other sections that consider objections to each of the *pramāṇas* as construed by Nyāya.

The sūtras consider two objections, one against comparison as a source of knowledge (2.1.44–45) and the other meant to reduce it to inference (2.1.46–48). The first argument is, yet again, a skeptical trope appealing to three exhaustive possibilities: comparison cannot be grounded by (i) scant similarity, (ii) significant similarity, or (iii) absolute similarity. Why options (i) and (iii) make for bad comparisons is likely obvious. The former wouldn't be enough to learn very much, while the later would amount to identity. What is wrong with option (ii) is not elaborated. The core point seems to cast doubt on similarity as something that could be used to truly discover something new. Someone is told that a water buffalo is like a cow, then sees something similar to a cow, leading to a eureka moment, "*That's* a water buffalo." If challenged to give a clear account of how much or, more pointedly, what sort of similarity is enough to underwrite such an event, it would seem difficult to do so. Vātsyāyana does not wade into the details of this objection but rather dismisses it as motivated by a misunderstanding. Comparison is grounded in "similarity with something that is well-known," as defined in 1.1.6. That we already have a handle on the relevant similarity is baked into the concept, and there is no need to specify in advance the "amount" of similarity required.

The second challenge is that as a process that starts with perceptible inputs and leads to imperceptible output cognition, comparison is nothing other than inference (2.1.47). Vātsyāyana's response is to argue for relevant differences between the two. First, comparison requires a perceptual encounter with the *output* side of the cognitive event. Only when one sees a water buffalo, after learning in general that water buffaloes are like cows, does one then have knowledge through comparison as understood here. Second, the primary input in comparison—an analogical statement that "*x* is like *y*"—requires a knowledgeable person such as a forester to inform the one who will eventually learn through comparison. Comparison does not occur autonomously in the way that inference functions autonomously for oneself. Finally, the content of analogical knowledge always involves similarity, unlike inferential knowledge.

It seems to me that this entire section shows comparison as understood by Vātsyāyana to be an amorphous and frankly convoluted notion. The above responses he makes seem to take the deep content of comparison to be knowledge of similarity itself. Yet similarity is typically framed as the *means* to analogical knowledge, which takes the form of "*x* is designated by naming term *y*." As noted under 1.1.6, I am sympathetic to those who argue that it could be reduced to another knowledge source or a combination of other sources.

2.1.49–56: Testimony

Testimony (*śabda*, literally "word," "sound," "language") is considered in these sūtras in a general sense, distinguishing this section from the immediately following one on sacred Vedic testimony. The debate in this section centers on reduction. An interlocutor offers three reasons that testimony reduces to inference (2.1.49–51):

1. Like inference, testimony involves knowing something unseen based on something directly perceived (i.e., a word or statement).

2. The output cognitions of testimony and inference are functionally identical.
3. Both testimony and inference function through an established relationship between two items, the indicator or sign and the indicated or signified.

As in the other cases, these objections may represent an abstract position rather than a distinct historical opponent. But they are consistent with the views of certain historical schools. Indeed, Nyāya's sister school, Vaiśeṣika, holds that testimony reduces to inference (*VS* 9.19). So, too, would later Buddhist Epistemologists who would become prominent in the generations following Vātsyāyana.

The core of Vātsyāyana's response is that the relation that underwrites testimony is fundamentally different from that which underwrites inference (2.1.52–56). A word does not generate cognition simply by being heard. It is only when words *that are spoken by authoritative speakers* are heard that testimonial knowledge arises. Testimony thus relies on an entirely different sort of relationship from inference. This is illustrated by the way sacred testimony can inform us about transcendent objects that we cannot know by inference alone (2.1.52). The output cognitions of testimony and inference are thus different in that the processes that generate them are distinct (2.1.52).

What is special about the relationship between words and their objects is that it is entirely based on convention (*samaya-kārita*):

> Convention is the employment of a rule that governs a referring term and its referent, "*This* object will be denoted by *this* word." (*Commentary* 2.1.55)

This relationship contrasts with the natural connections upon which inference is typically based (e.g., that between smoke and fire).[26] If one were to hold that words and their objects do have a natural relation, then uttering words like "cut" should injure one's mouth (2.1.53). More seriously, that different communities use different terms for the same objects undermines the theory of an inherent or natural relation (2.1.56).[27]

For Nyāya, the philosophy of language and the epistemology of testimony are inextricably fused. The power of words to refer to objects, and of statements to capture complex facts, flows from conventions that are followed within language communities. And the capacity of testimony to generate knowledge in the mind of a trusting hearer requires a further condition: that the speaker is an *āpta*, an authority. But the capacity for testimony to generate knowledge is simply a special instance of the general capacity for aptly used words to produce understanding.

2.1.57–68: Sacred testimony

This portion of the sūtras has three major subsections: 2.1.57–60 responds to an attack on the authority of the Vedas, 2.1.61–67 specifies types of Vedic statements, and 2.1.68 provides a final, comprehensive overview of how Vedic authority is justified by parity of reasoning with ordinary testimony.

This section corroborates Vātsyāyana's claim that Nyāya is the support for other Brahmanical intellectual disciplines, including Vedic study. We may recall that 1.1.8 spoke of testimony whose objects are imperceptible. Now this, too, will be filled out,

[26] Vātsyāyana uses the term *prāpti-sambandha* for natural connections lacking between word and object. I understand *prāpti-sambandha* to refer to the metaphysically real, discoverable relations that are fixed independently of human convention, namely, conjunction and inherence.

[27] This seems to attack a position associated with Mīmāṃsā, that there is an innate, natural tie between words and their objects (to be discussed below). The *Nyāya-sūtra* joins Vaiśeṣika in arguing against this position (see *VS* 7.2.18–20 and *MS* 1.1.5–23). But it is unlikely that the current section's interlocutor represents Mīmāṃsā.

as the sūtras defend sacred testimony in the form of the Vedas, specifically its hymns (*saṃhitās* or *mantras*) and ritual directives (*brāhmaṇas*).[28] *Saṃhitās* are hymns of glorification of deities such as Indra, Agni, and Soma:

> Let me now sing the heroic deeds of Indra, the first that the thunderbolt wielder performed. He killed the dragon and pierced an opening for the waters; he split open the bellies of mountains.
>
> Indra, who wields the thunderbolt in his hand, is the king of that which moves and that which rests, of the tame and of the horned. He rules the people as their king, encircling all this as a rim encircles spokes. (*Ṛg Veda* 1.32, stanzas 1,15)[29]

The authors of these hymns were inspired poets, "seers" who glorified the great divinities. In doing so, they encouraged and sustained the gods while beseeching them for reciprocal blessings and support. Jan Gonda (1975, 93) offers a capsule summary of their intellectual world:

> Vedic thought, the view of life and the world of the poets and their audiences, may briefly be defined as based on the belief in an inextricable co-ordination of what we would call nature, human society, ritual and the sphere of myth and the divine; on the belief also that these spheres influence each other continuously and that men have, by means of the ritual, to play an obligatory part in the maintenance of universal order and the furtherance of their common interests.

Vedic hymns are not, therefore, mere honorifics or recollections of ancient or primordial stories. They are re-creations of divine acts that continue to govern and structure the world.

[28] *Saṃhitās* and *brāhmaṇas* may be contrasted with the more speculative and philosophical portions of the Vedas, the *āraṇyakas* and *upaniṣads*.

[29] Translated by Donniger (1981, 149–151).

Table 9. The three defects imputed to the Vedas.

Defect	Example
falsehood	One may perform the sacrificial rite to have a son and still fail to have a son.
self-contradiction	Oblations (in the form of the Agnihotra rite) are enjoined at certain times (e.g., before sunrise), yet in other Vedic statements, performing oblations at that time is condemned.
redundancy	Certain mantras are to be repeated multiple times within a ritual act. Such redundancy is akin to the raving of a lunatic.

Brāhmaṇa texts are also "Veda" but are prose explanations of hymns and mantras in the context of a ritual culture. They offer instructions, explanations, and expositions on the nature and specificities of ritual obligations. Following an ancient pattern, *Nyāya-sūtra* 2.1.62–65 divides the teachings of the *brāhmaṇas* into the categories of *injunction* (e.g., "One who desires heaven should perform the fire sacrifice"), *explanation*, and *reiteration*.

A challenger argues that the Vedas lack authority (*prāmāṇya*) as they are beset by three defects: falsehood, self-contradiction, and redundancy (2.1.57). (See Table 9.) This criticism is consistent with multiple historical schools and traditions. From ancient times, Vedic ritualism was attacked on various fronts. Buddhists, Jains, and materialists all contended that the Vedic sacrificial culture and the scriptural sources that support it are unauthoritative.[30]

The first defect, falsehood, is illustrated by the rite to have a son. This ritual act has an observable result which sometimes fails to occur. It may be inferred that the promises of other unseen results

[30] Even the ancestors of "Hinduism" reflected in the Upaniṣads and the *Bhagavad-gītā* severely critique the culture of Vedic sacrifice. While they do not explicitly reject the sacrificial rites of the Vedas, they condemn those who fail to see a deeper purpose beyond them.

of Vedic rites, like a blessed state after death, are also false. We need to keep in mind that many of the rites were not just part of one's daily ritual obligations but special practices triggered by specific desires on the part of the sacrificer. They would have the basic form "if one desires *x*, then they should perform ritual *y*." This allows for what seems to be an easy test of the Vedas' efficacy, one that, in the interlocutor's view, they often fail.

Vātsyāyana's response is to argue that the promised results of Vedic rites may not occur for three major reasons: imperfections in the act performed, imperfections of the agent, and imperfections of the means employed. Failure to produce a son may be caused by imperfect performance of the ritual, an imperfection of the agent, such as sterility or barrenness on the part of the would-be-parents, or an imperfect means employed, such as impure ingredients used as offerings.

Vātsyāyana bolsters the case by noting that worldly actions are no different. The rule "If one desires fire, they should strike together pieces of wood" is widely and correctly accepted. Still, the promised fire may not arise if the wood is not properly struck together, the individual does not work hard enough, the fuel is wet, and so on. The result does manifest when all of the causal factors are faultless. Vātsyāyana concludes:

> The instruction that "A person who desires a son should perform the rite to achieve a son" is no different from ordinary practice. (*Commentary* 2.1.58)

The second charge, self-contradiction, rests on the fact that different Vedic statements enjoin or reject various times for ritual practice, disagreeing with each other. Vātsyāyana argues that the core point of such teachings is that once the practitioner fixes a time as their standard, then breaking *that* commitment is condemned. The varied statements simply speak to the fact that several times could be chosen for the sacrifice (2.1.59).

The third charge is that of redundancy, a rhetorical flaw identified in the *Nyāya-sūtra* itself.[31] The challenger points out that the Vedas often have instances of repetition. Vātsyāyana argues that there is a difference between meaningless repetition and purposeful repetition. Repetition in ritual prescriptions is purposeful, as it makes clear that a certain number of mantras are to be voiced (2.1.60).

Section 2.1.61–67 pivots to the *brāhmaṇa* portions of the Vedas, which specify and explain rituals. Vātsyāyana takes 2.1.61 to offer an independent argument for the authority of the Vedic scriptures: since the Vedic statements can be divided according to their purpose, they are meaningful or contentful. (See Table 10.)

The philosophical heart of the section, its major *positive* argument for the authority of the Vedas, is found in the concluding sūtra:

Table 10. The types of Vedic statements under 2.1.61–65.

Type of statement	Account	Vedic example	Ordinary example
injunction (*viddhi*)	a statement that enjoins an act	"One who desires heaven should perform the Agnihotra rite."	"Cook the rice."
explanation (*arthavāda*)	statements that (i) praise certain practices, (ii) condemn others, (iii) describe successful practitioners, (iv) describe mythical events	"The Sarvajit rite is the means to gain everything and conquer all."	"Food is the source of life, strength, happiness, and intelligence."
reiteration (*anuvāda*)	the restatement of an injunction and of its meaning	No example given; see 2.1.60.	"Cook! Cook!"

[31] Mere repetition (*punarukta*) is identified as a fault under *NyS* 5.2.1 and 5.2.15.

> Just like the authority of mantras or medical science, the authority of the Vedas comes from authoritative speaker(s). (*NyS* 2.1.68)

In his gloss, Vātsyāyana continues what has been a consistent theme: sacred testimony functions the same way as ordinary testimony, the difference being the special nature of its objects. The mention of mantras here is less about Vedic *saṃhitā*s than incantations directed to more "local" sorts of issues such as warding off evil spirits. But Vātsyāyana focuses on medical science when articulating the nature and source of testimonial authority:

> In what lies the authoritativeness of expert medical testimony? That when someone carries out its teachings—"Doing *this* helps you gain what is desired (health) and not doing *that* helps you avoid what is undesired (sickness)"—things happen accordingly. What it says is true, not false.
>
> Medical science is authoritative because it has authoritative speakers. What does their authority consist of? Direct knowledge of what they are talking about, compassion for the listeners, and a desire to effectively communicate what they know. Knowledgeable authorities are compassionate toward others, teaching them "*This* should be avoided; *this* is its cause; *this* is what removes it; *this* is the course of action to do so."[32]

Vātsyāyana's remarks expand upon the criteria for an *āpta* first given under 1.1.7. Speaking about an *āpta*'s compassion, he returns to the concern with success in action, a topic that motivates the entire Nyāya project:

> For ordinary living beings, who do not know these things on their own, there is no way to understand without being instructed.

[32] These are the four "therapeutic" categories mentioned in the introduction to the *Commentary*.

> And without proper understanding, they cannot effectively endeavor to gain the good and to avoid the harmful.

He concludes, "The instructions of an authority are thus *pramāṇa*, and the authorities themselves are thus *pramāṇa*."

Vātsyāyana's account of testimony and testifiers provides an empirical way to judge who are genuine authorities and who are not. Insofar as physicians make claims that are empirically verifiable, we have a way of discovering which ones know what they are talking about and which do not.[33] Likewise, insofar as the Vedas have some injunctions that are supposed to produce observable results, we may confirm their validity. This in turn leads us to trust their claims about matters that are not verifiable.[34]

We may take note of the way this section of the *Commentary* expands upon remarks earlier in this chapter that speak of *pramāṇa* identification as being based on reflection upon common experience (2.1.11). Part of that reflection consists in what we could call "track record arguments." Vātsyāyana here gives the most explicit account of such arguments that can be found in the *Commentary*. They (along with his remarks on 2.1.19) help set the trajectory for later Nyāya's emphasis on "extrinsic determination of veridicality." This means that while we have a default entitlement to trust apparently true cognition, we confirm its status largely through positive coherence with other things that are known. This approach is opposed to that of schools such as Mīmāṃsā, which hold that

[33] Antecedents of such tests are spelled out in the *Caraka-saṃhitā*, a text on medicine which predates and influences the *Nyāya-sūtra*. It discusses how to distinguish true physicians from the unqualified in Sūtrasthāna 9.15–27 and Vimānasthāna 4.4. True physicians are spoken of as *āpta*, the same term used for a testimonial authority in Nyāya, and they are also said to understand knowledge of the four therapeutic categories. Sūtrasthāna 11.18–19 puts forth a definition of *āpta* with respect to authoritative speakers in general.

[34] One interpretation of this argument frames it as follows: The medical portions of the Vedic corpus, which are testable, and the ritual portions about transcendent realities, which are not, have the *same authors* (presumably, the great sages). So if the former texts are authoritative, the latter should be as well.

whatever positive epistemic status cognition has is intrinsic to it, requiring no help from the outside.

This segues neatly to the final objection considered, voiced by a Mīmāṃsā ritualist:

> The authoritativeness of Vedic statements is due to their being eternal. It is wrong to say that it derives from the authority of a speaker.

This objection rests on background arguments that are fundamental to Mīmāṁsā, the most orthodox of the Brahmanical schools of philosophy. Mīmāṁsā was both a rival of and an ally to Nyāya, a rival in many details of epistemological analysis but an ally in respect to a shared metaphysical realism, acceptance of the Veda, and opposition to Buddhism. While both schools agree that putatively veridical cognition is (at least) prima facie justified, they differ over the grounds of such status. Mīmāṁsā champions a view called *svataḥ prāmāṇya*, "intrinsic determination of veridicality," best understood as the notion that the same causal conditions that give rise to the awareness of a knowledge episode also give rise to awareness of its high-grade positive epistemic status. There is no help needed from the outside.[35]

Mīmāṃsā's view seems to be motivated by a concern to account for the authority of the Vedas. Its major argument may be summarized as follows.[36]

1. Cognition is by nature revelatory and contentful. As such, it is prima facie justified.

[35] Taber 1992 is a classic article-length study of this concept.

[36] The foundation of this argument is found in Śabara's (c. 350) commentary on *MS* 1.1.2: "False cognition is that which, after arising, is then destroyed by the knowledge 'It is not like that.' Cognition derived from the Veda (e.g., that the fire sacrifice will bring future blessedness) is not destroyed in this way, at any time, for any other person, in any other condition or place. So, it is not false."

2. External considerations can only defeat this default justification; they are not required for positive support.
3. The Vedas are eternal and uncreated. There is nothing outside of Vedic statements, including any unique speaker(s), that confers authority upon them.
4. The central teaching of the Vedas consists in action-directing injunctions, teachings about *dharma*.
5. Vedic statements about empirical matters are not actually truth claims. Rather, they are subsidiary depictions meant to inspire practitioners. As such, there are no external "hooks" available to undermine Vedic teachings about *dharma*.

---

6. Vedic teachings about *dharma* are intrinsically justified and undefeated.

The first two premises apply to all knowledge sources. The final three establish the Vedas as a knowledge source for matters of *dharma* and *dharma* alone. By contrast with Nyāya, for which the status of the Vedas is derived from its speaker(s), for Mīmāṃsā it is literally *apauruṣeya*, "not by a person." Thus, Mīmāṃsā combines a notion of the Vedas as eternal, a theory of intrinsic determination of veridicality, and a non-cognitivist interpretation of seemingly empirical Vedic statements. All this is the background to the objection considered by Vātsyāyana.[37]

Vātsyāyana's response is to argue that eternality is irrelevant to the positive epistemic status accorded to testimony. And further, the eternality = authoritativeness claim makes little sense with respect to language. Central to language is that denotative terms are set by convention. This is clearly the case in ordinary life, where terms that are set by convention are authoritative if uttered by a knowledgeable speaker. In fact, without governing conventions, there would be no rules that restrict the use of term *x* for object *y*, and "every word would denote every object." Finally, it is legitimate

[37] See the discussion of *NyS* 2.2.13–39 below for further elaboration of related Mīmāṃsā positions.

to speak of the Vedas as "eternal" in deference to traditional claims, but such eternality amounts to an "uninterrupted succession of teachers and students," not an abstract timelessness.

Who exactly are the authoritative speakers of the Vedas, then? For Vātsyāyana, they are likely *ṛṣis* or sages, special beings with the rare capacity to intuit the religious truths expressed in Vedic statements. We see this under 1.1.8 and 4.1.60, where otherworldly and Vedic testimony is attributed to the sages (*ṛṣis*). He does speak of God, Īśvara, as an "authority" (*āpta*) under 4.1.21. But unlike later Naiyāyikas, he does not explicitly articulate the notion of God as the original speaker of the Veda.[38]

Part 2 (2.2.1–69)

The second part of Chapter 2 continues the discussion of knowledge sources and philosophy of language.

2.2.1–12: There are only four irreducible *pramāṇa* types

This section has three subsections: a consideration of candidate *pramāṇas* not included in the *Nyāya-sūtra* list (2.1.1–2), a defense of postulation (2.2.3–6), and a defense of absence (2.2.7–12).

An objector to Nyāya's wholesale epistemology argues that it is too restrictive, ignoring four legitimate knowledge sources that should have been included (2.2.1):

1. *Tradition (aitihya):* "An assertion that is passed down in the form 'they say . . . ' but for which the original speaker cannot be identified."

[38] In the subcommentary of Vācaspati, Nyāya's theory of testimony and its theism become united in the argument that the original teacher of the Veda and the original convention setter for language is God himself (*NyVT* 2.1.55; 2.1.68).

2. *Postulation (arthāpatti):* "The understanding derived from implication, from a consequence that obtains. When something is conveyed, some other fact is understood as a consequence. This is postulation."
3. *Inclusion (sambhava):* "Knowing that something is the case because something else is the true and that the two are invariably connected."
4. *Absence (abhāva):* "The opposition of nonexistence with what exists."[39]

Vātsyāyana's response is simply that while each of these is, indeed, a legitimate source of knowledge, they can all be reduced to more fundamental types. Tradition is ultimately testimony, while the other three are ultimately inference.

Vātsyāyana makes a number of remarks that enhance our understanding of these subtypes. He notes that the definition of testimony under 1.1.7 still applies to tradition. This makes clear that one does not need to first establish that a speaker is authoritative as a condition of accepting that their statement is true. At its core, testimony flows from an authoritative speaker, but it is often unlikely that we are in the position to gauge the original speaker's qualifications at all. Still, given the sorts of tests and observable indicators discussed in the immediately preceding section, tradition amounts to statements that have not been refuted in their long history. Furthermore, we see that in tradition, the authority behind the utterance includes trust in one's community, which preserves the assertion. This feature of tradition—that it rests on what may be called diffused authority—distinguishes it from ordinary cases of testimony, whose authority can be traced directly to a speaker.

Within classical Indian philosophy, postulation (*arthāpatti*) is often treated as something like inference to the best explanation or

[39] This is a quotation of *VS* 3.1.11.

a transcendental argument.[40] But interpretations by both classical philosophers and modern scholars are somewhat fluid. They range from the notion that postulation is simply inference under another name to its being a non-inferential capacity to unpack language according to context, akin to H. P. Grice's notion of conversational implicature. A paradigm example of postulation is: "Fat Devadatta does not eat during the day. He must, therefore, eat at night." I would suggest that Vātsyāyana's remark that it "functions through opposition" (2.2.1) captures the notion that it unpacks what is missing or presupposed for a statement to make sense.

Vātsyāyana also holds that postulation is a subspecies of *anumāna*, that by which we make immediate inferences:

> Postulation [*arthāpatti*] is something that follows [*āpatti*] from its meaning [*arthāt*]. "Something that follows" means a consequence that obtains. Postulation, then is the understanding that is a consequence of some other thing that is conveyed. Upon hearing "When there are no rainclouds, there is no rain," one understands "When there are rainclouds, there is rain." (*Commentary* 2.2.1)

This account of postulation is also a lens by which Vātsyāyana's notion of inference can be expanded and nuanced. See Appendix C for further discussion.

Vātsyāyana's defense of postulation looks familiar in broad outline, as it resembles the defense of inference under 2.1.37–38. In both cases, the challenger alleges that a putative knowledge source sometimes generates error and thus fails to be a true *pramāṇa*.[41] The response is likewise to appeal to a disjunctive conception of

[40] Keating 2020 is a recent collection of translations and analyses of *arthāpatti* throughout classical Indian philosophy.

[41] As pointed out by Tucci (1929), this argument against *arthāpatti* is found in the early Buddhist debate manual *Tarka-śāstra*, suggesting that Vātsyāyana was familiar with the text.

pramāṇa, where a true source always hits the mark and deviations are not the real thing. The challenger has misconstrued the characteristic output of postulation.

Sūtras 2.2.7–12 take up absence. The interlocutor alleges that absence does not establish anything positive; hence, it is unauthoritative. Vātsyāyana is probably right when he accuses them of mere impertinence, as the challenge seems sophistical: *absence by definition is negative, so it cannot directly establish something positive.* Still, this gives Vātsyāyana an opportunity to explain the way we learn from this ancillary knowledge source. The example used in the sūtras and *Commentary* seems to be that of a clothes washer, who must sort articles to be taken and those to be left alone. Those meant to be left alone are marked. When told to collect the unmarked pieces of clothing, an individual can identify them through the absence of the mark. What the objector misunderstands is the fundamentally relational nature of absence. Absence is always *of something* that the cognitive agent has in mind (2.2.11).

Vātsyāyana seems to be operating with a simple typology of absence, where it is either a prior absence of something yet to be created or a posterior absence of something that has been destroyed. A more robust typology may be found before him in Chapter 9 of the *Vaiśeṣika-sūtra*, which also mentions relational absence, "what exists is nonexistent (somewhere else)" (*VS* 9.1.4). Later Naiyāyikas include relational absence as a sui generis category. Here, in fidelity to the sūtras, Vātsyāyana argues that the relational absence found in the example is simply a subspecies of prior absence. Unmarked clothing and other such things are "yet to be marked," perhaps indefinitely (2.2.12).

The objection and the response within the sūtras depict absence as a means to know *something else*. The absence of specific marks lets us know which articles of clothing are meant to be taken. Should a student attend class at the normal time and find an empty room, she may then realize that class was canceled. Understood this way, it is fitting to reduce absence to a form of inference. It serves as the indicator by which we know something else. But this does not address how we apprehend an absence itself. How, for example, do I know that there is not a horse in my office right now? Given his explanation of the clothing example, Vātsyāyana seems to hold that we first know something positive, paradigmatically by seeing it. We see, for example, an article of clothing. We also have an explicit or tacit recollection of something else that could be present but is not. This is how we apprehend absence. This is in accord with his remarks in the introduction to the *Commentary*:

> When something visible is illuminated by light, something else that would be visible, but remains unseen, must not exist. One thinks "If it existed, it would be known, but since it is not known, it must not exist."

Knowledge of absence is thus grounded in knowledge of something positive (the location of the absence), assisted by a background instance of *tarka*, suppositional reasoning. I *see* the absence of the horse in my office when my perception of the contents of my office is aided by *tarka*.[42]

2.2.13–39: The impermanence of sound

This section of the sūtras transitions away from mainstream epistemology to issues within philosophy of language. For Nyāya, the two domains tend to overlap, as language is a way by which we learn about the world. Vātsyāyana starts by noting that there are various sorts of sounds (*śabda*). Insofar as it is uttered by a trustworthy communicator, *śabda* was spoken of earlier as testimony.

[42] Understood this way, there is no contradiction between the sūtra's claim that absence is reducible to inference and the traditional Nyāya notion, implied by Vātsyāyana here and made explicit by his subcommentator Uddyotakara (*NV* 1.1.4), that we can see absences directly.

Now sound will be considered in a more general sense, especially with respect to its metaphysical status. To motivate the discussion, Vātsyāyana illustrates significant disagreement, listing four incompatible positions on the metaphysics of sound (he does not name the associated schools, but I supply the most likely candidates in parentheses):

Sound is a quality of the ether (*ākāśa*). It is all-pervasive, eternal, and capable of being manifest (Mīmāṃsā).

Sound, along with other qualities like scent, preexists in specific substances and is capable of becoming manifest (Sāṃkhya).

Sound is a quality of the ether and, like cognition, subject to creation and destruction (Vaiśeṣika/Nyāya).

Sound arises when the elements are "jolted." It has no substratum, and it is subject to creation and destruction (Buddhism).

Although four positions are listed here, Mīmāṃsā receives almost exclusive attention.[43] Mīmāṃsā champions the thesis that "sound is eternal," while Nyāya denies it. The Nyāya/Mīmāṃsā debate over sound has been alluded to multiple times already in the *Commentary*, being the subject of the paradigm argument analyzed under 1.1.32–39 and used as an illustration for specific types of inferences (1.1.5), doubt triggers (1.1.23), and fallacies (1.2.9). Related Mīmāṃsā positions also seem targeted when Nyāya argues for the conventional basis of denotation (2.1.54–55) and for the basis of the Veda's authority (2.1.68).[44] Exactly why this issue is so important for the *Nyāya-sūtra* reflects both a historical debate

[43] By "Mīmāṃsā" I refer to the school as most likely known to Vātsyāyana, the *Mīmāṃsā-sūtra* (c. second century BCE) and Śabara's commentary (c. 350 CE), along with lost pre-Śabara works such as that of the Vṛttikāra he quotes under *MS* 1.1.5.

[44] It is also the context for many of the examples of dialectical rejoinders catalogued in Chapter 5.

about sacred sound in the form of the Vedas and an age-old philosophical problem regarding absences.

Mīmāṃsā's raison d'être is the defense and interpretation of the ritual teachings of the Vedas, and even its most sophisticated philosophical holdings are tethered to this directive. One way to understand Mīmāṃsā charitably is to start with what seems to be its fascination with the revelatory nature of language. In his *Bhāṣya* on the *Mīmāṃsā-sūtra*, Śabara compares Vedic statements to the vividness of direct experience. He remarks that "when the Veda is said to *assert*, this means that it reveals something; it causes something to be known."[45] The crux of Śabara's broader argument seems to be that the nature of cognition is to reveal information, and as such, there is incongruence between its revelatory nature and its being prima facie false or even doubted. Only in the light of external information does cognition become falsified.[46] This is the basis of Mīmāṃsā's theory of intrinsic justification (discussed under 2.1.68 above).

For utterances to generate understanding just by being heard requires certain conditions to be met. *MS* 1.1.5 holds that Vedic words (*śabda*) are sources of knowledge with respect to *dharma*, because Vedic words have an innate (*autpattika*) relationship with their objects or meaning (*artha*). Śabara glosses "innate" as *nitya*, a word that often means "eternal," adding that *autpattika*, which literally means "inborn," does not mean that Vedic words are "born" or created. It means that the relationship that Vedic words have with their objects is part of their nature: "the relationship between the word and its object is inseparable." Vedic statements about *dharma*

[45] *MSŚBh* 1.1.5; 1.1.2. More than a millennium earlier, such fascination is attested within the Vedas themselves, where sacred speech is personified as a goddess whose blessings were sought by poets, whose creative genius was spoken of as *seeing* and not merely *inventing* the contents of their works.

[46] This argument has some affinity to Burge's (1993, 471) argument for default trust in testimony: "The very content of an intelligible message presented as true" suggests a prima facie connection to truth, since "content is constitutively dependent, in the first instance, on patterned connections to a subject matter, connections that insure in normal circumstances a baseline of true thought presentations."

are non-contingently tied to their meanings and require nothing outside themselves as guarantors of this tie. In this, they are like ordinary words. Referring terms like "cow" are *nitya* in this sense. If not, they could not generate knowledge.

MS 1.1.6–23 responds to a number of objections to the notion that words are *nitya* while also offering a number of positive arguments. It, and the current section of the *Nyāya-sūtra*, seem to be targeting each other and responding to views presented by each other. Likewise, Śabara and Vātsyāyana target broadly similar expansions and developments of the opposed school's positions. Among the positive arguments offered by Mīmāṃsā is that words must exist beyond the mere seconds of their phenomenal availability if they are to serve the purpose of communicating:

> If a word is destroyed right after being uttered then it would be unable to generate knowledge for the other person. It would not be spoken for the sake of another. But on the view that it continues to exist, upon hearing it multiple times, one gains comprehension. (*MSŚBh* 1.1.18)

MSŚBh 1.1.19–20 further argues that common nouns like "cow" refer to the basic class (*ākṛti*) associated with (e.g.) cows and must do so inherently.[47] This avoids a vicious regress. If someone were to suggest that there was an original convention-setting event where it was decided that the term "cow" denotes a basic form or class of cows, the convention setter would *already* need a way to refer to that very form to be denoted by "cow." And akin to the way we speak of universals, we do not say there were (e.g.) eight *cow words* in someone's statement but rather eight instances of the word "cow."

Ambiguities in these arguments have led to divergent interpretations both in the classical tradition and among modern scholars. While the

[47] Also see *MS* 1.3.33. While Nyāya uses the term *ākṛti* for something's shape, Mīmāṃsā uses it for a class type.

original point of departure for this section of the *Mīmāṃsā-sūtra* is the claim that the *relationship* between a word and its meaning is *nitya*, the arguments collected under *MSŚBh* 1.1.6–23 often use the shorthand "Word is *nitya*." *MSŚBh* 1.1.6 ties the two issues together in an interlocutor's voice:

> You say that the relationship between the word and its object is eternal. That cannot be the case since the word itself is impermanent. A word is subject to destruction, and when it is again created, the relationship it has with its object is composed.

The term *nitya* is also beset by ambiguity. While it often means "eternal," it can mean "regularly occurring" and "fixed." Scholars have disputed the best reading in this context.[48] For that matter, *śabda* may mean "sound" in general, as well as "word" and "language." It clearly means "word" in the *MSŚBh* but slides into the more general sense of audible sound in this section of the *NySBh* (2.2.13–39). *MSŚBh* 1.1.17 distinguishes between a word and the "noise" one makes while speaking it. All of this is to say that the two sides run the danger of talking past each other.

The purely philosophical problem in the background concerns absences. When does something's absence entail its nonexistence as opposed to its merely being concealed to the observer? Obviously, from a phenomenological perspective, sounds and audible words as experienced are ephemeral. At the same time, there are many things that continue to exist while unmanifest to an observer, such as the color of a book that can only be seen in the presence of light. Could sound also exist in such a way?

[48] Freschi and Graheli (2005, 294–295) are exceptionally clear in disentangling these strands and argue that within the *MSŚBh*, *nitya* means not that words are eternal but simply that their relationship with their objects must be fixed or constant. Scharf (1996, 198–199) conversely argues that for Mīmāṃsā, words must be eternal.

In the face of disagreement and the wide range of philosophical issues outlined above, *Nyāya-sūtra* 2.2.13–17 articulates three reasons sound is impermanent:

1. It is caused.
2. It can be apprehended by a sense faculty.
3. It is commonly spoken of in a way that is consistent with impermanence.

The reasoning behind reason 1 should be fairly clear. Vātsyāyana (like other Indian philosophers) holds that "having been caused" entails "being impermanent." The *Vaiśeṣika-sūtra* defines something as being eternal when "it exists without being caused" (4.1.1). For Nyāya and Vaiśeṣika, eternal things include atoms and individual selves. Conversely, things that are created are bound by time and subject to eventual dissolution. With "conjunction" and "disjunction," Vātsyāyana speaks of things that cause sound such as striking a drum and breaking a stick, respectively.

Vātsyāyana interprets reason 2 in a nuanced way, seeing it as countering an objection to reason 1: sound is not caused but simply *manifest* by specific conditions.[49] Against this, he argues that we hear certain sounds such as the snap of an axe striking a tree after the actual conjunction of the axe with the tree has ceased. This distinguishes sound from other things such as visible color (e.g., the orange color of a book cover), which continues to exist even when unseen and is merely manifested by conditions such as the presence of light. Things like color must be co-located with their "manifester." Sound that is heard is the downstream effect of an original sound, which initiates a chain of cascading sound events expanding outward. This would not be possible if sound were merely *manifest* and consequently tethered to the locus of manifestation.

[49] *MSŚBh* 1.1.6; 1.1.12–13. *NyS* 5.1.29–31 identifies this argument as an instance of the dialectical rejoinder "by non-awareness."

Reason 3 is also significantly nuanced by Vātsyāyana. He takes it to refer to the way we commonly describe sound as intense or faint. Such descriptors only refer to things that are created and vary according to their causes. An interlocutor interjects that such variance may be due to adjustments in the *manifester*. Against this, Vātsyāyana argues that the experience of one sound drowning out another undermines the suggestion. For example, we notice loud drums drowning out the sound of a stringed instrument. This is because for each of them, the initial conjunction (of, e.g., a drumstick with the surface of the drum) creates cascading sequences of sound that range beyond their locus with varied intensity, such that they can override or be overridden by other cascading sounds.[50] By analogy with color, things that are merely manifest (as a book cover's color is manifest by light) remain tied to their loci, such that they couldn't come into conflict and drown each other out.

Sūtras 2.2.14–17 consider counterexamples to Nyāya's case. Against reason 1, the counterexample is absences, which may be caused and are yet eternal. That is, when (e.g.) breaking a pot, one causes an absence of that pot, which lasts forever. Thus, "being caused" does not entail "being impermanent." Vātsyāyana argues that to say that something is impermanent is to speak of the way something *positive* must come to an end. And something is eternal if it exists as a positive entity without cause or the possibility of destruction. This does not apply to absences. They are spoken of as "eternal" only in a secondary sense (2.2.15).

Against reason 2, the counterexample is universals, which may be apprehended by a sense faculty and are yet eternal. Indeed, while they are eternal, some universals, such as "redness," can be directly apprehended by the senses. Vātsyāyana responds that the correct reading of "can be apprehended by a sense faculty" is that this is not mere apprehension but apprehension of something disengaged

[50] This account of how sound travels is expanded under sūtras 2.2.35–39.

from its cause, which distinguishes it from "manifested" things that are bound to their loci (2.2.16).

Against reason 3, things that are permanent, such as selves or the ether, are sometimes said to have "parts."[51] Such nonliteral talk is common, so that might be the sort of discourse in play when sounds are spoken of as contingent and varied. Vātsyāyana responds that "part-speak" is nonliterally applied to selves and the ether, while statements about the fluctuating intensity or weakness of sounds are literally true (2.2.17).

Sūtras 2.2.18–21 restate the creation/manifestation debate outlined above. Nyāya's view is summarized by Vātsyāyana:

> Sound is heard when it is uttered. Being heard, we infer that it did not exist prior to that point. And after being uttered, we no longer hear it. Having occurred, it no longer exists, and therefore, we do not hear it anymore. It is said that this is so [in sūtra 2.2.18] because we do not identify any obstructors (which would prevent our ability to hear something that is still existing but unmanifest). (*Commentary* 2.2.18)

The final subsection (2.2.22–39) offers several further arguments by the proponent of the thesis that sound is eternal, with rebuttals from the Nyāya camp. "Sound is eternal, because it is intangible" (2.2.22–24), which is refuted in that intangibility *deviates.* Atoms are tangible yet permanent, while actions, which are intangible, are impermanent. Vātsyāyana was apparently so taken by the fault of this argument that under 1.2.5, he uses it as an example of the counterfeit reason the *deviant*.

Others argue that as they are transmitted, sound or words must be "shared" and thus endure beyond the act of sharing.[52] Thus, "Sound is eternal because it is bestowed" (2.2.25–28). This

[51] *NySBh* 4.2.22 gives an account of ether as impartite.
[52] See *MSŚBh* 1.1.18.

argument fails because words are significantly unlike other things that are shared and that clearly persist throughout the process.

Further, "Sound is eternal because it is repeatedly recited" (2.2.29–32). This echoes *MSŚBh* 1.1.19–20 which was reviewed above. We speak of a single word as being recited ten times, not ten different words being recited. This is rejected on the grounds that the word "repetition" may apply to distinct actions. To say that someone danced three times does not mean the dance is each time a single entity, which continues to exist when uninstantiated.

Finally, there is another appeal to ignorance, "Sound is eternal because a cause of its destruction is not apprehended" (2.2.33–39).[53] Here Vātsyāyana unpacks more fully his protoscientific account of "sound streams" and how they travel though the ether, with each sound instance created by an immediately preceding sound instance.

2.2.40–57: Phonemes and their transformation

This section consists of a debate over the status of phonemes (a rough translation of the Sanskrit *varṇa*). Vātsyāyana opens by noting that *śabda* has two forms, that composed of phonemes and that which is mere noise, and he tells us that the current discussion is restricted to the former. He does not provide an explicit conceptual connection to the previous section, but one may be found in *MS* 1.1.10 and 1.1.16, where an interlocutor argues that the fact that certain phonemes seem to transform motivates the position that they are impermanent. As phonemes are the fundamental units of words, the interlocutor argues that the latter must then be

[53] Gangopadhyaya's translation of the introductory *Commentary* on 2.2.36 (1982, 149, lines 16–17) is missing a crucial negation, which obscures the passage. It should read, "Impression in the form of an auxiliary cause is not apprehended. Because of its non-apprehension, it does *not* exist."

impermanent. We find a similar claim in *NyS* 2.2.50, "If phonemes were eternal, there could be no transformation."

Sanskrit has rules that govern "euphonic combination" (*sandhi*), how vowels and consonants transform and combine when they come into contact with each other. Often, these rules allow for smoother recitation, akin to saying "come'ere" for "come here" and "nex'time" for "next time" in English. Vātsyāyana uses a stock example (also used by Śabara in *MSŚBh* 1.1.10): *dadhi* + *atra* = *dadhyatra*.[54] Here, *i* turns into *y* when the two terms are joined within speech. The reason for doubt in this case is that some take the *i* to be transformed into *y*, while others hold that the *y* replaces *i* (2.2.40).

It is not obvious which thinker or camp the current interlocutor represents. Mīmāṃsā largely agrees with the Nyāya arguments about the facts on the ground, holding that in these cases, what occurs is substitution, not transformation. The subcommentator Vācaspati Miśra suggests that the opponent is from the Sāṃkhya camp. This is plausible in that a central aspect of Sāṃkhya metaphysics is that material causes transform without being destroyed, and possible transformations exist latently within their material causes.

Philosophically, this section is not especially sophisticated. It does, however, give Vātsyāyana an opportunity to reflect on issues of metaphysical identity in the context of change or transformation:

> Transformation is spoken of in the following way: When some kind of substance composed of clay or gold retains its nature, but its earlier configuration ends and a new configuration arises. (*Commentary* 2.2.46)

> What is eternal is not caused, nor does it cease. Something eternal has the property of being neither created nor destroyed. (*Commentary* 2.2.51)

[54] *Dadhi* is coagulated milk, and *atra* means "here." The two form a sentence, "Curd is here."

Vātsyāyana concludes by pointing out that "transformation" may be used as a nonliteral shorthand for various ways we replace certain phonemes with others (2.2.57).

2.2.58–69: The meaning of common nouns

This section reflects on a question in the philosophy of language that can be traced to the landmark *Eight-Chaptered Treatise on Grammar* (*Āṣṭādhyāyī*) by Pāṇini (late fifth century BCE), along with subordinate works such as the "Great Commentary" (*Mahābhāṣya*) of Patañjali (c. 150 CE).[55] Grammarians (*vaiyākaraṇas*) were akin to "ordinary language" philosophers in that their point of departure in understanding language is usage. While articulating rules and schemas that govern proper Sanskrit usage, the grammarians would sometimes identify and advocate for philosophical views as related to linguistic commitments. Categories developed by grammarians were also used as analytic tools by later thinkers of various stripes.[56]

The sūtras themselves provide a bridge between the former section and this one:

> Phonemes become words [*pada*] when case endings are added to them. (*NyS* 2.2.58)

Vātsyāyana explains:

> Phonemes that are appropriately transformed take on case endings and are then designated "words." There are two kinds of case ending, nominal and verbal. For example, "The

[55] The following discussion is a revised version of Dasti 2020.
[56] See *NySBh* 2.1.16; 4.1.16.

> Brahmin cooks" (where both the noun and the verb have appropriate case endings). . . . Here the motive is to understand what is apprehended through words. And, having taken up nouns, there is investigation. The example is "cow." (*Commentary* 2.2.58)

Grammarians divide words into four types—nominals, verbs, preverbs, and particles—and then subdivide nominals into general terms, property terms, action terms, and what may be called proper names. As noted by Vātsyāyana, the topic of this section is general terms, or common nouns. Like the grammarians, Nyāya has a referentialist theory of meaning. Meaning is the object(s) denoted by a term. There are varieties of secondary meaning and figurative speech as well, but in ordinary usage, the meaning of a term is the object it denotes.[57] The question here is, what exactly is the object (*padārtha*) of a common noun such as "cow"? This section examines arguments for three alternatives: individual, shape, and universal (2.2.58–65), followed by Nyāya's settled answer (2.2.66). It concludes by offering definitions and analyses of individual, shape, and universal (2.2.67–69).

In the characteristic style, the sūtras introduce doubt to stimulate inquiry:

> There is doubt owing to usage that is directed to the individual [*dravya*], form [*ākṛti*], and universal [*jāti*], which are inseparably connected. (*NyS* 2.2.59)

Before Vātsyāyana, and likely before the *Nyāya-sūtra* itself, various thinkers had argued for specific candidates among these three options. Ancient grammarians took different stances on this issue, some advocating the individual, others

[57] Vātsyāyana investigates secondary meaning at length in *NySBh* 1.2.12–14, while taking up the fallacy of equivocation (*chala*).

the universal, and others both.[58] Mīmāṃsakas advocate the universal (*MS* 1.3.30–35).[59]

Following the sūtras, Vātsyāyana sympathetically unpacks the rationale for each option:

> It's the individual, since the usage is for an individual in the case of the word "which" as well as with words for group, offering, possession, number, growth, reduction, color, compounds and offspring. (*NyS* 2.2.60)

Vātsyāyana elaborates that taking the individual to be the meaning is the only way to account for usages that require granular specification. In phrases such as "The cow that is standing" or "The cow that is sitting," only individuals can account for usage. Because universals are singular and undivided, they cannot serve as the meaning of usages that require plurality or specification. Vātsyāyana remarks that "individual" (*vyakti*) is here synonymous with "substance" (*dravya*).

Next, the rationale for the object's being a universal is given: in its absence, a bare individual could not play any role within language.

> No, it is not the individual since there would be nothing to ground usage. (*NyS* 2.2.61)

Vātsyāyana elaborates that bare, unqualified substances cannot be the meaning of the word "cow" even in the usages mentioned above. Even when speaking of specific cows, what is referred to is

58 Scharf 1996, 21–150, is an excellent study of this issue and provides translation of Patañjali's commentary on Pāṇini 1.2.58 and 1.2.64, major loci of grammatical debate on this subject.

59 In the *MS*, the term *ākṛti* is used for the object of common nouns, but in Mīmāṃsā usage, *ākṛti* is a universal and not merely a shape or configuration as it is for Nyāya. In pre-Vātsyāyana grammatical texts, *ākṛti* is used in both senses.

something that is being distinguished or qualified *as a cow*. The universal is baked into the reference, so to speak.

In response to the problems of individuation, the advocate of the universal suggests:

> There is usage of certain words (like "stick"), with reference to things like Brahmins . . . because of conditions like association, even though these are not what the words primarily refer to. (*NyS* 2.2.62)

On this account, the meaning of a term is the universal, but individuals maybe spoken of through secondary, figurative use (*upacāra*). Vātsyāyana accordingly provides a list of stock examples of secondary usage, where nonstandard meanings are affixed to terms by the force of context. (See Table 11.) On behalf of this option, Vātsyāyana notes that this solves the problem of individuation: "A word denoting a universal is directed toward the individual through association or connection."

The case for the third option, form, is cleverly motivated by taking seriously the rationale provided for the universal:

> It is the form [*ākṛti*] that is the primary meaning, because determination of what exists depends upon it. (*NyS* 2.2.63)

Vātsyāyana explains that the primary referent for common nouns must be something that makes it possible to distinguish between types of things when we communicate. While universals provide a metaphysical basis for making such distinctions, they don't provide an epistemological basis. Our knowledge of objects as belonging to certain classes is itself dependent on our ability to identify repeatable forms or shapes:

> Something's form is a fixed arrangement of its parts along with its sub-parts. When form is grasped, what exists is determined, and

Table 11. The grounds for figurative use under 2.2.62.

Ground	Example
association (*sahacaraṇa*)	"Feed the sticks" means "feed the Brahmins" because the latter are associated with the sticks they carry.
location (*sthāna*)	"The stands are shouting" means "the people in the stands are shouting."
purpose (*tādarthya*)	"They're weaving a mat" refers to the straw being used to make the mat before the mat is completed.
comportment (*vṛtta*)	"The king is Kubera [the god of wealth]" because the king conducts himself in a way that we associate with Kubera.
measure (*māna*)	"That is an *āḍhaka*" for a bag of grain that weighs an *āḍhaka* (roughly eight pounds).
holding (*dhāraṇa*)	"Scale paste" means sandalwood paste on a scale to be weighted.
proximity (*samīpya*)	"The cows are roaming the Ganges" refers to the tracts of land near the Ganges.
connection (*yoga*)	"The black one" means a cloth that has black color.
cause (*sādhana*)	"Food is life" means that food allows one to live.
importance (*ādhipatya*)	"This person *is* the family" means that this person is the most important member of their family.

we say, "That's a cow," "That's a horse." Without this being grasped, such instances of knowledge would not occur. The rule is: the thing that is properly denoted by a word is that which, through its being grasped, results in what exists being determined. That is its meaning. (*Commentary* 2.2.63)

Word use depends upon distinctions and, hence, universals, but to know something as possessing a universal itself usually requires the recognition of a particular form. Therefore, it is argued, such forms or shapes are the primary referents of common nouns.

What problems are faced by this third entry? The core problem advanced is that form is metaphysically inessential compared with the universal and individual. Vātsyāyana argues that if we take a word to denote something that is connected to a universal such as cowhood, then form seems superfluous in contrast with the individual, which is the locus of cowhood. "What is connected to the universal, then? A thing, an individual substance that has a fixed arrangement of parts." A metaphysical basis for use of common nouns is what is needed, but form is ultimately an individual feature of an individual substance. The next sūtra amplifies this point by noting that a cow shape can exist in an individual without the corresponding universal, and thus it cannot play the role that is needed:

> The primary referent is the universal, because a clay cow, though endowed with individuality and shape, cannot be the subject of the consecrating ceremonies of washing, and so on. (*NyS* 2.2.64)

Vātsyāyana makes the case plain:

> "Wash the cow," "Bring the cow," "Donate a cow"—these would not be used for a cow made of clay. Why? Because a clay cow would not belong to the proper class; it lacks the appropriate universal.

The final salvo in this debate is fired on behalf of both the individual and the shape against the universal. In effect, an interlocutor stamps his foot to the ground while reiterating that it is epistemic priority that matters here, not metaphysical priority (2.2.65).

Before looking at Vātsyāyana's response, let us take stock of reasons for and against each of the candidates. (See Table 12.)

The Nyāya solution to this apparent trilemma is to propose that all three serve as the complex object(s) of reference:

> Nevertheless, the individual, the form, and the universal constitute the word's meaning. (*NyS* 2.2.66)

Table 12. The three candidates for the meaning of common nouns.

Meaning	Case for	Case against
individual (*vyakti*)	Provides grounds for fine-grained, granular reference; is epistemically fundamental, even when grasping universals.	Is incapable of providing grounds for regularities of reference.
universal (*jāti*)	Provides metaphysical basis for regularities of reference; accounts for usages that distinguish between real members of a class and objects that merely have their shape (e.g., a cow vs. a clay cow).	Is epistemically secondary, as it is only grasped after grasping an individual and its shape.
shape (*ākṛti*)	Accounts for what is epistemically immediate when identifying class membership; accounts for usage pertaining to similarly shaped artifacts (a clay cow is still called "cow").	Is as much an individual as the substance it qualifies; is thus also incapable of providing grounds for regularities of reference. Things with "cow" shapes but lacking the universal *cowhood* are sometimes outside the scope of the word "cow."

Vātsyāyana explains:

> There is no rule about which of the three would be the meaning element that is predominant or subordinate in any given case of a word's usage. For when one wants to talk about a distinct thing to be understood in a specific manner, then it is the individual that is the predominant meaning and the universal and shape subordinate. But when one does not want to talk about distinctness or difference but is speaking in the mode of generalization, then it is the universal that is the predominant meaning and the individual and shape subordinate. All of this is richly illustrated in common usage. The predominance of shape may be likewise understood. (*Commentary* 2.2.66)

I would suggest that the best reading of *NyS* 2.2.66 is as a disjunction, not a conjunction. The meaning consists in the individual or the universal or the form, with the "or" being inclusive. In paradigm cases, all three disjuncts are present even as some are primary and some are subordinate. But in non-paradigm cases, fewer than three are directly denoted. This is supported by Vātsyāyana's remarks under 2.2.68:

> When a universal is not made known by means of a form, in cases like clay, gold, and silver, form is excluded. The condition of being the object of the term is vacated.

Clay, gold, and silver are malleable; their observable form is not what indicates their nature. Therefore, the common noun "gold" is used to refer only to an individual piece of gold and the universal gold-ness. This is an explicit admission that in non-paradigm cases, the object of reference need not include all three disjuncts, even as they are all typically present in paradigm cases.

This is consistent with the view advanced throughout the *NySBh* that real objects are typically multifaceted complexes that endure changes of properties. For example, when we refer to a cow, we speak of a substance (*dravya*), possessing a distinct shape (*ākṛti*), and a universal (*jāti*) inhering in all cows. Even when some properties of an object are secondary, latent, or merely dispositional, they are still metaphysically integrated with the object. From the epistemic perspective, some properties may be at the forefront of a cognitive event, with no need to consign others to nonexistence.

This section concludes by offering definitions of individual, shape, and universal:

> The individual is something tangible which is the bearer of specific qualities. (*NyS* 2.2.67)

> Form is that by which a universal or its indicators are known. (*NyS* 2.2.68)

> A universal is that which produces knowledge of commonality. (*NyS* 2.2.69)

Vyakti (translated here as "individual") is not a standard term found in Nyāya-Vaiśeṣika lists of metaphysical reals but is inherited from earlier debates about language by grammarians and others. Vātsyāyana's gloss of sūtra 2.2.67 presents an opportunity to connect the notion to Nyāya's referentialist philosophy of language in a deeper way. He clarifies that an individual is a substance, but not all substances are "individuals" in this linguistic sense. Only those that are compounds, built up out of parts, and that locate qualities such as color, taste, and touch. (Again, Vātsyāyana here appeals to Vaiśeṣika categories, and its list of qualities in particular.) In short, "individuals" can be apprehended by the senses.

This seems to go hand in hand with the fact that the individual is arguably the most basic object of reference. Universals and forms must metaphysically inhere in substances (or, for some universals, in properties or actions that inhere in substances). And the substances that we most immediately apprehend, which are *vyakti*, are objects of "knowledge by acquaintance," to borrow Bertrand Russell's (1910–1911) phrase. Insofar as they are not objects of immediate sense perception, substances such as atoms or abstract selves are not *vyakti*. We refer to atoms or selves through description or by appeal to other manifest things with which they are connected (in the case of a specific self, its body and behavior, as well as its mental states that are evident through bodily indicators).

3

Objects of Knowledge

Part 1 (3.1.1–72)

Chapter 1 of the *Nyāya-sūtra* lists and defines the sixteen major topics of the system. Chapter 2 provides special investigations into knowledge sources. Chapter 3 now examines the "objects of knowledge" (*prameyas*) introduced and listed under 1.1.9:

> Self, body, senses, sense objects, cognition, *manas*, purposeful action, vice, rebirth, karmic results, suffering, and liberation are the objects of knowledge. (1.1.9)

3.1.1–26: The self (*ātman*)

This section argues that the self is an irreducible, genuine feature of reality. It has five major subsections: self as other than the senses (3.1.1–3), self as other than the body (3.1.4–6), the unity of the visual faculty (3.1.7–14), self as other than the *manas* (3.1.15–17), and the eternality of the self (3.1.18–26).

We have seen under 1.1.10 that a self is an enduring psychological substance which is the substratum of properties such as cognition and desire, co-locating these properties in a way that allows them to collectively constitute an individual person. A self's continued existence is the basis of an individual's identity through time. The question of the self is taken up again here, particularly in light of reductionist opposition. Vātsyāyana starts with a question:

Vātsyāyana's Commentary *on the* Nyāya-sūtra. Matthew R. Dasti, Oxford University Press.
 DOI: 10.1093/oso/9780197625927.003.0003

> Is the self nothing more than the aggregate of body, senses, *manas*, cognition, and feeling? Or is it rather something distinct? (*Commentary* 3.1.1)

Vātsyāyana recognizes that in ordinary language, people are said to "see by means of their eyes," presupposing a view where an agent (self) employs instruments (senses) to perform an action (perception). He notes that this fails to provide a clear answer, however, since we speak of agents as being entirely separate from their instruments ("She cuts with an axe") but also as collections whose parts are instruments ("The tree stands with its roots").

While this subsection of the sūtras is specifically concerned to distinguish the self from the senses, the *Commentary* tends to target bundle theories of personhood more generally. With respect to agents and their properties, Ganeri (2001a, 641) suggests that the operative distinction is between the "is" of predication, which favors Nyāya's substance self, and the "is" of constitution, which favors a reductionist approach. On the substance view, a self has qualities and features that are predicated of it. On the reductionist view, there is nothing except bundles of qualities and features.

Vātsyāyana depicts the proponents of the aggregate view as Buddhist philosophers. We have already seen him identify "those who deny the self" as the opponents in his argument for the diachronic unity of the self under 1.1.10. Under 2.1.33–36, mereological nihilists likely associated with Buddhism deny the reality of composite wholes. This broadly anti-substantialist, reductionist approach finds psychological expression in the historical Buddha's view that personhood is reducible to five aggregates (*skandhas*):

1. material form (states of the body)
2. sensation (hedonic states such as pleasure, pain, and indifference)
3. perception (sensations such as a patch of red)

4. volition (affective states including those that initiate activity)
5. self-consciousness (awareness of one's own bodily and mental states)

These aggregates are collections of fluctuating event states that cause other event states. Collectively, a chain of these may be spoken of as a "stream." On this account, there is no underlying self that is the basis of personhood but rather contingent, causally interacting clusters of event states, which we mistakenly reify into a substantial self or person. The Buddha claims that such reification is a fundamental cause of suffering:

> Material form, monks, is not-Self. Now were this material form Self, it would not lead to affliction, and one would be able to effectively say, "Let my material form be like this or not like this." But inasmuch as material form is not-Self, therefore, it leads to affliction, and one cannot effectively say, "Let my material form be like this, or not like this." [The same is restated for each of the other *skandhas* in order.] (*Discourse on the Characteristic of Not-Self*)[1]

Recall the famous chariot metaphor within *The Questions of King Milinda*, which I cited under 2.1.33. The passage concludes with the following statement attributed to the nun Vajirā:

> Just as, with an assemblage of parts,
> The word "chariot" is used,
> So, when the aggregates exist,
> There is the convention, "a being." (*QKM* 2.1.1)[2]

By the time of Vātsyāyana, major Buddhist philosophers had developed various arguments to illustrate why substances, including

[1] Translated by Peter Harvey, in *BPER*, 269.
[2] Translated by Peter Harvey, in *BPER*, 274.

the psychological substance called "self," were philosophical fictions.[3] Abhidharma thinkers in effect replaced substances with a trope metaphysics. All that exist are *dharmas*, momentary property particulars. In the ninth chapter of his *Abhidharmakośa*, Vasubandhu (c. 350–430 CE) argues that the same reduction holds for material objects and non-material selves:

VASUBANDHU: So how, then, is the self a support of mental states?
Advocate of the self:In the way that the earth is the support of qualities such as scents, and so on.
VASUBANDHU: We are greatly pleased with this! It's this exactly that is our reason for saying "There is no self." In the same way, we say that earth is not different from scents and so on. Gentlemen, which one of you can pick out a stuff called "earth" that is distinct from scents, and so on?[4]

Against this background, the *Nyāya-sūtra* here offers one of its most famous arguments:

> Because a single object is known through sight and touch. (*NyS* 3.1.1)

As explained by Vātsyāyana, this sūtra appeals to the evidence of cross-modal cognition. An object presented by both sight and touch is immediately and intuitively recognized as the same. This entails that sense experiences are not merely "local." There must be something capable of standing above and unifying distinct sensory inputs. While the context of this argument concerns all of the senses, it is no accident that the senses chosen for it are sight and touch. These two allow us to apprehend shape and size, deep

[3] *BPER*, 261–308, collects anti-self arguments by Buddhist philosophers preceding and contemporaneous with Vātsyāyana. See Siderits 2015 for an important philosophical study of Buddhist reductionism.
[4] (Slightly modified) translation by Charles Goodman, in *BPER*, 302–303.

structural features of an object, as opposed to qualities at some remove (e.g., the scent of a flower):

> Two separate cognitions that have the same object are tied together by a single agent. And neither the aggregate [of body, *manas*, etc.] nor the senses could serve as such an agent. Therefore, the very being who grasps a single object through both sight and touch, who brings together cognitions that have the same object and agent but different instrumental causes, is distinct from the body, mind, and senses; it is called "self." (*Commentary* 3.1.1)

This argument mirrors that of 1.1.10:

> The desire to obtain something occurs because different perceptions are tied together by a single experiencer who sees multiple things of the same type. It is thus an indicator of the self. (*Commentary* 1.1.10)

In both arguments, the phenomenon that Vātsyāyana appeals to is *pratisaṃdhāna*, the connecting of multiple cognitive inputs in a single act of awareness. This "tying together" is sometimes translated as "recognition" or "synthetic cognition" and requires a single agent who spans multiple cognitive events. The earlier argument of 1.1.10 focuses on the diachronic identity of the self, with recognition spanning temporal boundaries. The argument of 3.1.1 is about cross-modal awareness that spans boundaries between different sense modalities. We can experience the same object through multiple sense modalities, recognizing it as one and the same.

As unpacked by Vātsyāyana, the argument of 3.1.1 may be reconstructed as follows:

1. Cross-modal awareness occurs.
2. Individual sense faculties are restricted to their own proper contents.

3. The agent of cross-modal awareness must be able to grasp and synthesize the inputs of all the senses.

---

4. The agent of cross-modal awareness cannot be reduced to any of sense faculties.

This conclusion is meant to settle the opening doubt about agents, instruments, and actions. Vātsyāyana makes explicit that it has a broader application than the senses themselves: any part of a fluctuating bundle of cognitive events would lack the capacity to stand above and engage in acts of synthetic cognition. Whatever is the bearer of cross-modal awareness amounts to a self as understood by Nyāya, a cognitive agent that stands above the senses and cannot be reduced to any particular part within a bundle of mental events.

Crucial to the argument is the widely held view that sense faculties are restricted to their own proper objects. Sight scopes only visible form, hearing scopes only sound, and so on. No two sense modalities overlap such that one of them could apprehend the objects of the other. The interlocutor of 3.1.2, however, appeals to this very fact as if it were a rebuttal:

> No, since the sense faculties are restricted to their proper objects. (*NyS* 3.1.2)

It would be odd for an objection to merely reiterate a premise of the argument it is trying to refute. Given Vātsyāyana's expanded account of 3.1.1's argument, it makes more sense to read this objection as asserting a *metaphysical* conclusion about the demarcations between the sense faculties, while premise 2 of Vātsyāyana's argument under 3.1.1 relies on *phenomenological* demarcations between sense faculties. The interlocutor attacks premise 3 by claiming that there is settled evidence against it. On this reading,

3.1.2 would give voice to a long-standing Buddhist rejection of "self," broadly consistent with Hume's celebrated fruitless search, which takes sense experiences to be irreducibly "local."[5] From *The Questions of King Milinda*:

MILINDA: Is there, Nāgasena, such a thing as the self . . . the living principle within, which sees forms through the eye, hears sounds through the ear, experiences tastes through the tongue . . .?

NĀGASENA: I will tell you about the five doors, great king. Listen and give heed attentively. If the living principle within sees forms though the eye in the manner you mention, choosing its window as it likes, can it not then see forms not only through the eye, but also through each of the other five organs of sense? . . .

MILINDA: No, Sir.

NĀGASENA: Then these powers are not united to one another indiscriminately. . . . It is by reason of the eye and forms that sight arises . . . and a similar succession of cause and effect occurs when each of the other five organs of sense is brought into play. And so, herein there is no such thing as self. (*QKM* 2.3.6)[6]

Further:

MILINDA: But if there is no such thing as a self, what is it then which sees forms with the eye, and hears sounds with the ear, and smells odors with the nose, and tastes tastes with the tongue, and feels touch with the body, or perceives qualities with the mind?

[5] In *NySBh* 3.1.12, Vātsyāyana speaks of this view as the idea that "consciousness belongs to the senses" (*indriya-caitanya*).

[6] (Slightly modified) translation by Davids (1890, 86–89).

NĀGASENA: If there is a self which does all this, then if the door of the eye were thrown down (if the eye were plucked out) could it stretch out its head, as it were, through the larger aperture and see forms much more clearly than before? Could one hear sounds better if the ears were torn away, or smell better if the nose were cut off, or taste better if the tongue were pulled out, or feel touch better if the body were destroyed?

MILINDA: Certainly not, Sir.

NĀGASENA: Then there can be no self inside the body. (*QKM* 3.17.15)[7]

As presented in these texts, the *ad absurdum* argument is that a self that stands above the senses would be homuncular, the senses little more than windows, and the self would have another level of senses built into itself so that it may "look" through those windows. Understood along these lines, the metaphysical restriction between the senses claimed by the interlocutor of 3.1.2 would militate against premise 3.

It is possible to frame the objection of 3.1.2 alternatively, as denying the data of premise 1. In effect, it would claim that cross-modal awareness is nothing more than a projection or fancy, and as such, there is no data to be explained. This reading would resonate with certain Abhidharma views cataloged by Vasubandhu. They argue that shape is not real, since if it were, it could be cross-modally apprehended, an impossibility (on Buddhist presuppositions).[8] Soon after Vātsyāyana, Dignāga would also argue that cross-modal synthesis is not possible, since that would violate the restriction of each sense to its proper objects and obviate the need for more than

[7] (Slightly modified) translation by Davids (1890, 132–133).

[8] *ADhKBh*, Chapter 4, "Understanding Action," translated by Poussin and Sangpo (2012, 1291–1292).

one type of sense modality. His solution is also to treat cross-modal awareness as a form of error.[9]

It seems to me that the best reading of the interlocutor is that they are arguing in consonance with the passages from *The Questions of King Milinda* and attacking premise 3. As explained by Vātsyāyana, the interlocutor appeals to a methodological principle put forth elsewhere in the *Commentary*, by which causes are identified.

> If *x* is absent when *y* is absent but occurs in *y*'s presence, then *x* belongs to *y*.

Here *x* is a type of event or occurrence, and *y* is its cause. Thus, grasping of color "belongs to" the visual organ, grasping of scent to the olfactory organ, and so on. By this principle, we have all the evidence we need to account for sense experience of every type, as localized to each sense faculty. The interlocutor concludes, "What's the point in positing something else as the experiencer?"

The response of the *NySBh* has two facets. First, Vātsyāyana argues that the causal principle put forth fails to settle the issue, as it is consistent with two scenarios: (i) the senses are independent causes of sense experience (the Buddhist account), and (ii) they are necessary as instrumental causes but insufficient for sense experience in the absence of a conscious being (the Nyāya account). Second, as reiterated in sūtra 3.1.3, this very restriction only helps the Nyāya case. Though the data under scrutiny are all *sensory*, cross-modal awareness is not reducible to a *specific* sense modality. The restriction of the senses thus makes plain the explanatory need for something else:

> This undeniable proof of a conscious self's functioning can be illustrated. One who sees the color of a ripe piece of fruit infers the taste and scent with which it was previously associated in their

[9] *PS*, Chapter 4, "Examination of Vaiśeṣika," translated by Hattori (1968, 45–46).

> experience . . . it [the conscious self] also allows one to know the various objects of cognition in the form of perception, inference, testimony, doubt, and illumination, having recognized them as due to its own agency. And having heard the authoritative texts [*śāstra*], which covers all topics, a self comes to know things that range further than the ear can hear. For having heard sequential phonemes, putting them together in the form of words and sentences, and remembering the meanings of each word, one comes to grasp complex content that none of the senses could grasp working independently. (*Commentary* 3.1.3)

Vātsyāyana offers examples of the self as the basis of synthetic cognition in five major dimensions of cognitive life:

1. cross-modal recognition
2. states of knowledge generated through *pramāṇas*
3. doubt
4. understanding language (by holding individual ordered letters within standing memory and recognizing words, sentences, and their content in turn)
5. understanding systematic treatises about specialized topics

One aspect of the self that is highlighted here is what we could call "cognitive agency," that insofar as the self is a knower, it participates in a wide range of features we associate with agency: responsibility, ownership, goal-directed activity, and success or failure with respect to goals. All these require the agential self to be an enduring entity, which directly bears the normative weight of its actions. Unpacking the contours of agency, in debate with both Buddhists and Hindu schools such as Sāṃkhya, is a major theme of this third chapter of the *NySBh*.

It is worth pausing to consider some of the attention that contemporary scholars have paid to the cross-modality argument as put forth here. Arindam Chakrabarti (2020, 10) stresses that the cross-modality argument presents us with a biconditional, "Selves over and above experiences are real if and only if objects over and above experiences are real."[10] He argues that without a substantival self, whose self-knowledge involves self-predication, we could not even recognize bundles of red, sweet, and roundish properties as *apples*. In the other direction, "reductive anti-realism about the external world will lead to unavailability of the notion of a self which can re-identify itself across different successive experiential states" (16). Chakrabarti makes clear that in his opinion, the antecedents of each conditional holds. He adds to the argument of 3.1.1–3 by bringing out an interpersonal dimension: mere bundle selves lack a deep principle of individuation among them, such that there is a blurring of personal identity among persons. This generates another departure from external-world realism in that intersubjective agreement about something—"[its] being the common target of many strictly distinct centers of experience"—is the primary criterion for something external being real (14). This point might be thought of as something new or added on to the Nyāya argument. But I would suggest that it appropriates the reasoning by Vātsyāyana elsewhere, namely, that flux theories cannot account for the demarcation of distinct individuals (under *NyS* 1.1.10).

Jonardon Ganeri (2001a, 647) argues that the most cogent reading of the cross-modality argument has a weaker conclusion than that offered by Chakrabarti, "refuting not reductionism about the self but only a reductionist account of the sense of self." Ganeri points to what he calls a "commensuration requirement": if one is to think of one's own perceptions in different modalities as converging upon the same object, with seamless integration between the representations of spatial properties, one must oneself occupy a stable, singular vantage point. "One can make sense of that expectation only if one thinks of the perceptions as locating

[10] Originally published as Chakrabarti 1992.

the object with respect to a single spatial map, and hence of all the perceptions as one's own" (652).

Richard Sorabji includes the cross-modality argument in his expansive work, *Self: Ancient and Modern Insights about Individuality, Life, and Death*, remarking, "I think the controversy on this subject between Buddhists and Hindus is much more sophisticated than what is found in the ancient Greeks, as well as extending beyond the point at which discussion has so far reached in current anglophone philosophy" (2006, 278). Without taking a final stand on who wins the debate, Sorabji sees the cross-modality argument, and Nyāya's enduring self which owns various mental states, as allied to defensible commitments.[11]

Sūtras 3.1.4–6 transition to a separate issue that we might call karmic or moral continuity. Like 1.1.10, sūtra 3.1.4 seems to present a commonsensical case for a self that Vātsyāyana reinterprets in the context of anti-Buddhist dialectics:

> There must be a nonmaterial self, since otherwise, when there is burning of the body, there would be the absence of sin. (*NyS* 3.1.4)

This sūtra alludes to cremation, suggesting that if there is no self beyond the body, then sin, "bad karma," would be inoperative, destroyed along with the body which is cremated at death. There would be nothing to carry karmic traces across embodiments, and the nearly pan-Indian notion of karma ensuring moral continuity across lives would be destroyed. Vātsyāyana, however, reads "burning the body" in a more specific way, as an illustration of harming someone (*prāṇi-hiṃsā*, "injuring a living being"). He goes on to assert that notions of the person that reduce it to a fluctuating

[11] Kisor Chakrabarti (1999, 93–133), we might also mention, does not offer a distinct interpretation of the cross-modality argument but does helpfully unpack it in the light of the broader theses about the self in the *Nyāya-sūtra* as a whole. His illustrations of the way Nyāya's dualism does not fall prey to many of the fatal flaws of René Decartes's dualism are particularly noteworthy.

aggregate, without a stable continuing self, undermine karmic continuity and moral responsibility:

> There would be no sin, because there would be no connection between the agent of any particular act and its results. Conversely, the results would be connected to someone who was *not* the original agent. For, in the continuous series of body, senses, cognition, and feeling, one aggregate arises and another is destroyed. And the fact that the series is a connected sequence of creation and destruction does not mitigate the problem of the agent's *otherness*, since each individual aggregate of body and the rest is an entirely different location of mental states. For the *otherness* of the location is proclaimed by you [a Buddhist interlocutor]. (*Commentary* 3.1.4)

This passage strongly supports the assumption that Buddhism is Vātsyāyana's target here. He alludes to both the Buddhist notion of momentariness and a standard Buddhist response to the problem of moral continuity, namely, that causal connections between time slices of a momentary stream are sufficient to underwrite continued personhood.[12] Vātsyāyana continues:

> This being the case, the living being in the form of an aggregate of body, etc., who causes harm would not be connected to the karmic fruits of harm; the one who would be connected would not be the agent of the harm. Thus, on the view that each aggregate is a different being, there would be the unacceptable consequence of losing what has been done [*kṛtahāna*] and gaining what has not been done [*akṛtābhyāgama*].

[12] Cf. *QKM* 2.2.6. In his subcommentary, Vācaspati insists that the only real candidates for the opponent here are Buddhists or materialists and remarks that the latter would not mind at all if "sin" and karmic justice were rendered null and void philosophically.

The notions of "losing what has been done" and "gaining what has not been done" concern moral responsibility and moral continuity, broadly understood through a "karmic" lens. If someone is a completely different being at the time that they receive the karmic consequences of an action from what they were at the time the karmic seeds were planted by virtuous or vicious acts, then moral responsibility and moral continuity would be null and void.[13] If *b* is the one who "owns" the results of *a*'s moral acts, this would be both morally and metaphysically untenable. Vātsyāyana further mentions religious ways of life such as celibacy that are engaged in for the sake of long-term soteriological benefit. These also presuppose the karmic and moral continuity that a self provides.[14]

The interlocutor's response is quite reasonable and resonates with critiques of dualism articulated throughout history: an eternal self could not be injured, and *this* would itself undermine morality (3.1.5). Insofar as the self is eternal, standing above the fluctuations of matter and mind, things like "harming" and "killing" would be meaningless, and the immorality and religious demerit attached to such acts would be delusion. This might be a case of *tu quoque*, but more charitably it could be seen as making the case that a problem that besets two competing views is not a specific problem for one alone.

Vātsyāyana's response is to argue that there is a third way to understand harm that is, in fact, Nyāya's view. He identifies three positions:

1. There is no enduring self, and the person is a fluctuating stream of aggregates (rejected under 3.1.4).

[13] Also see *NySBh* 4.1.10; 3.2.72.

[14] Uddyotakara reasonably interprets Vātsyāyana as specifically alluding to Buddhist monasticism here.

2. There is an enduring self, and it cannot be harmed. As such, sins of harming and killing are null and void (rejected under 3.1.5).
3. Harming and killing involve destruction or injury to the body and senses, which are the receptacles of the self's experiences and sensations (accepted under 3.1.6).

The interlocutor failed to consider this third option, imputing a radical dualism to Nyāya. But Vātsyāyana stresses that there is a profound intimacy between body and self—again, laying out an "integrationist" dualism of Nyāya in contrast with what we might speak of as Cartesian or Sāṃkhya variants that fail to integrate matter and consciousness. The body is the receptacle for the self's experiences of pain, pleasure, and the like, and the senses are the instruments of cognition.

This reading requires Vātsyāyana to understand the word *kartṛ* in sūtra 3.1.6 as referring to the senses, which are instruments of cognition. From a strictly grammatical perspective, this is legitimate although perhaps unusual. In Sanskrit grammar, an agent is simply the "independent" contributor to an action that is described in a sentence.[15] In "The car rolls down the hill," a car is the agent of rolling down a hill even if left in neutral, with no driver present. At the same time, Vātsyāyana's interpretation is somewhat forced from a metaphysical perspective, since for Nyāya, the only true agent is the self, the locus of intention and volition. That the senses are not independent agents *in this sense* was argued immediately above.

Perhaps mindful of such inconsistency, he offers an alternative reading of the sūtra in the second half of his commentary, which interprets the word "agent" in the sūtra as referring to the body through figurative meaning. This allows him to read the sūtra in a

[15] Vātsyāyana reflects extensively on the grammatical *kāraka* system under 2.1.16 and engages with it under 3.1.1, 4.1.16, and 5.2.7. See Cardona 2014 for an examination of the *kārakas* in relation to agency.

grammatically straightforward way, "No, because of the injury to the 'agent' and the locus of effects." Under this interpretation, he gestures slightly to something that is frankly underdiscussed by classical Hindu philosophers, the differences between *selfhood* and *personhood* proper. For Nyāya, a person is a self *plus* fluctuating world-directed mental and physical states. While the self is the true agent, it is only when integrated with a body/*manas* complex that its agency can manifest such that it can have the panoply of qualities and activities that we collectively call *personhood*. This integrated dualism is expanded upon and nuanced throughout the third chapter of the *NySBh*.

Sūtras 3.1.7–14 return to the view that consciousness rests in the senses themselves and offer a new reason to reject it. While a bit arcane, the discussion provides context for Vātsyāyana to reflect further on the nature of recollection and memory. There are two major portions: on the duality of the visual faculty as a further reason that there must be a self (3.1.7–11) and on memory as a quality of the self (3.1.12–14). The latter portion could be thought of as an entirely separate section, but there is enough continuity that I will keep it nested under the broader discussion of the visual faculty.

The argument of 3.1.7 is simple: we are able to see something with the left eye, then the right, while recognizing it as one and the same. This shows that even within a specific sense modality, there is need of a higher-level agent of synthesis and recognition. In his explanation, Vātsyāyana offers a definition of recognition (*pratyabhijñāna*), which he glosses as a temporal version of synthetic cognition, the "tying together" of cognitive events that we have seen him talk about as early as 1.1.10:

> Recognition is a synthetic cognition that targets a single object of earlier and later awareness: "That object I saw before is the very one that I am seeing now." "This very object is the thing I knew in the past." Since there is recognition of something through the

> right eye that was formerly seen by the left eye, here, too, "The object I saw before is the very that one I am seeing now." If the senses themselves were the loci of consciousness, then there would be no recognition by one sense of something experienced by another. Recognition would be impossible. But since such recognition occurs, the conscious experiencer must be something distinct from the senses. (*Commentary* 3.1.7)

The opponent retorts that in fact, there is simply one visual faculty that seems to be two as it is physically divided by the nose. In response, the *NySBh* offers multiple rebuttals. One eye may be destroyed while the other still functions (3.1.9). If the interlocutor argues that the visual faculty is thought of as a composite whole with two major parts, still, when the parts of a whole are destroyed or removed, the whole no longer continues (3.1.10–11). The skull of a dead person has two separate orbits where the eyes are located (3.1.11). Pressing on one eye distorts the image of an object that both eyes are looking at (3.1.11).

The subsection beginning with 3.1.12 cites another event that spans sense modalities but is not, strictly speaking, recognition or synthetic cognition: upon seeing a ripe piece of fruit, one's mouth begins to water. Again, the phenomenon requires a locus of awareness and memory that stands above and unifies inputs.

The interlocutor's response leads to deeper scrutiny of the nature of memory:

> No, there is no self, since the object remembered is the content of memory. (*NyS* 3.1.13)

This objection is obscure in the sūtra, but as interpreted by Vātsyāyana, it seems to be of a kind with classical Buddhist notions that the object of a cognitive state (here, memory) is part of its causal conditions, and there is no need to posit a self as a further cause. Vātsyāyana interprets it as being offered by a Buddhist flux theorist who claims that the content of memory is simply the object remembered.

In response, Vātsyāyana reflects deeply on the nature of memory, more so than anywhere else in the *Commentary*. Following sūtra 3.1.14, he argues that memory makes sense only as a quality of the self and not any "local" cognitive process. If it were merely local, then recollection and allied events would be impossible. Or one would have to deny the restriction of senses to their own proper domains. That there is a self, therefore, remains the best theory. The self is cognitive agent, the senses its instruments, and memory a quality that inheres in the self.

Vātsyāyana next pivots to phenomenology, claiming that the objector of 3.1.13 "failed to fully account for the content of memory." His passage is worth quoting at length:

> For something not currently apprehended, the content of the memory "I knew that object" is not merely an object without qualification. Rather it is an object known in the past as qualified by both the cognition and the knower: "I was the knower of that object," "That object was known by me," "The prior cognition of that object belongs to me." Although these are four ways of speaking about the object of memory, they are ultimately synonymous. In every case, one is aware of a knower, a cognition, and the thing known.
>
> So, for an object that has been seen, memory ties together three cognitions pertaining to it, whose agent is the same. They could not have different agents or no agent. What then? They have the same agent. Thus, "That object I saw in the past is the very one I am seeing now." The phrase "I saw in the past" conveys both seeing [*darśana*] and awareness of one's own seeing [*darśana-saṃvit*]. If there was no awareness of the seeing as one's own, a person could not entertain the thought "I saw in the past." These two cognitions are joined by a third in "The very one *I am seeing now*," which is directed to the same object. Thus, three cognitions

converge with single object. Recollection could not have no agent or different agents. What then? It has the same agent.

The objector thus fails to account fully for the content of memory and tries to refute something well known to be real when claiming that there is no self "since the object remembered is the content of memory." For it is not that the content of the three cognitions is just bare memory or the bare object itself. Rather, there is a synthesis of memory [*smṛti-pratisaṃdhāna*], just like synthesis of cognition belonging to one being who ties together the varied contents.[16] And this single knower of all the varied contents ties together the cognitions: "I will know that object," "I know that object," "I knew that object." Desiring to remember a specific object that it hasn't thought about in a while, the knower determines "That is the thing I knew," synthesizing a memory that is qualified by the three times [past, present, future] and qualified by a desire to remember.

But if a knower is nothing more than a stream of connected mnemonic impressions [*saṃskāra-santati-mātra*], such traces are destroyed as others arise. There is no single impression existing that could be aware of cognition or memory spanning the three times. Without such awareness, there would be no synthesis of cognition or memory involving "I" and "mine," just as we cannot recollect something known by a different embodied being.

Therefore, we infer that there is a single being who grasps all contents and ties together the connected experiences within his own body and connected memories, and who could not recollect something known by a different body, since the being is not present there. (*Commentary* 3.1.14)

Vātsyāyana's position is that while the self is not the *object* of memory, it is part of the *content* of memories in the form of the fixed and recognizable locus or perspective that spans all of them.

[16] See 1.1.10 and 3.1.1.

The next subsection, 3.1.15–17, entertains an objection that Nyāya's arguments to prove the self prove instead that there is a *manas* or "inner faculty." That there is a self remains unproven. Vātsyāyana's response highlights a significant distinction between classical Indian philosophy and mainstream Western thought, where the former tends to distinguish between a self proper and a "mind," in the form of *manas* or another candidate mental faculty. In Western thought, "mind" and "self" are often interchangeable.

Sāṃkhya, a Brahmanical school, tends to be the most radical in this regard, taking all features of mental life besides consciousness itself to be properties of the "inner organ," not the self.[17] Nyāya has a much more restricted role for the *manas*, but Vātsyāyana follows the sūtras in arguing here that the objector's claim simply amounts to a terminological distinction (3.1.16). By parity of reasoning, as there must be distinct sense modalities for distinct types of sensory contents (touch, taste, etc.), there must be an instrument of mental impressions and selective attention, whatever we call it, that can be employed by the agent of cognition (3.1.17). If we want to call the self *manas* and its faculty the *mati-sādhana* (instrument of mental perception), it makes little difference.

The last major discussion of the self is over its immortality (3.1.18–26). Vātsyāyana gives voice to an interlocutor who offers a reason for doubt: since something's genuine existence is compatible with its being either eternal or non-eternal, the existence of the self does not guarantee immortality. Parallel to the concern voiced by Simmias and Cebes in Plato's *Phaedo*, the doubt here is that arguments already advanced might prove that a self must exist prior to death, but that it survives the destruction of the body remains dubious.[18]

[17] *SK* 19, 20, 23.
[18] *Phaedo* 86a–88b.

In response, a similar three-step dialectic is repeated three times in this section. Step one is a positive reason for the self's eternality by appeal to the behavior of newborns and infants:

> 3.1.18: Because a newborn experiences happiness, fear, and unhappiness, and these stem from memories connected to earlier repeat experience.
> 3.1.21: Because of a drive toward the breast, generated by repeated experience of eating in a prior existence.
> 3.1.24: Because all beings have desires (even newborns), and desire is informed by previous experience.

Step two is an objector's attempt to see these phenomena as nothing but brute, insentient physical processes, citing possible counterexamples. Each sūtra below addresses the immediately preceding one:

> 3.1.19: Such changes in a newborn are like the changes of lotuses and other flowers, opening and closing their petals.
> 3.1.22: The movement of a newborn toward the breast is like the movement of iron toward a lodestone.
> 3.1.25: It arises in the same way a substance is produced along with its qualities.

Step three is a response that such counterexamples fail:

> 3.1.20: No, because changes in things constituted by the five elements are due to causes like heat, cold, and the rainy season.
> 3.1.23: No, because nothing other than iron moves toward the lodestone (and thus, it is a restricted, ungeneralizable case).
> 3.1.26: No, because emotions like desire are caused by deliberation.[19]

[19] Under this sūtra, Vātsyāyana cites *VS* 6.2.13 and 6.2.16, which account for emotions such as attachment.

In each instance, Nyāya's core case is that newborns exhibit behaviors (desire, intentional action, emotions such as fear) that have, as a causal condition, memory informed by prior experience. And since they have not yet gained such experience in the present life, it must have occurred in prior embodiments:[20]

> The very same self, upon leaving the former body, takes on a new body. Suffering from hunger and remembering former instances of eating, the child is driven toward the breast. (*Commentary* 3.1.21)

> The former body presupposes yet another former body and so on . . . and therefore the eternality of the self is proven. (*Commentary* 3.1.24)

We should note that "remembering" here need not be self-conscious propositional memory but only the sort of memory that governs motor functions such as riding a bicycle or eating food, that is, "knowledge-how."

The debate centers on whether the principle about memory may be refuted by examples drawn from the natural world such as the movements of plants and magnetized iron. In this regard, Vātsyāyana makes several points about argumentation and causal reasoning. As noted earlier, he seems to have a pet project of addressing the sloppy use of examples. Here he argues that examples disconnected from reasons fail to be probative. And for the matter at hand, the analogues offered fail to refute the fact that human emotions are informed by prior experience, something widely observed (3.1.19).

With respect to causal reasoning, Vātsyāyana argues that we have a handle on the basic causal relations that govern things such as the opening of flower petals or the movement of iron shards toward

[20] The parallels here with Plato's argument for preexistence by appeal to recollection (*Phaedo* 72e–76e) are striking.

a magnet. He is not claiming deep scientific knowledge of such things but rather that we are aware of such events as being causally rule-bound. "An action's cause is indicated by the action itself. And the rules which govern an action's cause are indicated by the rule-bound nature of the action itself" (*Commentary* 3.1.23). Here Vātsyāyana appeals to a view of causes that he expresses fairly often in the *Commentary*. Causes account not merely for why *b* follows from *a* but for why *c*, *d*, and *e don't*. (The term for causal rule, *niyama*, is the same as that used for ethical or religious self-control and other types of constraint.) Actions occur in rule-bound ways, and we often have at least a broad sense of the correlations that govern their occurrence. On this basis, we identify causes through inference and generalization. By the same token, things such as human affective states do not just happen but are governed by comprehensible causal conditions. Therefore, again, the cases offered as counterexamples fail to be probative (3.1.20).[21]

3.1.27–31: The body

Vātsyāyana begins this section by connecting it to the former: "An individual's body is caused by their own previous actions (karma) and is the receptacle for their experiences of pleasure and pain. It is now the subject of inquiry." The core issue is whether the body is composed of a single type of element or a combination of elements. The sūtras argue that it is composed of earth only, by appeal to a theory of elements and their unique qualities (3.1.27) and the authority of sacred testimony, *śruti* (3.1.31).

The theory of five elements and their special qualities is alluded to under 1.1.13–14. The special quality of ether is sound; of air, tactility; of fire, visible form; of water, taste; of earth, scent. If

[21] For a developed analysis of the major argument of this section, centered on Udayana, see Phillips 2005.

something has odor, this is because of the presence of earth atoms. Later in this chapter, Vātsyāyana remarks: "We observe that each of the elements like air manifests a specific quality in a fixed way" (3.1.60). Presumably, as the human body is possessed of odor, it is constituted particularly by earth. Trying to make sense of the sūtras, Vātsyāyana notes that "the other elements lack scent, and if the body were made only of them, it would have no scent." But at the same time, he concedes that "if the human body were created *only* out of earth, without being mixed with other elements, it could not serve its purpose as the locus of pleasure, pain, and bodily movements."[22] Therefore, he concludes, "the body exists as a conjunction of the five elements together."

The crucial distinction here is composition (*tatprakṛti*) versus mere conjunction (*saṃyoga*). Under 3.1.30, Vātsyāyana argues that a body is composed of earth but exists in conjunction with the other elements, just as an earthenware jar is composed of earth but exists in conjunction with water, fire, and so on. This is held to be a better account than that of the body's being composed of all five elements together, because on the latter view, "The body would lack the qualities of odor, taste, visible form, or tactility, in conformity with its material cause."

Vātsyāyana does not unpack the claim any further. As explicated by later commentators, his point is about atomic combinations and ensuing perceptible qualities.[23] In brief, earth atoms must combine with other earth atoms to create something that on a macro-level has the quality of scent. Likewise for the other atoms and their distinct qualities. According to Vaiśeṣika physics, if atoms combined heterogeneously with other types of atoms on a micro-level, they could not produce a uniform product with a perceptible quality. The object would have a fundamentally "mixed" and irregular composition.[24] This argument is beset by the compositional fallacy that

[22] As defined in *NyS* 1.1.11.
[23] *NyV* and *NyVT* 3.1.30.
[24] *VS* 4.2.2–4.

infects a number of ancient atomisms.[25] One also wonders why Nyāya could not choose, say, water as the element the body is composed of (since any part of the body has "taste"), while holding that the other elements participate through mere conjunction.

3.1.32–50: The sense faculties

Vātsyāyana introduces this section: "Now, the senses will be considered, according to the order of *prameyas*. Are they produced from primordial matter [*avyaktika*] or from the elements [*bhautika*]?" The alternatives have to do with two major competing metaphysical systems, those of Sāṃkhya and Nyāya-Vaiśeṣika, respectively. *Avyakta*, "the unmanifest," is an epithet for primordial matter according to Sāṃkhya. It is basic stuff of the world, prior to transformation into any objects.[26] For Nyāya, atoms of the four elements earth, water, fire, and air, along with the all-pervasive ether, are the bedrock of the world. To say that the senses are "elemental" for Nyāya means that each one is composed of a primary elemental type, which determines its perceptual domain.

As is often the case, the sūtras introduce doubt to initiate the topic:

> Since perception arises only when an eyeball is present, but also at a distance, there is doubt. (*NyS* 3.1.32)

The point of the doubt is that if the eyes are damaged, perception does not occur, suggesting that the visual faculty is physically, or "elementally," constructed. And yet vision can seemingly act at a distance, without being in direct contact with its objects.

[25] However, *NySBh* 4.1.11 attempts to justify the notion that atoms share the qualities of the objects composed of them.

[26] *SK* 10, 16.

Acting at a distance, Vātsyāyana tells us, "would be possible if these sense faculties are non-elemental and all-pervasive." That is, if the senses were directly products of the *avyakta*, then they could act at a distance, with no need to "touch" an object in order to grasp it. Elemental things function through direct contact. But if the senses were constructed out of more subtle variants of matter, contact would not be necessary.

The notion of the senses as products of *avyakta* is a general way of speaking of Sāṃkhya theories, where a non-elemental subtle form of primordial matter is what "reaches out" to connect with perceptible objects. Below, *NySBh* 3.2.3 presents a Sāṃkhya view that cognition consists in modifications of the "inner instrument," *buddhi*, which extends outward and takes the form of external objects.[27] *Buddhi* in Sāṃkhya metaphysics is more subtle than sense objects and is "all-pervasive," spanning the distance between the physical body of an individual and objects external to them.[28]

The mainstay of Nyāya's position is that its view allows for an elemental conception of the visual faculty that also makes sense of its ability to seemingly operate at a distance. Sūtras 3.1.33–35 put forth Nyāya's view of the senses—perception in particular—as elemental; 3.1.36–43 defend the Nyāya theory that the eyes could emit invisible rays of light to perceive objects; 3.1.44–50 debate the issue of whether glass or other transparent objects should be able to block eyesight.

What is Nyāya's view exactly? In summary, it is that the eyes can perceive things at a distance, as well as things much larger or smaller than themselves, because they emit rays of light that contact visible objects. This account is supported by inference: the visual

[27] Cf. *YS* 4.23–24.

[28] The commentator Vācaspati suggests that the "mental" faculty of *ahaṃkāra* is what connects to perceptible objects according to the interlocutor's view. Like *buddhi* (on the Sāṃkhya account), it is more subtle than a physical object and is not limited by spatial distance.

faculty can be obstructed by objects that are in the way. If it were non-elemental and all-pervasive, that would not occur (3.1.34).

The interlocutor objects that we never see such rays (3.1.35), leading Vātsyāyana to reflect on non-apprehension and the limits of its evidentiary force. I count four major responses to the argument from non-apprehension:

1. When something is proven by inference, non-perception is not enough to refute it (3.1.36).
2. Something's perceptibility may vary according to differences between property (*guṇa*) and substance (*dravya*) (3.1.37). Vātsyāyana gives the example of water, which may be imperceptible as a distinct substance when "clinging to other things," though it can still be felt. With respect to the eye's rays, he catalogs various permutations of fire and its properties: "There is perceptible fire which has manifest form and touch, like the rays of the sun. And there is perceptible fire with manifest form and non-manifest touch, like the rays of a lamp. And there is manifest touch and non-manifest, imperceptible form, like the fire atoms mixed with water. The rays of the eye are thus imperceptible as they have unmanifest form and touch."
3. The senses are constructed according to an individual's karmic merit and for the sake of serving "human purposes" (3.1.38). "Human purposes" translates *puruṣārtha*, a common term for the goals of life recognized by classical Hindus: virtue, wealth, pleasure, and liberation.[29] More basically (as expressed by Sāṃkhya), the human purposes are twofold: to enjoy the world but also, if desired, to seek liberation from it. As a response to the initial objection, this sūtra seems to be arguing that the eyes are constructed to serve

[29] Vātsyāyana mentions these under 2.1.20.

human purposes effectively. That their rays are invisible but sensitive to obstruction makes sense. Presumably, if everyone had visible rays emitting from their eyes, ordinary life would get convoluted and disrupted.

4. Special conditions may impede something's perceptibility (3.1.39–44). For example, a meteor at midday is invisible due to its radiance being overwhelmed by the brighter light of the sun (3.1.39–41). While the eye's visual rays are not perfectly analogous to the meteor, they may be unperceived because they fail to meet the conditions of perceptibility (3.1.42–43).

The final subsection returns to the issue of obstruction and materiality. Appealing to the principle that "being physical [or 'elemental,' *bhautika*] is to function by means of direct contact," the interlocutor argues that the visual faculty cannot be physical as it can see through obstructions such as glass, a sheet of mica, and quartz (3.1.44). Vātsyāyana responds that while eyesight is obstructed by many physical things, some physical objects do not obstruct the passage of fire atoms. Fire atoms in the form of sunlight can, for example, heat the water in a jar, through the jar's walls, just as the cooking fire can pass through a pan to heat food. Certain physical objects have special properties such as transparency, which allow for the passage of light through them (3.1.45–49). There is no absolute principle. The opponent's insistence that all material objects behave the same way with respect to their capacity to obstruct sight leads to Vātsyāyana's final reflections on methodology:

> It is inappropriate to make demands upon or dismiss things established by perception and inference. (*NyS* 3.1.50)
>
> *Commentary*: By nature, *pramāṇa*s target the truth. For objects that have been investigated by perception and inference, one cannot simply demand, "Be like this" or "Don't be like that." It is inappropriate to say, "Let scent be visible, just like form" or "Let form be invisible, just like scent." It is inappropriate to say,

"Let water be indicated by smoke, just like fire" or "Fire should not be indicated by smoke, just like water." Why is this? Because objects are known by *pramāṇas* as they are, according to their true nature, their own qualities. *Pramāṇas* apprehend things as they really are. The demands and dismissals you have put forth are "Let there be no obstruction by things like walls, just like glass or sheets of mica" and "There should be no failure to obstruct by glass or sheets of mica, just like walls, etc." These are not the properties of these substances as discovered by perception and inference.[30]

3.1.51–60: The multiplicity of the senses

This section continues the examination of the objects of knowledge as well as the themes of metaphysical composition and reduction. Here the senses are under scrutiny. The discussion starts with reflection on mereology: a composite whole has different parts in different locations, and yet insofar as it is a composite, it is one single thing throughout (3.1.51). An interlocutor argues that the skin, the locus of the sense of touch, covers the entire body, including the loci of the other putative sense faculties. As such, all the senses may be reduced to the sense of touch.

Vātsyāyana responds that we have good reasons to dispute such a claim: blind persons cannot apprehend color through touch (3.1.52). Elements such as earth pervade each of the loci of the distinct sense faculties, and in their absence, sense experiences do not occur. This makes doubtful the theory that one sense faculty, touch, could account for all sense experiences (3.1.52). We

[30] These reflections connect to Vātsyāyana's epistemological musings under 2.1.11, where he argues that knowledge sources should be conceived in accord with experience, not a priori theoretical categories.

do not perceive all perceptible objects at the same time, which is best explained by a plurality of sense faculties and a gatekeeper, the *manas* (3.1.53). The single-sense theory would require the sense of touch to work only through direct contact, as it does with tactile objects, but also without direct contact as with vision (3.1.54). The different senses serve different functions in terms of generating experience (3.1.55–56; 3.1.59).

NySBh 3.1.59 acts as a coda by arguing for the distinctness of each of the senses on five separate grounds:

1. They produce different kinds of cognition.
2. They are located in different places.
3. They have different causal processes by which they engage objects.
4. They have different sizes.
5. They have different material causes.

The sūtras conclude by expanding upon the fifth reason, unpacking the way each sense is associated with a distinct element:

> Each is made up of one of the elements, as each apprehends the special qualities of an element. (*NyS* 3.1.60)

This last argument makes explicit a consideration that has been largely implicit so far. Nyāya endorses something akin to the notion "Like perceives like," associated with Greek thinkers such as Empedocles and Aristotle:

> We find a principle that the elements like air each manifest a distinct quality . . . a certain substance like earth manifests a certain quality like scent. And from this principle, we understand that a sense faculty is composed of the very element whose distinct quality it grasps, and is not composed of those which remain unmanifested to it. (*Commentary* 3.1.60)

We will see this principle developed in the next section.

3.1.61–72: Objects in general

The concluding discussion of Chapter 3, Part 1, is about "objects" (*artha*), in this case, the five major elements. They will be considered largely insofar as they are the basic objects of sense perception.

As mentioned earlier, each element has a special property (*viśeṣa-guṇa*). For example, earth has scent. The sūtras now address a possible misconception, namely, that each of the special properties is the *only* sensible property of each respective element. A notion of nested qualities is presented, expanding as one moves down the list from air to earth (ether is a special case). (See Table 13.)

The list unfolds straightforwardly, with the exception of ether. Air can be felt (in the form of blowing wind) but not seen. Fire can be felt and seen. Water can be felt, seen, and tasted, and earth can be felt, seen, tasted, and smelled. What makes ether an exception is that according to Nyāya-Vaiśeṣika physics, ether is a ubiquitous

Table 13. The elements and their qualities according to *NyS* 3.1.61–62.

Element	Qualities			
air	touch			
fire	touch	visible form		
water	touch	visible form	taste	
earth	touch	visible form	taste	scent
ether				sound

field which locates sound waves.[31] Were I to throw a clump of clay against a wall, it would create sound through a forceful conjunction. The sound is not located in the clay or the wall but rather in the ether, and it travels through the ether to my ear as I hear it.

The interlocutor of this section insists that each element has only a single distinct property. To support this, they appeal to sense experience and the implicit principle "Like perceives like" discussed above. For example, we do not perceive touch through our sense of smell when we apprehend the fragrance of moss. And if the olfactory organ is composed of earth atoms, then, since earth has each of the four qualities besides scent, the faculty should be able to feel (3.1.63–64). In response to the question of why we are able to apprehend more than one quality in earth, Vātsyāyana has the interlocutor appeal to the same principle he himself advanced while explaining that the body is *composed* only of earth while also *mixed* with other elements (3.1.64). On this view, when we see or taste, for example, a piece of clay, we see fire atoms and taste water atoms mixed with earth atoms (3.1.65).

Vātsyāyana follows the sūtras in arguing that the position has several fatal flaws (3.1.66). He offers ten separate reasons against it by interpreting the "perceptibility of earth and water," mentioned in the sūtra in multiple ways.

1. The correct criteria for being visible are (i) having intermediate size (being neither atomic nor ubiquitous), (ii) being a composite formed out of atoms, and (iii) being the locus of manifest color.[32] The visibility of substances made of water or earth is explicated on this standard.

[31] Nyāya speaks of waves not in the modern sense but as the "flow of sound" through ether. See *NySBh* 2.2.13.

[32] Cf. *VS* 4.1.6.

2. The criterion that admixture with fire elements is what makes something perceptible would mean that warm air should be perceptible.
3. Earth has six "tastes," while water has one, sweetness. On the opponent's view, earth would only taste sweet, like pure water.[33]
4. On the opponent's view, when something like earth is seen, its visible color would be manifested by the color of fire atoms mixed with it. The unacceptable consequence of this view is that fire itself would only serve to manifest earth's color and would not have its own color.
5. On the opponent's view, color is present only when fire atoms are intermixed with other elements. But earth has many different colors, while water has one basic color. This cannot be accounted for on the view that color is due only to mixture with fire atoms, since the color of fire is uniform.
6. Likewise, earth's touch is temperate, while fire's is hot and air's cool. On the view that touch is due only to mixture with air atoms, such variation between fire and earth is inexplicable.
7. As we perceive four qualities in macro substances made of earth, three in those made of water, and so on, it is reasonable to infer that this is due to the qualities of their causes (namely, their constituent atoms).[34]
8. It is possible to distinguish substances made of earth versus other elements, while still noticing that they have more than one quality.
9. There is no legitimate inference in support of the view that the elemental types are fundamentally mixed together (as

[33] The number of irreducible tastes was debated by ancient Indian medical theorists. *CS*, Sūtrasthāna 26, 1–9, portrays a legendary debate over the issue, concluding that six is the correct view.

[34] *VS* 4.1.2–3 is cited as a proof text.

argued by the interlocutor under *NyS* 3.1.65), either now or at the time of creation.

10. At times, the qualities of some elements in a mixture overwhelm the qualities of others. Heated air is hot; the added fire atoms overwhelm the naturally cool feel of air. But on the opponent's account, fire has only the property of touch because of admixture of air atoms. This leads to the consequence that in the case of heated air, the quality of air would overcome the quality of air, an absurdity.

Vātsyāyana wraps up the section by providing a few details about how the senses function. Responding to the challenge voiced in 3.1.63, that on Nyāya's theory of qualities, a sense faculty should be able to grasp all the qualities nested in its cognate element, he follows the sūtras in arguing that there is not a perfect one-to-one correspondence. Rather, a sense faculty is restricted to apprehending the qualities that are *predominant* with it. For example, the quality of scent, associated with earth, is predominant within the olfactory sense (3.1.67–68). Finally, that sound is a quality of the ether, and is apprehended by the portion of ether in one's ear, is supported by an argument by elimination (3.1.72); there is no better account available.[35]

Part 2 (3.2.1–72)

Continuing the examination of the objects of knowledge, Part 2 begins with *buddhi*, cognition, a topic that dominates this part of the *Nyāya-sūtra*, up to 3.2.55. As each subsection under *buddhi* is concerned with significantly different issues, I will use entirely separate section headings.

[35] Cf. *VS* 2.1.24–26.

3.2.1–9: Against Sāṃkhya's notion of *buddhi*

Sūtra 3.2.1 voices doubt about whether cognition is eternal or temporary: *buddhi* is intangible. This makes it akin to both action and ether, but action is impermanent, while ether is eternal. Therefore, on grounds of intangibility, we remain doubtful whether *buddhi* is eternal or impermanent.[36] Vātsyāyana points out that this question is really settled. It has been made clear that cognition is impermanent. That it arises through external causes is stated explicitly in 1.1.4 and 1.1.16. Vātsyāyana suggests that this issue is a pretext to critique the notion of *buddhi* advanced by Sāṃkhya:

> The purpose of this section is rather to refute a certain view that is put forth. After investigation, Sāṃkhya philosophers say that *buddhi* is eternal and exists in the form of the inner instrument [*antaḥkaraṇa*], which belongs to the self. (*Commentary* 3.2.1)

Here we find a terminological difference about *buddhi* which reflects a significant metaphysical debate. Sāṃkhya disagrees with Nyāya about the nature of the self and its relationship with psychological faculties. Nyāya holds that the self is the locus of psychological states such as desire and cognition and that a self employs the *manas* as an instrument of selective attention. Sāṃkhya, too, accepts that there are a self and a *manas* but conceives of a much more robust tripartite inner instrument consisting not only of *manas* but also of *ahaṃkāra* ("false conceit") and *buddhi*.[37] The latter is the most subtle form of matter aside from prime matter itself (sometimes called *pradhāna* in its untransformed state). It

[36] This would be an example of doubt due to a shared property according to *NyS* 1.1.23.

[37] Vātsyāyana also accepts a notion of *ahaṃkāra*, not as a distinct faculty but as a deep misconception concerning oneself. In Nyāya's metaphysical scheme, it would simply be a type of error (*NySBh* 4.2.1).

Table 14. Differences between Nyāya and Sāṃkhya on *antaḥkaraṇa* and the self.

Function or property	Locus for Nyāya	Locus for Sāṁkhya
consciousness (*caitanya*)	self	self
propositionally structured cognition (*adhyavasāya; jñāna*)	self	*antaḥkaraṇa*
memory (*smṛti*)	self	*antaḥkaraṇa*
desire/aversion (*rāga/dveṣa*)	self	*antaḥkaraṇa*
volition/agency (*prayatna/kartṛtva*)	self	*antaḥkaraṇa*
moral responsibility/karmic merit (*dharma/adharma/adṛṣṭa*)	self	*antaḥkaraṇa*

takes on the affective and cognitive states that Nyāya consigns to the self. (See Table 14.)

In essence, Sāṃkhya holds the self to be nothing more than an unchanging quantum of consciousness. There are various traditions and permutations of Sāṃkhya philosophy, but despite different shadings in their accounts of primitive reals, mainstream Sāṃkhya at the time of Vātsyāyana appears consistent on this point:

> The *buddhi* engages in determinate cognition. In its most pure form, it has merit, knowledge, non-attachment, and power. When corrupt, it has the opposites. (*SK* 23)

> Along with the rest of the inner organ, the *buddhi* comprehends all contents. (*SK* 35)

Sāṃkhya's self is a "spectator," watching the *buddhi* while remaining ever unchanged.[38] It emits consciousness, which enters

[38] *SK* 65.

and illuminates the *buddhi*. But the *buddhi* is the locus of all propositionally structured cognition, somehow "reflecting" the consciousness of the self:

> Although it is unchanging, consciousness becomes aware of its own *buddhi* by means of entering into the forms assumed by the *buddhi*. (*YS* 4.22)

> The inner instrument knows all objects, colored both by the objects and by the knower. (*YS* 4.23)

The self, in contrast, is "a witness, isolated, indifferent, a seer, and a non-agent" (*SK* 19).

What motivates such a radical dualism? Sāṃkhya, like Nyāya, sees the ultimate good of life as unearthing one's hidden self, a quest whose roots go back to the Upaniṣads. The deep self is something more fundamental than our current psychophysical circumstances, and it is our true essence. It is the very content of liberation. The motivation for Sāṃkhya's dualism seems to be to make sense of liberation by conceiving of the self as truly changeless, divorced from the fluctuations of matter:

> If happiness and distress were the qualities of the *ātman* ("self"), there would be the undesirable consequence that the *ātman* could never attain liberation from them. (*Yuktidīpikā* commentary on *SK* 19)[39]

This view is likely supported by reports of *yogīns* that in deep meditative experience, discursive thought ceases. *Yoga-sūtra* 1.2–3 takes such experiences to be states of disassociation from the inner instrument, where the self's pure awareness "abides in its own nature." Sāṃkhya's dualism is thus radical and uncompromising, far more

[39] Translated by Bryant (2014, 23).

exacting even than Descartes's. Any and all modification occurs on the "matter" side of the self/matter divide. "Mental" faculties such as *buddhi* are merely subtle forms of materiality.

We might conceive of Sāṃkhya's view of the self as one pole on a continuum, with Buddhism as the other pole. Buddhists see a person as a stream of fluctuating mental and physical states, with no self to serve as a locus of continuity. Sāṃkhya rather sees the core of each individual as a self that is divorced from the fluctuations of the world, an unchanging quantum of consciousness that is contingently associated with an insentient mental faculty. Nyāya stands in the middle, conceiving of a person as an eternal self that is the location of impermanent, world-directed mental states.

Vātsyāyana's positive argument under 3.2.1–3 is that an account that divides consciousness *simpliciter* and propositionally structured cognition between two separate locations is untenable. The division collapses under scrutiny:

> If cognition belongs to the *buddhi*, the inner instrument, what then is the nature of the conscious being, what are its basic characteristics and reality? And what exactly does the conscious being do with the cognition that exists in the *buddhi*? (*Commentary* 3.2.3)

Vātsyāyana argues that the Sāṃkhya responses to this question fail because they don't adequately distinguish the two loci and their functions. If the self "becomes conscious of" (*cetayate*) the presentations of *buddhi*, this is synonymous with cognition. If *buddhi*, rather, is said to "cause the self to know" (*jnāpayati*), this is nothing other than Nyāya's own view that *buddhi* means "cognition" and the self knows through cognition.

I would argue that Vātsyāyana's core case is to see cognition as an instance of agency, cognitive agency. In his first discussion of knowledge under sūtra 1.1.1, he spoke of an individual as an agent of knowledge (*pramātṛ*), who employs *pramāṇas* as instruments. From this perspective, the Sāṃkhya dualism of *consciousness* (a property of the conscious being alone) and *activity* (a property of matter alone) fails. The standard Sāṃkhya metaphor for this is found in *SK* 21:

> The connection of self [*puruṣa*] and matter [*prakṛti*] is like that of a lame person and a blind person.

The lame person can see but not walk, and the blind person can walk but not see. That is, consciousness is a function of the self, the "lame person," while agency and change are a function of matter, the "blind person." Without mentioning it in particular, Vātsyāyana frames this sort of image as misleading. He stresses the incongruity of claiming that for a single cognitive event (e.g., seeing an object in the distance), one entity provides consciousness, while another unconscious entity is the substratum of cognition. *To cognize* means to be conscious of a particular fact or object, while *being conscious* means having the capacity to undergo experience.

Sūtras 3.2.4–9 return to basic problems with Sāṃkhya's notion of *buddhi* as something that is unchanging and ubiquitous and yet also responsible for fluctuating cognitions. By contrast, Nyāya holds that the *manas* is atomic and rapidly "moves" between different sense channels to allow for selective attention and the flow of cognitions over time. A major subtext includes a critique of Sāṃkhya metaphysics, insofar as it does not distinguish substances and properties.

In a final attempt to address these issues, the Sāṃkhya interlocutor offers the analogy of a crystal. Changes of color in a crystal do not signify deep changes of the crystal itself. So, too, the modifications of *buddhi* in the form of cognition do not threaten its eternality.[40] Vātsyāyana finds this yet another use of an example without proper supporting argumentation. But the analogy does set the stage for the ensuing discussion of momentariness.

[40] *YS* 4.23.

3.2.10–17: Against momentariness and *satkāryavāda*

This section departs from sūtra 3.2.9's example of a crystal, and it concludes by returning to the issue of *buddhi*. But it functions as a sidebar concerned with the question of diachronic identity. Nyāya again finds itself between Buddhism and Sāṃkhya, this time between Buddhist accounts that deny endurance and Sāṃkhya accounts that deny metaphysical significance to creation and destruction. The section has two halves accordingly. The first is a refutation of the Buddhist theory of momentariness (*kṣaṇikavāda*) (3.2.10–14), and the second is a refutation of the Sāṃkhya theory of the preexistence of the effect (*satkāryavāda*) (3.2.15–17).

Structurally, there are some anomalies with Vātsyāyana's interpretation of this section (and hence, the ensuing commentators following him). In his reading, a third interlocutor, a Buddhist, interjects during the Nyāya/Sāṃkhya dispute over *buddhi* to introduce a tangential topic. After Nyāya's response, they disappear immediately, and the conversation returns to debate with Sāṃkhya. This and the fact that the sūtras do take up the question of momentariness later under 4.1.25–28 have led some scholars to suggest that Vātsyāyana's interpretation is a misreading; the original meaning of the sūtras here is simply a continued dispute with Sāṃkhya.[41]

Noting that the term *kṣaṇikatva*, "momentariness," is used by the interlocutor in sūtra 3.2.10, Vātsyāyana takes them to be a *kṣaṇikavādin*, "an advocate of the view that things are momentary." This is an epithet for Buddhist philosophers who defend an anti-substantival, flux metaphysics. While the historical Buddha did not directly articulate a theory of momentariness, he planted several conceptual seeds that latter Buddhists would develop. Two deserve mention: (i) impermanence is a fundamental feature of existence, and (ii) things arise dependent upon a complicated web of fluctuating causes:

[41] Prasad 1930, 31–37.

> Bhikkus, form is impermanent. The cause and condition for the arising of form is impermanent. As form has originated from what is impermanent, how could it be permanent? [The same is stated for the four other *skandhas* in turn.] (*Saṃyutta Nikāya* 3.18.7)[42]

In the Abhidharma philosophies developed after the Buddha, we find explicit arguments for momentariness. Departing from the Buddha's claim that things arise due to causes and adding that a cause discharges its capacity as soon as it generates an effect, momentariness amounts to the notion that instability is built into things. Destruction is due not to outside causes but to the nature of reality itself:

> What is this "moment"? Immediate cessation upon having obtained existence. What exists in this fashion is momentary. Indeed, nothing conditioned exists later than its acquisition of existence. It perishes just where it was born. (Vasubandhu, *Abhidharma-kośa-bhāṣya* 4.2c)[43]

Buddhists hold that the appearance of continued stability is due to our unenlightened projection of underlying stuff such as substances, when what is truly real is a variety of property tropes in flux. For things such as fire, what looks like a single moving entity is a sequence of entirely separate states. So, too, it is argued, for all other things. Vātsyāyana's interlocutor argues:

> For a crystal, individual instances arise, and others are destroyed in sequence. Why? Because the instances are momentary.

[42] Translated by Bodhi (2000, 870).

[43] Translated by Siderits (2021, 174). For translation of the entire passage, see Poussin and Sangpo 2012, 1287–1290.

> A moment is the smallest interval of time. Things lasting for a moment are momentary. (*Commentary* 3.2.10)

The argument that Vātsyāyana offers on behalf of the Buddhist is fairly simple, an induction from cases like the body, which despite seeming to be stable, is perpetually in flux, to *all* substances being so.[44]

Vātsyāyana responds by arguing that the opponent is requiring the data to conform to the theory and not the other way around. "There is no rule that for all individual things, there is a chain of growth and decay like the body . . . it is unsupported by perception or inference." To extend such a rule to stones or minerals "is as absurd as arguing that since a certain plant is bitter, every substance is bitter" (3.2.11). Furthermore, this view seems to assert causal chains unknown to experience, where creation and destruction occur constantly and imperceptibly, without the standard indicators of parts being destroyed or added, as seen in earthenware, anthills, and the like (3.2.12). The interlocutor does claim that we find examples in nature of spontaneous transformation, such as milk into curd, but Vātsyāyana argues that even this example is faulty, since we do identify special causes for this change through inference (3.2.13–14).

It is the phenomenon of milk transforming to curd that brings the Sāṃkhya adherent back to the discussion:

> No, since the milk is only transformed or it only has a new quality. (*NyS* 3.2.15)

The example of milk turning into curd is found in classical Sāṃkhya and is used in this section to illustrate two separate ideas: (i) spontaneous transformation and/or destruction without a cause, as

[44] Vasubandhu's own arguments are far more sophisticated. Siderits (2021, 172–179) and Westerhoff (2018, 75–79) both offer acute, concise studies.

argued above under 3.1.13, and (ii) continuity despite change, as argued under 3.2.15.[45] The current interlocutor disagrees with the former and asserts the latter. Vātsyāyana explains that the notion of transformation that they advocate has two variants:

> Some say that the milk is transformed, not destroyed. Transformation [*pariṇāma*] is when a property that belongs to an abiding substance departs and another property arises. Others say that transformation is simply the manifestation of a different quality, and the substance endures when the former quality ceases and the other quality arises. (*Commentary* 3.2.16)

What these two variants share is that significant change does not destroy the substance. As opposed to the Buddhist doctrine of momentariness, which denies stability, this view denies destruction. Apparent creation and destruction are transformations of an underlying stuff which endures. In Sāṃkhya and also Vedānta metaphysics, this doctrine is known as *satkāryavāda*, "the view that the effect preexists in the cause." As argued in the *Sāṃkhya-kārikā*, prime matter has all possible effects or states existing latently within it. Even effects produced out of more refined matter such as a lump of clay (e.g., pots, plates, and statues) are already existing within it. As such, creation is not really producing something entirely new, nor does it involve the destruction of the old. Rather, it is the manifestation of latent, already-existing effects through transformation, while other effects return to the latent state.

Sāṃkhya argues for this principle as the best account of causation, starting with the principle of sufficient reason, "since nonbeing is not a cause" (*SK* 9).[46] As something must come from *something*,

[45] Gauḍapāda (c. 500 CE) uses the example of milk and curds while commenting on *SK* 9 and the restriction of distinct effects to distinct sorts of causes. The example is also found in *Brahma-sūtra* 2.1.24 (c. 200 CE).

[46] We find this in the proto-Sāṃkhya of the ancient Upaniṣads. "And some say . . . 'being arises from nonbeing.' But how could this be true? How could something come from nothing?" (*Chāndogya Upaniṣad* 6.2.1–2)

even in the earliest, most primordial acts of creation, there must have already been matter that serves as its basis.[47] Beyond this, *satkāryavāda* is motivated by the fact that causal regularities demand that an effect is in some way anticipated within its material cause.

> Since a material cause is required;
> Since it is not the case that all things come from all things;
> Since something is capable of causing what is possible for it to cause;
> The effect exists within the cause [*satkārya*]. (*SK* 9)

The view is that when an effect occurs, this is merely a potentiality of the cause coming to full manifestation. As such, just as the effect already exists in the cause, the cause continues to exist after the production of the effect. Without denying that creation occurs, Sāṃkhya denies that being is ever bracketed by nonbeing. There is simply matter in various modes or states existing latently within it.

Vātsyāyana's response is again to argue that we have a good handle on the criteria for the creation and destruction of material objects, one that allows us to recognize that material things are often destroyed while new things are built from them. When the underlying components are separated and reformed into a new arrangement, a new substance is produced (3.2.16). The Buddhists are therefore wrong by not recognizing that a stable configuration of component parts allows for the endurance of material substances, while Sāṃkhya is also wrong for denying that change involves genuine creation and destruction.

With respect to Sāṃkhya's arguments for *satkāryavāda*, Vātsyāyana's responses show that the need to account for causal

[47] Sāṃkhya offers versions of what we could consider cosmological arguments, not for God but for the existence of prime matter as the material cause of the world. See *SK* 14 and 15. Also see Guha, Dasti, and Phillips 2021, 9, 16–17, for discussion of one such argument "from delimited measurements."

regularities can be addressed without such a radical view. Possible effects in the form of macro-objects are indeed limited by the possibilities allowed for by their material causes and the combinations that they may take. But this does not entail that creation and destruction are merely terms for "manifestation" and "non-manifestation" of objects that exist within their material causes. They do not exist prior to their creation, nor does a previous object continue to exist after its structure has been reconfigured.

Vātsyāyana does not explicitly locate such structure (*vyūha*) within Nyāya's categorical schema, but he does mention it as identical to "form" (*ākṛti*) under 2.2.68: "Form is nothing more than a fixed configuration [*vyūha*] of something's parts and sub-parts." A form is a non-repeatable quality inhering in a material object, one that often indicates a universal. As such, it is best understood as a special kind of *conjunction*, a quality shared by multiple substances in contact.[48]

Finally, Vātsyāyana returns to the issue of examples that fail to be probative without proper grounding. In the language of informal fallacies, he suggests that both the crystal and milk cases mentioned above are instances of *proof by select instances*.

3.2.18–41: Cognition as a property of the self

Moving on from the critique of Sāṃkhya, this section focuses on *buddhi* according to Nyāya. As stated under 1.1.15, the word *buddhi* is in Nyāya a synonym for terms such as *jñāna* and *upalabdhi*, which mean "cognition," an episode of awareness. This section defends the view that metaphysically, cognition is best understood as a property of a self. It also amplifies the arguments about the self

[48] Uddyotakara makes this explicit in his commentary on 2.1.33: "For us [Naiyāyikas], a particular arrangement of parts is conjunction, and conjunction itself is something distinct from the parts themselves."

that began under 1.1.10 and featured prominently in the first half of this chapter of the *Nyāya-sūtra*. There are three subsections: a response to the problem of simultaneous cognition (3.2.18–33), a rejection of loci of mental states other than the self (3.2.34–39), and a summary of the argument centering on recollection (3.2.38–41).

Let us pause and consolidate the idea of the self as a unique psychological substance. I would suggest that what is being expressed with this notion is that the self is a *location*. Any particular self is an irreducibly unique, stable location of mental states. In the Vaiśeṣika metaphysical toolkit used by the *Nyāya-sūtra*, the category of substance accounts for the loci of qualities:

> The characteristics of a substance are its possession of actions and qualities, and that it is an inherence cause (*VS* 1.1.4).[49]

Material objects such as a pot possess a particular color, for example, *an instance of tan*. If dropped, they possess the action *falling*. Selves, too, possess certain qualities, a few of which were mentioned in sūtra 1.1.10: *desire*, *aversion*, *effort*, *pleasure*, *pain*, and *cognition*. The self is is therefore a substance, albeit a unique psychological substance.[50]

As people speak of physical space, logical space, the space of possible worlds, and the like, we may also imagine a range of *experiential space*. Each self is a unique point within experiential space, a unique perspective or locus of experience. My experience of, say, a tree in the distance is located in me, while yours is located in you. Vātsyāyana has already argued that part of the content of memory

[49] An inherence cause (*samavāyikāraṇa*) is the preexisting stuff in which effects inhere. For material objects such as a pot, this would be the portions of clay out of which it is made. Loosely, an inherence cause is akin to a material cause in that it is the material basis of effects. But "inherence cause" is a broader category, where a self is the inherence cause of every mental state predicated of it.

[50] Halbfass (1992, 105) notes: "In debates between Hindus and Buddhists, the *ātman* is the substance par excellence, the most representative, and most controversial exemplification of a 'substratum,' a durable 'center of change,' and a core of irreducible identity."

is oneself as a locator of experience (3.1.14). With arguments from recollection and synthetic cognition, he has also stressed the way a self permits the co-location of varied states, diachronically and synchronically. We could say that when such co-location is sufficiently robust, there is full-blown personhood, as opposed to the somewhat abstract and bare notion of selfhood.

Nyāya's philosophy of self is, therefore, a substance dualism but of a very lean sort, quite different from Descartes's *res cogitans.* A self is a nonmaterial substance locating mental qualities; when appropriately tethered to a body/mind complex, it is the seat of agency for actions and cognitive processes. But on its own, the self is not a person, nor can it think or undergo experience without a body/mind complex (argued under 3.2.30 below).[51]

The sūtras begin this section by arguing that the sense organs could not be the loci of *buddhi,* since cognition continues after a sense faculty has been destroyed. Memories pertaining to visual experience continue even after the visual faculty has been destroyed. They must be housed somewhere else (3.2.18). The *manas*, too, fails to be an appropriate locus. Its basic function is to sift between inputs such that one is not overwhelmed with simultaneous, unintegrated cognition (3.2.19). If *manas* were the locus of cognition, it could not serve this purpose. Here Vātsyāyana returns to the notion of the self as cognitive agent. The *manas*, like the sense faculties, is instrumental in the production of cognition, allowing for selective attention as well as our capacity for introspection and apperception. As an instrument, it cannot be the agent of cognitive acts:

> The controller is the knower, and the controlled is an instrument. If it were to possess cognition as its own quality, the *manas* would cease to have the nature of an instrument. (*Commentary* 3.2.19)

[51] Dasti (2014, 120n27, 131n50) discusses Nyāya's self as possessing capacities for agency and the like that are actualized only under certain conditions.

Repeating the argument of 3.1.16, Vātsyāyana suggests that if the interlocutor thinks the *manas* is the agent of cognition and employs other instruments to know, this amounts to its being a self. There would be nothing more than a terminological difference.

This response triggers the objection in the next sūtra, which returns to the problem of simultaneous cognition:

> Even if it were a quality of the self, the problem still holds. (*NyS* 3.2.20)

To understand this obscure charge, we must return to some of the framing comments above. Like Descartes, Nyāya-Vaiśeṣika recognizes that the self is not easily circumscribed within three-dimensional space. But the school moves in the opposite direction, so to speak, with this datum. The seventh chapter of the *Vaiśeṣika-sūtra* considers the size of fundamental reals and claims that the self, like ether, is "all-pervasive." It is not atomic in size or intermediate-sized like the composite macro-objects of ordinary experience. It is literally unbounded by physical limits.[52]

We might understand the reasoning behind this idea as an argument from elimination. There are, broadly speaking, three possible sizes: atomic, intermediate, and all-pervasive. The smallest possible things are atomic. Intermediate things are composite objects, tables, chairs, and the rest, but also living bodies, trees, and mountains. All-pervasive things have no physical boundaries, like ether. The self could not be atomic, as then it could not be in contact with the body and the senses. Nor could it be intermediate, because only material composites have this size. The only remaining option—and one consistent with its being a single, non-composite substance—is that it is all-pervasive.

Nyāya has a more nuanced palate than Descartes for what counts as "material" and "nonmaterial," as well as for the properties of each. For Nyāya, we might distinguish between "physical" or "elemental" entities

[52] *VS* 7.1.28–9.

and a host of "nonphysical" entities, one of which is the self. Things that are constructed out of the elements are physical, and a mark of the physical is that it is obstructed by other physical things.[53] But there are also nonphysical substances that have extension without impingement, most notably ether, time, and self. As Kisor Chakrabarti (1999, 26) points out, "although the self has extension, it is not solid and does not prevent other physical objects from occupying the same space."

This idea of the self as all-pervasive is what animates the current objection: "The self is all-pervasive, in contact with all the senses. As such, there is the unacceptable consequence that cognition would arise simultaneously" (*NySBh* 3.2.20).[54] If cognition is a property of the self, which is all-pervasive and in contact with all the senses, we should be flooded with multiple types of cognition all the time. The answer to this challenge is that a connection between *manas* and the senses is still required for sensory cognition, and this is what regulates and restricts cognitive inputs (3.2.21–22).

A second objection is that if the self is eternal and no grounds for the destruction of cognition are observed, locating cognition in the self would entail that cognition itself is eternal, a patent falsehood (3.2.23). In response, Vātsyāyana does stress that the impermanence of cognition is something "every embodied being witnesses inside themselves." It is a fact of experience. But destruction can be accounted for in the way that a sound may be overridden by another sound or one quality may overwhelm another. Cognition at $time_t$ could be overridden by an ensuing cognition at $time_{t+1}$, and so on (3.2.24). This view of cognition helps to make clear why terms such as *buddhi* or *jñāna*, which refer to such fleeting, episodic states, are not synonymous with "knowledge" as used in everyday English.[55]

[53] "Obstruction is a feature of physical objects" (*Commentary* 3.1.38). The term for "physical" here is *bhautika*, "composed of the elements."

[54] This, too, is background for Vātsyāyana's aside about the *yogīns* under the former sūtra. *Yogīns* are commonly said to have wide-ranging awareness, even spanning multiple bodies. This would be impossible if cognition were a property of the atomic-sized *manas*.

[55] This will be discussed at length under 3.2.42 below.

Sūtras 3.2.25–34 advance a third objection, centered on memory (*smṛti*). Since mnemonic traces are themselves qualities of a self, and the *manas* is always connected to the self in some way, the view that cognition is a quality of the self would lead to the absurdity that we would be constantly experiencing our memories.

The primary response is that remembering is constrained by other causal factors:

1. Beyond contact between a self and *manas*, other factors are required for mnemonic cognition, including focus (*praṇidhāna*) and inferential marks that trigger transitions between ideas. These other factors are non-simultaneous and allow for the orderly flow of mnemonic cognition (3.2.33). (A partial list of indicators is provided under 3.2.41 below.)
2. Instruments that produce awareness function sequentially. In the case of memory, the operative instrument is *manas*, while the agent is the self (3.2.33).

Many of Vātsyāyana's arguments in this section are directed against specious, prima facie views purportedly supporting Nyāya but which he finds lacking (under 3.2.25 and 3.2.31). Against the view that the *manas* must move to those "portions" of the self where specific memories are stored, he argues that despite the self being all-pervasive, the *manas* is confined to space delimited by the physical body. Therefore, this model of recollection will not work (3.2.26–32).

In this context, we find interesting digressions about embodiment and cognition:

> Being alive [*jīvana*] is understood to be the conjunction of an embodied self with a *manas*, a conjunction accompanied by karmic merit that is fructifying. (*Commentary* 3.2.26)

> The effort [*prayatna*][56] born of the contact between a self and *manas* is twofold: that which sustains the body and that which impels bodily movement. (*Commentary* 3.2.28)

> Independent of connection to a body, the connection of a self with a *manas* would not be enough to cause remembering, since the nature of a body is to be the receptacle for experience [*upabhoga*]. That is, the body is the seat of experiences for the self, who is the knower. Therefore, the mere connection between a self and a mind which has [ex hypothesi] set out beyond the body would not be capable of generating mental states like cognition or pleasure. If it were, there would be no use for a body. (3.2.30)

These passages help provide a picture of embodied life on Nyāya's view. Life involves the self connected to several ancillary causal factors. Fundamentally, a self that is connected to a *manas* and qualified by karmic merit that is in a state of fructification. Karmic merit provides parameters that tether a self to a specific embodiment.[57] Connection to a *manas* allows for the self to exhibit a distinct sort of effort. Typical examples of effort would be something like the impetus to move one's arm and hand to pick up a drink. This is a state of the self that impels bodily action. The other kind of effort, which sustains the body, motivates sub-volitional processes such as circulation and digestion. As I've pointed out elsewhere, for Nyāya and Vaiśeṣika, this notion of "effort" is meant to capture the innate capacity of a self to provide organization and direction to matter in accord with an individual's karmic merit.[58]

Final remarks on the need for a body as the seat of experiences show again how modest Nyāya's interactive dualism truly is. While the self is an "all-pervasive" locus of experience, the body "localizes"

[56] 1.1.10 lists *prayatna* as one of the qualities by which we infer a self.

[57] Cf. 3.2.60–72.

[58] Dasti 2014, 115.

the self to provide it with a discrete, determinate context for both action and experience.

Sūtras 3.2.34–37 consider other candidates for loci of cognition. The first is a hybrid position as envisioned by Vātsyāyana, perhaps reflecting an ancient iteration of Sāṃkhya. He frames sūtra 3.2.34 as a rebuttal directed to an unmentioned interlocutor:

> Some hold the view that cognition is a property of the self, while desire, aversion, effort, pleasure, and pain are properties of the inner instrument [*antaḥkaraṇa*]. (*Commentary* 3.2.34)

This view fails for reasons already developed: an individual's cognitive and affective lives are inextricably fused. Initiation and cessation of bodily activity observed in someone's body flow from their cognitive and affective states.

At the end of his remarks, Vātsyāyana reflects on the problem of other minds, noting that initiation (*ārambha*) and cessation (*nivṛtti*) of activity are indicators that other people exist within material bodies. We might see a friend walk over to pick up a mug of coffee, take a sip, and then sit down (my example). Vātsyāyana suggests that we know about ourselves that initiation and cessation of movements are impelled by our states of desire and the like. We therefore infer the same for other embodied beings.

An epistemological problem motivates the next interlocutor, depicted as "one who holds that consciousness belongs to the elements" (*bhūta-caitanya*). *Bhūta-caitanya* is an epithet that evokes materialism in the philosophy of mind: there is no need for a nonmaterial self, since material objects can serve to locate cognition.[59] This objector agrees that the initiation and cessation of activity are indicators of conscious life, but on those grounds, consciousness belongs to "things made of earth and the like."

[59] Gokhale (2015, 123–135) connects this principle to ancient Indian materialists.

Vātsyāyana offers two arguments on their behalf by interpreting sūtra 3.2.35 in two ways:

1. Material bodies made of earth and the other elements engage in alternating activity and rest. As these are indicators of desire and aversion, hence of consciousness, material things are conscious (*Commentary* 3.2.35).
2. Material elements like earth *in the bodies of living things* initiate activity, as indicated by the specific arrangements of their parts. Therefore, they possess consciousness. This is a specific type of action that is not exhibited in things like stones, which lack consciousness (*Commentary* 3.2.36).

Vātsyāyana rejects argument 1 through the counterexample of instruments like axes. These, too, go through periods of activity and rest, but that alone does not show that they are conscious. Argument 2 attempts to avoid easy counterexamples. Material bodies of living things undergo structural change, as indicated by their distinct arrangements (*vyūha*). They possess a special kind of activity, which prompts the inference to consciousness. Despite this nuance, Vātsyāyana argues that counterexamples remain. A clay pot, for example, is a material composite, with a distinct structure. But that does not prompt an inference to it or its constituent elements bearing consciousness.

To settle the debate, more is needed than conflicting examples. Vātsyāyana offers the following principle:

> For a conscious being, activity and rest are caused by desire and aversion, but these do not reside in the same locus. Activity and rest reside in the instrument that is employed. They exist only within the physical elements that are employed. (*Commentary* 3.2.37)

He also identifies the principle put forth by the materialist:

> Since the material elements are conscious, activity and rest are caused by desire and aversion that is restricted to the *same* locus.

Vātsyāyana responds that the materialists' rule would entail that in any given body, there are countless, separate loci of awareness, as there are countless material elements in varied combinations and processes. By contrast, Nyāya's notion of a nonmaterial self (one that synthesizes experience as amply illustrated) makes more sense of the singular nature of consciousness in each living body.

Vātsyāyana further subsumes the opponent's argument 2 within Nyāya's scheme. Since movement in things like axes is due to a special quality of the knowing agent, along with the adjunct cause of karmic merit, so, too, the configuration of living bodies. This "special quality" includes both the sub-personal "effort" and karmic background for embodiment spoken of under 3.2.26 and 3.2.28. What axes and bodies have in common is that they are "employed for the sake of the goals of life" and belong to the nexus of karmically influenced objects. Karmic merit influences teleological dimensions of life, even those dimensions seemingly unrelated to human choice and agency.[60]

Under 3.2.38–40, Vātsyāyana summarizes many of the arguments about self that have been offered in this chapter, countering alternative views that have both Sāṃkhya and Buddhist elements. As made explicit in 3.2.39, Nyāya's is an argument from elimination. A nonmaterial self is the only remaining option to make sense of our lives as agents, knowers, moral beings, and, for some, seekers of ultimate liberation over a multi-lifetime journey.

[60] See 3.2.60.

3.2.42–45: Cognition as ephemeral

This section expands upon the discussion of cognition's ephemeral nature under 3.2.24, where Vātsyāyana remarks that it is a patent fact of experience. Under 3.2.42, he gives two reasons to support the observation:

1. Movements (such as the flight of an arrow) are experienced in a sequence of brief segments, where each segment is the object of a distinct cognition.
2. Perceptual experience of a lasting object (such as a water jar) stops when the object is blocked. This shows that standing perception is not a single long-lasting state but a sequence of connected cognitive events.

None of this is particularly controversial or surprising. But Vātsyāyana's further remarks on recollection show that *jnāna*, "cognition," is not identical with "knowledge" as normally used in English:

> Memory does not prove that cognition endures, since mnemonic impressions [*saṃskāras*] generated by cognition are the cause of memory. (*Commentary* 3.2.42)

"Knowledge" typically refers to a dispositional state, something whose content remains latent within memory until brought to conscious awareness. In contemporary philosophy, this content is often expressed as a proposition, knowledge that something is the case. I know that my younger daughter was born in March, but such standing knowledge is triggered only on occasion. By contrast, *buddhi* or *jñāna* occurs in the present moment and is ephemeral. It is an information-bearing intentional state directed toward whatever my attention is on at this very moment. The stream of consciousness flows from perceptual cognition, to inferential cognition, to apperception of one's own mental contents (cognition of cognition), to remembering, and so on.

In Nyāya's categories, the standing knowledge that my younger daughter was born in March is held as a memory trace which may be accessed by the *manas* as directed by the self. When it is accessed, a fresh instance of remembering occurs. It is for this reason, incidentally, that memory is not a *pramāṇa* for Nyāya. Memory does not generate new information but retrieves information stored from what would ideally be an earlier *pramāṇa* token.

3.2.46–55: Cognition as distinct from bodily properties

As Vātsyāyana admits at the end of this section, the view that the body is the locus of consciousness was considered and rejected earlier. He sees this section of the sūtras as taking up special points of consideration, since "the truth is understood more securely when it is examined in various ways" (3.2.55). Three arguments are offered to refute the thesis that consciousness (*cetanā*) is a property of the body:

1. An argument from non-consciousness (3.2.46–47). Consciousness is not a constant property found in a body. Bodies can exist without consciousness, in contrast with their always having visible form and other qualities truly their own. Therefore, consciousness is found in the body because of the presence of something else that joins with it, akin to the way the warmth of water is due to fire atoms mixed in with water atoms.
2. The problem of multiple knowers (3.2.50). Akin to the argument already seen under 3.2.37, Vātsyāyana observes that consciousness is a single quality spread throughout the various parts of the body. But on the thesis that the body is the

locus of consciousness, there is no reason for there to be only a single locus of awareness. In fact, there should be many conscious beings existing within the same body, as distinct sorts of actions and responses are found in different parts of the body.

3. Consciousness is radically different from physical properties (3.2.53). Unlike physical properties of the body, consciousness is imperceptible by the physical senses but uniquely perceptible though introspection.

The most interesting objection is found under 3.2.47, where an interlocutor asks, "Why couldn't consciousness be like an impression [*saṃskāra*]?" *Saṃskāras* are most familiar to students of Indian philosophy through yoga psychology, as memory traces that perpetuate one's mental fluctuations (*citta-vṛtti*). Vātsyāyana does use the term in this way[61] and also, in a connected sense, as a designator for the unseen karmic merit that is stored in an individual self.[62] He also speaks of *saṃskāra* in relation to physical things, as a quality that inheres in macro-objects,[63] to explain a sound wave's movement,[64] and to explain how the force of wind is transferred to a tree's branches as it moves them.[65] What all of these have in common is that a *saṃskāra* is a dispositional property that carries or transfers content. For example, a memory trace is a standing property that is triggered only under certain conditions. When triggered, one's memory of (e.g.) a childhood home becomes manifest to consciousness through memory. The momentum of a thrown rock is also a *saṃskāra*, which carries some of the force of the thrower's arm as it hurls the rock. The interlocutor thus asks

[61] 3.2.25; 3.2.31; 3.2.33; 3.2.41; 3.2.42.
[62] 3.1.68; 3.2.37; 3.2.60; 4.1.47.
[63] 2.2.67.
[64] 2.2.35–36.
[65] 5.1.9.

why consciousness could not be a dispositional property of the body manifest under certain conditions.

Vātsyāyana's response is to argue that dispositional properties may not be triggered due to a stoppage or destruction of a relevant cause. A body remains, however, after consciousness is gone. So the body itself cannot be the cause of consciousness. Vātsyāyana moves from this to an argument from elimination: no other candidate material cause will solve this problem, whether thought of as something that (i) exists within the body, (ii) exists outside the body, or (iii) is a hybrid of both.

Consciousness is not, therefore, an emergent feature of physical bodies. But before we turn our back on the notion that it is emergent, it might be helpful to consider these remarks along with Vātsyāyana's arguments under 3.2.26–30. There he makes clear that while consciousness, cognition, and affective states such as desire are all properties of the self, they are possible only when a self is tethered to a body/*manas* complex. The body "localizes" the self physically and provides an arena for experience and action. Because of this, it would not be wrong to speak of consciousness and the panoply of qualities we associate with personhood to be emergent properties. But when they emerge, they are borne by a nonmaterial self and not the body or *manas*. This, again, is why a liberated self exists in a sort of stasis, according to Vātsyāyana, far from the states of bliss and discovery proclaimed in the Upaniṣads. Indeed, Nyāya's liberated self is, in a way, *less than* an embodied self in that various dispositional features and potentialities of the liberated self remain permanently unactualized.

3.2.56–59: On *manas* ("the inner instrument")

This section offers little that is new by way of arguments for the nature of the *manas*. *Manas* is held to be a singular, "atomic"-sized instrument of selective attention on the grounds that something must sort through the varied sense inputs to allow for the orderly sequence of cognition that we experience as knowers. An important addition to the conception of *manas* that is brought out here is that our ability to seemingly attend to more than one thing at the same time is due to the *manas*'s rapidity in switching between various inputs. A challenge is offered, that we can indeed do various things at one time, and therefore, there must be more than one *manas* for a single person. The sūtras respond that *manas* can move at the proverbial speed of thought. Therefore, our occasional sense of simultaneous thoughts is due to our inability to resolve distinct episodes that occur in rapid sequence. The sūtras offer the analogy of a spinning firebrand, while Vātsyāyana puts forth the example of verbal comprehension:

> We fail to notice the sequence when we cognize phonemes, words, sentences, and their meanings, because it happens so rapidly. When phonemes, the basis of sentences, are uttered, first individual phonemes are heard. One then connects them together as individual units or as collections in the form of words. Having done this, one resolves each word and then remembers their meanings. Connecting them all together as a single unit, one determines the sentence. And finally, by understanding the meanings of the connected words, one grasps sentence meaning. We do not notice this sequence because all these cognitions occur so rapidly. From this, we may infer that other instances of cognition or action that occur in rapid sequence are mistakenly thought of as simultaneous. (*Commentary* 3.2.58)

3.2.60–72: Embodiment as determined by karmic merit

This section is a detour from the ordering of the objects of knowledge, which lists *purposive action* after *manas*. The focus is on what we could call "karmic causality." Within the overall framework of the *Nyāya-sūtra*, I see it as a return to the topic of the body (the second on the list of objects under 1.1.9, discussed under 3.1.27–31), since it is an examination on the role of karmic merit within embodiment.[66]

Vātsyāyana has appealed to karmic merit as a contributing factor to biological life (3.2.26). He now develops arguments for this claim in the face of opposing views:

> There is doubt about this due to disagreement: Is the creation of one's body due to the causal influence of their prior acts? Or rather, do the elements act alone, with karma playing no causal role? Conflicting claims are heard on this point. (*Commentary* 3.2.60)

Throughout the section, Vātsyāyana uses a handful of related terms for the hidden influences that carry the momentum of one's prior acts. These include *puruṣa-karma* ("a person's actions"), *karma* ("actions"), *dharma-adharma* ("merit and demerit"), and *adṛṣṭa* ("unseen force"). He will argue that not only is one's current body structured according to such forces (3.2.60–65), but they are the fundamental tie between the self and the body/*manas* complex that makes experience possible (3.2.66–72).

While explaining and defending Nyāya's view, "the body is created from a connection with the results of former acts," Vātsyāyana unpacks the way actions generate karmic merit, which leads to future embodiment. What is noteworthy is that this is one of the few places in the *Commentary* where he explicitly appeals to teleology:[67]

> When one's body dies, a new body is created by these impressions [*saṃskāra*] in the form of merit and demerit along

[66] I here follow Uddyotakara.
[67] Others include 3.1.38 and 3.1.68.

> with the material elements. And, as with the former body, one acts to achieve the goals of life [*puruṣārtha*] with the new body. . . . We observe that the creation of things like chariots—which are effective in helping people act to obtain the goals of life—occurs when the material elements are connected to effort, a special quality belonging to a person. From this we infer that the body—which is also made to be effective in helping people act to obtain the goals of life—is produced by elements that are influenced by a special quality belonging to a person. (*Commentary* 3.2.60)

The argument may be reconstructed as follows:

1. If something is instrumental in achieving the goals of life, its material constituents come together because of a special quality belonging to persons.
2. Human bodies are instrumental in achieving the goals of life.

---

3. Therefore, the material constituents of human bodies come together because of a special quality belonging to persons.

Basic features of this argument are familiar from teleological arguments: in ordinary life, structured effects related to the human good require agency; so, too, for other "natural" effects such as bodies, trees, and so on. A fascinating difference is that here the output conclusion is not for a creator God or cosmic designer but rather a "personal quality" that influences insentient material elements in the construction of such effects. Similar to some of the arguments for the self, the conclusion is something that will be filled according to the best explanation available. One is then found within the Vaiśeṣika toolkit. While the "personal quality" involved in the construction of artifacts is human effort (*prayatna*), this will not work for the construction of bodies. But some quality must be there, as random chance will not do. A different personal quality is available, however, one that is held to permeate human choices and intentions and also to govern the movements of atoms as they come together in constructing the world, namely, karma or *adṛṣṭa*.[68] The teleological element of this reading is further amplified under 3.2.66 below. There Vātsyāyana provides a description of just how complicated the human body is, underscoring that it is "something that is constructed with the greatest difficulty" and therefore unlikely to be composed due to mere luck.

Vātsyāyana represents a transitional position between nontheistic schools that accept karmic causality, such as Mīmāṃsā and Buddhism, and the natural theology famous in later Nyāya. A theist who holds that God influences the creation of the world in accord with karmic causality (4.1.21), he also holds that karmic merit itself has an inherent teleology that affects the world. It is the next major commentator, Uddyotakara (as well as authors whose works are largely lost to us, such as Aviddhakarṇa) who develops a full-blown teleological argument for God by making the case that karma needs an intelligent being who stands above it and governs it.

The opposing position, that unaided material elements create human bodies, is attributed to a "denier" (*nāstika*), who argues that there are ample illustrations of material elements coming together on their own to effect macro-objects.[69] Such objects (e.g., mineral deposits) are then used by people for their purposes. The body would be just one more case of such causality (3.2.61).

The sūtras offer four arguments in response:

1. Since Nyāya is arguing that ordinary elements coming together to effect human ends are influenced by karma,

[68] See also Vātsyāyana's final comments on *NyS* 2.1.30.

[69] The term *nāstika* is often used for one who rejects the Vedas along with the cultural authority of derivative works and tradition traced from it. In the *Commentary*, however, Vātsyāyana uses it for a general sort of skeptic (1.1.1) and speaks of views associated with "deniers" as detrimental mental formations (1.1.2).

citing them as counterexamples is begging the question (*sādhyasama*) (3.2.62).[70]

2. Human bodies differ from the examples offered in that they are produced by biological reproduction (3.2.63).
3. Human bodies differ from the examples offered in that they are created in utero by metabolized food and drink of the mother (3.2.64).
4. Unseen karmic influences help explain why some instances of intercourse lead to conception and others do not (3.2.65).

Sūtra 3.2.66 transitions from bodies to embodiment in general. Here Vātsyāyana makes use of the principle of sufficient reason:

> Since each self is qualitatively identical, in the absence of a causal factor that is related to each individual, bodies produced of earth and the like would be equally connected to all selves. And since there is no restricting factor that belongs to earth or the other elements, being a locus of sensations of pleasure or pain would hold for all selves equally. And yet such sensations are restricted in different ways for different individuals. Therefore, we understand that the same karma that causes the production of bodies is also what tethers individuals to different bodily conditions. (*Commentary* 3.2.66)

This argument is expanded under 3.2.67, where Vātsyāyana speaks of people born into various life conditions, with beautiful or unattractive bodies, sick or healthy bodies, and so on. I would suggest that it is a misreading to take Vātsyāyana to use the notion of karma here as a kind of theodicy. That is not his current project. His concern is to explain the radical disparities found in the conditions

[70] This is a precursor to a standard strategy in Nyāya's later natural theology (in both Uddyotakara and Vācaspati), arguing that the status of trees, mountains, and the like are part of the dispute and, hence, cannot be used as counterexamples to the proof. See Dasti 2011, 7–8.

of each person's birth. These demand explanation, and the karmic momentum of the past provides an explanation, unlike anything on the "matter" side of the equation. It is something in the vicinity of the principle of sufficient reason that is operative and not a concern to justify God's ways.[71]

Vātsyāyana's commentary on the remaining sūtras of this stretch develops the argument that the quest for liberation makes sense only if karmic merit is a property that directly belongs to individual selves (3.2.68–72). By reading *adṛṣṭa*, "the unseen," in 3.2.68 as meaning *adarśana*, "non-perception," he interprets this subsection as directed primarily toward Sāṃkhya, as opposed to materialism. In mainstream Sāṃkhya, an individual's enmeshment in matter is spoken of as due to "non-discrimination" between the true self and what is not the true self.[72] The Sāṃkhya position is that worldly entanglement is perpetuated by a failure to disentangle the self and matter, especially subtle "mental" matter such as *buddhi*.

Unlike Nyāya, which sees karma and other qualities such as cognition and desire as properties of the self, Sāṃkhya's self is untouched by fluctuation or content of any kind. Only *buddhi* and other insentient faculties, which somehow "reflect" the consciousness of the self, undergo modification and change. This is explicitly said in Sāṃkhya; its dualism is so uncompromising that the entire march to liberation is carried out by the *buddhi*:

> The *buddhi* brings forth experience of every sort for the self and also distinguishes the subtle difference between self [*puruṣa*] and matter [*pradhāna*]. (*SK* 37)

> No one is therefore ever bound, released, or the subject of transmigration. It is *prakṛti* [matter] alone, in its various modes of being, that is bound, released, and undergoes transformation. (*SK* 62)

[71] For a paradigm example of a karma-based theodicy, see Śaṅkara's commentary on *Brahma-sūtra* 2.1.34–37, translated in Guha, Dasti, and Phillips 2021, 72–74.
[72] *SK* 14.

Vātsyāyana targets what we might call Sāṃkhya's agential or moral dualism in his critique. For Sāṃkhya, agency is on the side of *prakṛti*, and the self is ever and always a passive witness. The self cannot be a locus of moral or karmic information, so all of the karmic information that governs an individual's tie to the world is on the "matter" side of the self/matter divide. For these reasons, Vātsyāyana argues that on Sāṃkhya's view, there should be little confidence to trust that after liberation, an individual self will not be snatched up again by matter and its machinations. There is nothing to prevent this from happening, since there is nothing about an individual self that reflects its status as liberated, worldly, moral, immoral, or whatever (3.2.68).

The rest of the *Commentary* in this chapter reiterates this basic point, that placing karmic merit in anything but the self results in the loss of any trust that liberation is possible or stable. Doing so also leaves one without an explanation for the radical differences between different lives. Vātsyāyana's exhaustive commentary on the final sūtra argues that the opponent's view allows one "to acquire consequences for things they haven't done." While this notion is typically associated with a need for moral continuity, here it is about the need for an appropriate account of differences among people:[73] "This observable disparity in pleasure and pain has no basis [on their view]."

[73] 3.1.4.

4

Objects of Knowledge and the Insight That Leads to the Supreme Good

Part 1 (4.1.1–68)

The first part of Chapter 4 continues the special investigations into the *prameya*s, covering the seventh to the twelfth (and final) objects of knowledge on the list given in 1.1.9. The second part will focus on knowledge of the truth (*tattva-jñāna*), an fundamental insight which is said to produce the supreme good.

4.1.1–9: Purposive action (*pravṛtti*) and vice (*doṣa*)

Purposive action and vice are intimately connected in Nyāya's action theory. The former are goal-directed activities, and the latter are traits that prompt one to act in ways that perpetuate worldly entanglement:

> The striving of someone possessed of desire or aversion is purposeful action. (*Commentary* 1.1.1)

> Purposeful actions are undertakings by means of speech, *manas*, or the body. (*NyS* 1.1.17)

> Vices are characterized as impellers. (*NyS* 1.1.18)

The sūtras decline to take up *pravṛtti* here for extensive investigation, noting that "purposive action accords with what has already

Vatsyāyana's Commentary *on the* Nyāya-sūtra. Matthew R. Dasti, Oxford University Press.
 DOI: 10.1093/oso/9780197625927.003.0004

been discussed" (4.1.1). Vātsyāyana sensibly suggests that this is a reference to the discussions of the self, body, and so on, in Chapter 3, where questions of agency, responsibility, and karmic/moral merit emerged as central to selfhood. It is useful to remember that while *pravṛtti* typically means purposive or intentional action, Vātsyāyana reads it in a restricted way under 1.1.2, as synonymous with *dharma* and *adharma* (merit and demerit). This is likely why he now refers to the self as "that which is the locus of merit and demerit" (*Commentary* 4.1.1).

The sūtras tell us that *doṣa*, vice, is also to be understood in accord with what has been discussed already (4.1.2). Vātsyāyana's summary account blends together various elements from Chapter 3 and the early reflections in sūtras 1.1.1–2:

> Vices are qualities of the self, as they are co-located with cognition. They are a cause of repeated birth and death, since they trigger purposive actions and have the capacity to span rebirths. They exist as a beginningless chain, since repeated birth and death is itself beginningless. Misconception is removed by knowledge of the truth, and when misconception is gone, there is liberation, breaking the chains of attachment and aversion. (*Commentary* 4.1.2)

Sūtras 4.1.3–9 are concerned with the criteria for individuating vices. Following sūtra 4.1.3, Vātsyāyana argues that a wide range of vices may be grouped under three basic headings: attachment, aversion, and ignorance. (See Table 15.) Attachment is characterized by clinging; aversion, by an inability to endure; ignorance, by misconception.[1] The three are all distinct causes of unhealthy behaviors. Still, ignorance is significantly different from the other two. It is a cognitive

[1] In Table 15, I translate *amarṣa* as "impatience." But here I would like to invoke a more general sense of the term, "inability to endure," as the vice is supposed to encompass all the others.

Table 15. A typology of vice under 4.1.3.

Fundamental type:	attachment (*rāga*)	aversion (*dveśa*)	ignorance (*moha*)
Subtypes:	lust	anger	misconception
	jealousy	envy	cynicism
	covetousness	malcontentment	pride
	thirst (for pleasure)	malice	negligence
	greed	impatience	

vice, as opposed to the others, which are affective. Misconception about what is truly valuable leads to world-directed deliberation (*saṅkalpa*), which then triggers the other vices. Thus, ignorance is the most dangerous of the three, as it is causally fundamental to the other two, and it must be targeted to break the chain of worldly existence (4.1.6).

A question that some readers may have is not addressed in this section. While vices impel one to unhealthy actions, what about ethically positive actions that are likewise associated with positive character traits? Are the sūtras—and Vātsyāyana in turn—presupposing that *all* actions are in some way vicious? One would perhaps be justified in thinking this, since the view of liberation they have presented is of an inactive, peaceful stasis. But from early on, Vātsyāyana has distinguished between healthy, virtuous actions and the vicious actions mentioned here:

> Apart from vicious actions, there are auspicious acts of charity, protection, and service though the body. Through speech, there is truth-telling, speaking in ways that are beneficial and kind, and recitation of sacred literature. Through the mind, there is compassion, non-covetousness, and faith. (*Commentary* 1.1.2)

In his commentary on 1.1.2, Vātsyāyana makes clear that positive acts, leading to merit and higher, better births in the future, are *purposive actions*, as are the vicious acts that lead to demerit and lower births. Without mentioning a correlate to "vice" by name, in Indian thought, it is typically contrasted with virtue (*guṇa*). Vātsyāyana seems to presuppose positive character traits or virtues that motivate healthy behaviors. In his final comments on 4.1.68 below, he also notes that actions that are not impelled by vice are of a different sort and fail to generate future entanglements.

While virtuous acts are distinct from those stemming from vice, in relation to Nyāya's overall soteriology, Vātsyāyana does suggest that the highest goal of liberation would require that one transcend *both* virtue and vice. With this, he is consistent with a deep thread running from the Upaniṣads through the *Bhagavad-gītā* and other yogic literature, that the yogic quest leads one to forsake not only selfishness but *mere* piety as well.

4.1.10–13: Rebirth (*pretyabhāva*)

Like the other topics considered so far in this chapter, the discussion of rebirth does not go far beyond the extensive discussions of self and embodiment in Chapter 3. Vātsyāyana does make clear, however, that given that the self is eternal (and, we could add, spatially unbounded), ordinary talk of it "dying" or even "departing" at the time of death must be understood in a secondary sense. Birth occurs when an eternal self becomes conjoined to a particular living body, and death is when it becomes disassociated from that body.

With sūtra 4.1.11, the discussion of rebirth triggers expansive consideration of various models for causation. Vātsyāyana frames sūtras 4.1.11–13 as departing from the topics of rebirth and how bodies are created. But even here, we see a very broad causal principle that will be mirrored by many of the theories put forth in the next section (4.1.14–43):

> Manifest effects come from manifest causes, since this is established by perception. (*NyS* 4.1.11)

Compare this to rules considered later on, including "things arise from nonexistence" (4.1.14) and "things arise without a cause" (4.1.22). In each case, human bodies and other objects are examples mentioned to illustrate universal causal principles. The rule of 4.1.11 is accepted by the sūtras and interpreted by Vātsyāyana as pertaining to atoms of the elements, earth, water, air, and fire:

> From *manifest causes*, spoken of as elements like earth that are supremely subtle and eternal, are produced the *manifest objects*, substances that are understood to belong to bodies, senses, objects, and related things. (*Commentary* 4.1.11)

This account presents a prima facie contradiction. "Manifest" means "available to the senses," and yet atoms are said to be "supremely subtle" and beyond the range of sense perception. Vātsyāyana therefore interprets their being "manifest" as their having a certain similarity with objects built out of them. Both possess certain qualities, such as color. He interprets the sūtras' claim that this is "established by perception" to mean the rule that causes (such as clay) must have qualities in common with their objects (such as clay pots) is perceptually established. The rule is then extended through inference to non-perceptible reals.[2] Of course, the relevant similarity is not absolute. As an interlocutor rightly notes, a pot is not produced by a pot (4.1.12–13).

[2] Cf., *VS* 2.1.24: "The qualities of the effect are found to be preceded by the qualities of the cause."

That the sūtras claim the causes to be *manifest* is likely another shot directed toward Sāṃkhya, which contends that the ultimate cause of the world is the *unmanifest* (*avyakta*), a state of materiality in its most abstract, unqualified form.

Here Vātsyāyana engages with a methodological concern to which he often returns: the reasonable extension and application of induction from ordinary experience. In accord with his improvements upon the sūtras case-based method of inference, he tries to advance principles of legitimate extrapolation, while also justifying and making sense of the Vaiśeṣika metaphysical inheritance he accepts.

4.1.14–43: Various theories considered and critiqued

The Upaniṣads provide evidence of ancient investigations into the fundamental cause of existence. Not unlike the pre-Socratic search for an original *arche*, the *Śvetāśvatara Upaniṣad* reflects on candidates for "the cause . . . from which we are born, by which we are established":

> Is it time, inherent nature, necessity, chance, the elements, the Womb, the Person? (*Śvetāśvatara Upaniṣad* 1.1–2)

By the time of the *Nyāya-sūtra*, such investigation was explicable in the form of reasoned views (*dṛṣṭis*) attributable to the burgeoning traditions and schools of classical philosophy. Vātsyāyana introduces the current section as following from the preceding reflections on causation. It is an extended consideration of views or theories put forth by numerous interlocutors and camps. Many of these identify a cause that stands above all else, offering reductive "singular accounts" according to Vātsyāyana (4.1.29).[3]

[3] Gopinath Kaviraj's introduction to Jha 1919 (xviii–xxiii) speculates on historical analogues to each of the views presented in this section.

There are eight subsections: that nonexistence is the foundation of created things (4.1.14–18), that God independently creates with no regard to human agency (4.1.19–21), that things arise by chance (4.1.22–24), that all things are impermanent (4.1.25–28), that all things are permanent (4.1.29–33), that everything is unique or a heterogeneous heap (4.1.34–36), that all things are "empty" as alleged by Buddhists (4.1.37–40), and that all objects can be reduced to a few kinds (4.1.41–43). Vātsyāyana shows us that in some cases, the Nyāya view incorporates a flawed position with slight modifications, while in others, it rejects the view entirely.[4]

The first subsection, 4.1.14–18, considers the view that nonexistence (*abhāva*) itself is the cause of created things, since a material cause (e.g., a seed) must be destroyed for an effect (e.g., a sprout) to arise. Vātsyāyana ultimately accepts this view in a modified sense. Two theses of the interlocutor are accepted: (i) creation involves the reconfiguration of the material cause such that the prior object is destroyed and a new object is created, and (ii) we do, in fact, speak of prior and future things as causes in a figurative sense, despite their current nonexistence (e.g., a son who is yet to be born is said to cause joy).

The mistake of this view as proposed by the interlocutor is to overstate the role of nonexistence, which is not a *cause* that precedes an effect but rather a byproduct of the causal process. The view endorsed by Nyāya here is that while material causes do span the gap between pre- and post-causal states, their reconfiguration is enough to ensure that something wholly new arises. In Nyāya's metaphysical categories, "reconfiguration" is a modification of an object's structure (*vyūha*), which itself is a type of *conjunction*,

[4] Bronkhorst (1985) remarks that sūtras 4.1.11–40 do not "organically fit" with the broader text, being an extensive tangent about causal theories appended to the sūtra on rebirth. This, along with other considerations, leads him to suggest that Vātsyāyana, or some unknown intermediary before him, added this section to the sūtras. With regard to "fit," it is true that 4.1.11–40 is tangential to the main course of the sūtras. But so, too, are the *Nyāya-sūtra*'s celebrated arguments for holism (2.1.33–36), as well as others on the philosophy of time (2.1.39–43) and karmic merit (3.2.60–72).

nested within the category of *quality*. "We find that parts of an object and their mutual conjunctions are the causes of a sprout's arising" (4.1.18). The core idea that is accepted is in many ways definitive of Nyāya's mature view (contra Sāṃkhya) that in causation, wholly new things do arise, despite a dependence upon preexisting material causes and their qualities.

The next subsection is concerned with the relationship between God's causal power and human agency (4.1.19–21). Nyāya is famous for a natural theology developed through the early commentators,[5] but the place of theism in its earliest stratum is controversial. Like its sister text and precursor, the *Vaiśeṣika-sūtra*, the *Nyāya-sūtra* does not explicitly list God (*īśvara*) among the fundamental objects of inquiry (under, e.g., *NyS* 1.1.1 and 1.1.9). This lacuna, along with the testimony of classical works such as the *Yuktidīpikā*, has led some scholars to conclude that in its earliest period, Nyāya-Vaiśeṣika was not theistic.[6] They suggest that for various possible reasons, whether to solve problems of cosmology or epistemology or simply owing to the influence of popular religious movements, the twin schools became theistic over time and robustly so in the post-sūtra period.

A problem with some of these speculative histories is that while the *Vaiśeṣika-sūtra* was likely not theistic in its earliest stratum, this does not justify speaking of Nyāya-Vaiśeṣika as a single entity for which theism was a later add-on by commentators. Despite its temporal posteriority and deep Vaiśeṣika allegiances, the *Nyāya-sūtra* is a distinct work from the *Vaiśeṣika-sūtra*, differing from it on several important points. Speaking of Nyāya-Vaiśeṣika as a single tradition obscures this fact, as well as the fact that the *Nyāya-sūtra*

[5] Chemparathy (1968, 79): "The Nyāya-Vaiśeṣika system . . . can be said to be the foremost Indian system of philosophical theism in the first millennium of the [Common Era]."

[6] The *Yuktidīpikā* (c. 550 CE) is a polemical commentary on the *Sāṃkhya-kārikā*, which claims that the theism of Vaiśeṣika in its post-sūtra period is an "invention of the Pāśupātas" and grafted onto Vaiśeṣika philosophy. The Pāśupātas are an early Śaivite sect. See Chemparathy 1965; Chemparathy 1968; Balcerowicz 2010, 330–337.

does appear to accept a God-like being, albeit one introduced in a somewhat tangential fashion.

The argument of this section of the sūtras presents a dialectical movement in three steps:

1. Assertion: God is the sole cause of the unfolding of the world, since human actions are sometimes found to be fruitless (4.1.19).
2. Rejection of the assertion: No, since without human actions, the relevant results do not occur (4.1.20).
3. Affirmation of a hybrid view: Human actions are necessary for relevant results, but only when God actuates them. God is a more powerful, supervisory causal factor in the unfolding of the world, who exerts his influence in conjunction with human behaviors and their proper outcomes (4.1.21).

This seems to me to be a straightforward reading of the sūtras themselves.[7] They affirm that God is an instrumental cause in the continued unfolding of the world. But exactly what "result" (*phala*) means in this context is ambiguous. It could refer to the commonplace success of intentional actions (e.g., whether someone is hired for a job they've interviewed for). "Result" also can refer to *karmic* results generated by the moral weight of actions, which fructify across embodiments. As interpreted by Vātsyāyana, the sūtras might be understood to address either notion, but they shade toward the former:

> The Lord [*īśvara*] shows favor to an individual's actions. That is, for some person striving to attain some result, the Lord bestows it. When he does not bestow it, then the desired result does not occur. (*Commentary* 4.1.21)
>
> If one were to claim that the Lord brings forth consequences that ignore the results of an individual's actions, this would be subject to

[7] See Bulcke 1968, 27–35, for an examination of the sūtras in their own context, as well as the major early interpretations starting with Vātsyāyana.

> the same refutations as the view that bodies are created with no regard to karmic merit given under 3.2.60–72. (*Commentary* 4.1.21)

In this reading, the observation of sūtra 4.1.19, that human actions are sometimes fruitless, is not about *karmic* continuity as much as more commonplace results of intentional actions. Still, Vātsyāyana clearly sees God as the overseer and administrator of karmic merit as well. This nuances and complicates the role of karmic merit as outlined within the earlier sūtras. While a sort of moral and metaphysical "glue" that connects an individual self to its body/*manas* complex and allows for a certain range of bodily circumstances that conform to moral parameters set by earlier actions, karma is overseen and administered by an intelligent, personal being. Vātsyāyana's interpretation again may be seen in a developmental vein, as taking hints or seeds in the sūtras and providing directions that prove decisive for later Nyāya philosophers. Uddyotakara and Vācaspati Miśra do indeed argue that karmic merit *requires* God to function, as it is an inert informational state. For his part, Vātsyāyana rejects the notion that karmic law is subject to gaps or failures, and arguably, this consistency is because of the oversight of a being with God's knowledge and power.

Vātsyāyana also leads the way for ensuing commentators by appending to sūtra 4.1.21 an excursion on theology that goes well beyond explaining the sūtra itself. Following a familiar pattern, he seeks to find a place for God within the Nyāya-Vaiśeṣika categories. Thus:

> It makes little sense to think that God is something other than a self, since he fits best within that category.

And yet God is no ordinary self:

> God is distinguished from other selves in that demerit [*adharma*], misconception, and delusion are absent, while he is

> endowed with merit [*dharma*], knowledge, and perfect concentration [*samādhi*].

Vātsyāyana seems to be looking for a vocabulary to express God's unique power. He borrows from yogic traditions to do so:

> As a result of his merit [*dharma*] and perfect concentration [*samādhi*], he possesses lordliness in the form of the eightfold yogic powers, such as the ability to make oneself as small as an atom.[8]

That he speaks of the *īśvara* as possessing *dharma* seems strange, since *dharma* is something that typically arises by obedience to religious and ethical rules. If God oversees karma, it makes little sense to hold that he gains merit by observance of karmic law. Vātsyāyana remarks, however, that God's *dharma* "conforms to his intention." God's *dharma* is not generated by submission to a larger ethico-religious system of rules but flows directly from his intent. My reading is that Vātsyāyana takes *dharma* here in a wide sense, as a sort of occult power to influence the world. Again, he seems to be looking for a vocabulary to express God's creative power.[9]

God is, furthermore, an "authority," *āpta*, the same term used for an authoritative speaker under 1.1.7. His relationship to created beings is like "a father to his progeny." These ideas both suggest that there is more to the *īśvara* than being a cosmic bureaucrat.

Given the history of later Nyāya natural theology, which finds provers to establish God as the maker of bodies, trees, and other

[8] Vātsyāyana already shows a familiarity with Vyāsa's commentary on the *Yoga-sūtra* in *NySBh* 1.2.6. The eightfold yogic powers are mentioned in *Yoga-sūtra* 3.45. The *Caraka-saṃhitā* also mentions eight yogic powers under Śarīrasthāna 1.138–141, though "making oneself as small as an atom" is not on that list of eight.

[9] Later Naiyāyikas deny that *dharma* applies to God at all; they see his capacity to control matter as his own inherent potency.

such things, it is noteworthy that Vātsyāyana does not offer an argument for God. He does somewhat cryptically suggest that "apart from cognition [*buddhi*], there is no quality whatever capable of serving as an inferential mark for him." What would it mean to use cognition as an inferential mark to prove the existence of God? *Starting* from God's cognition to prove God's existence would be circular. Indeed, the most famous proofs offered by later commentators begin with structured effects found in nature, to *conclude* that their cause must be intelligent (*buddhimat*, "possessed of cognition"). Again, however, there is a likely antecedent in Vyāsa's commentary on the *Yoga-sūtra*. Under *Yoga-sūtra* 1.25, Vyāsa notes that knowledge, like other personal attributes, comes in degrees. As such, he contends, there must be a most complete instance of knowledge, where "the seed of omniscience is unsurpassed." He argues that the being who has the highest degree of knowledge is *īśvara*. The similarity to Thomas Aquinas's "Fourth Way" is patent, though this argument focuses on a spectrum of cognition, not goodness.

Sūtras 4.1.22–24 entertain and reject a reductive maxim, that things arise "without a cause." Vātsyāyana argues that natural structures that seemingly have no observable cause fall within the range of karmic causation, as discussed under 3.2.60–72.

Sutras 4.1.25–28 address universal impermanence, that all things "have the condition of being produced and destroyed." While this resonates with Buddhist theories of momentariness, the view entertained here is the less specific claim that nothing is eternal. Sūtras 4.1.26–27 suggest that the thesis of universal impermanence falls to self-refutation, as it requires that the impermanence itself is an eternal fact. Vātsyāyana adds that these sorts of claims require careful investigation. Rarely are metaphysical truths determined by a simple a priori calculus:

> When knowledge sources show that something has the condition of being produced and destroyed, it is impermanent. If it is

> shown not to, then it is the opposite. And things such as atoms, ether, time, self, *manas*, and some of their qualities, as well as universals, individuators, and inherence, are not found to have the condition of being produced and destroyed. Therefore, they are eternal. (*Commentary* 4.1.28)

Sūtras 4.1.29–33 entertain the contrary of the previous claim, that all things are eternal. Here, too, we find a superficial resemblance to a view already encountered; Sāṃkhya's *satkāryavāda*, but again, the current position seems distinct. The proponent says that ultimately, the five basic elements are real, and everything is reducible to them. While claiming that "everything" is eternal, this view denies full existence for macro-objects. As unpacked by Vātsyāyana, the interlocutor holds that what is truly real about (e.g.) a clay pot is the clusters of elements that constitute it:

> Everything that exists is nothing more than material elements. (*Commentary* 4.1.29)

> We do not find an object to be anything other than the material elements, as though they could possess properties the elements lack. (*Commentary* 4.1.31)

Vātsyāyana offers a number of arguments to support the view that creation and destruction are real phenomena, as are the objects subject to them (4.1.32):

1. Identifiable causes for the creation and destruction of macro-objects are patent facts of experience.
2. There are shared properties in common between a macro-object and its material causes.
3. Individuals' efforts are concerned with things that engender creation and destruction. If these two were not real, human activity would effectively cease.

4. Composite wholes (*avayavins*) have been established philosophically and are subject to creation and destruction by combination and disunion of constituent parts.
5. The reductive criterion (of 4.1.29 and 4.1.31) is flawed, since impermanent things such as sound, action, cognition, and other mental states are not reducible to any or all of the five elements.

Anticipating the transition from reductionism to wholesale subjective idealism under 4.2.26–32, the opponent suggests that ordinary experience of causes and effects is nothing more than error, akin to a dream. While more concise and simpler than his response in that later passage, Vātsyāyana's response here also appeals to self-refutation: if macro-experience can be doubted and rejected by skeptical analogy with dreams, then by parity of reasoning, so, too, can our experience of material elements such as earth.

The final salvo of the interlocutor slightly shifts their thesis in such a way that it is reminiscent of Sāṃkhya's *satkāryavāda*. On this view, a latent property of the material cause is simply *manifest* during creation and continues to exist in a latent state after destruction.[10] For Vātsyāyana, this fails for four major reasons:

1. We would not be able to distinguish between creation and destruction, since any particular property would exist at all times.
2. We would not be able to make distinctions between specific occurrent properties, since all properties would exist at all times.
3. We could not make distinctions with respect to the present time, since we could not contrast it with nonexistent past and future states.

[10] Cf. 3.2.15–17.

4. Likewise, distinctions with respect to the past and future would be undermined, as they are grounded in events that have gone out of being and will come into being, respectively.

Sūtras 4.1.34–36 give voice to an interlocutor who alleges that everything is just a heterogeneous heap. "We find that nothing whatever is a single object" (4.1.34). Vātsyāyana frames the objection as akin to Abhidharma reductive empiricism:

> A term used to express an object is a designating term [*samākhyā-śabda*]. Such terms scope heterogeneous contents. Every designating term for an object refers to a cluster. Take, for example, "jar." This term designates a cluster of sensible qualities, scent, taste, form, and touch, as well as parts, like its base, sides, neck, and so on. (*Commentary* 4.1.34)

Vātsyāyana's response to this echoes that found under 2.1.33–36. Taken as a universal claim, the view contradicts itself, since "a cluster is simply the aggregation of *singular things*." If there are *no* singular things, the position collapses entirely.

Sūtras 4.1.37–40 consider a thesis of universal nonexistence. We might think of the argument here as naturally following the former, which was concerned with the characterization of objects and the use of naming terms. The transition between the interlocutors of these two sections neatly mirrors the historical transition from Abhidharma Buddhism to the Madhyamaka Buddhism of Nāgārjuna.[11] Abhidharma reductionism stops with individual property tropes such as an instance of color or touch. These basic units of experience are the only things that survive analysis. They are not conceptually constructed, and therefore they have genuine

[11] This is one of the parts of the *Nyāya-sūtra* that complicate the question of influence from and to Nāgārjuna. While Nāgārjuna is aware of the *Nyāya-sūtra* and responds to some of its arguments, this section seems to be a direct response to him.

being, *svabhāva* ("intrinsic nature," "essence").[12] Though a fellow Buddhist, Nāgārjuna takes issue with Abhidharma and seeks to go even further. He argues that *nothing* has *svabhāva*, due to the interdependence of *all* things. He teases out various forms of dependence: causal, linguistic, and conceptual. To be dependent in any of these ways is to lack *svabhāva*. Reflecting on basic ways in which our concepts depend on each other, even explanatory concepts such as "cause" and "effect," he suggests that the dependence is mutual, not unidirectional:

> If something is established dependently and it, in turn, establishes the very thing upon which it depends, then what depends upon what? (*MMK* 10.10)

Nāgārjuna often tries to reduce various forms of realism to absurdity, arguing that the notion of something that exists intrinsically leads to inescapable contradictions. He provides a wide array of arguments to the effect that various phenomena championed by philosophers (e.g., causation, motion, indwelling selves, substances that bear properties) lack *svabhāva*. Many of his arguments have the following form:

1. *X* enters into relations with other nodes of causal, conceptual, and linguistic networks.
2. *X* possesses intrinsic existence (*svabhāva*).
3. If something possesses intrinsic existence, then its identity is isolated from the network of conditions within which it is embedded.
4. If something's identity is isolated from the network of conditions within which it is embedded, then it does not enter into relations with other nodes of such networks.

---

[12] Westerhoff 2009, 19–52, is an excellent study of the concept of *svabhāva* in Buddhist sources.

5. Therefore, *x* does not enter into relations with other nodes of causal, conceptual, and linguistic networks.[13]

The contradiction between the conclusion and premise 1 leads to the rejection of premise 2.

Nāgārjuna's arguments target both Abhidharma Buddhism and Hindu schools such as Nyāya. We have reviewed his attack on Nyāya's *pramāṇa* methodology under 2.1.17–20. The interlocutor of this section of the sūtras argues against realism in a broad sense:

> Anti-realist argument 1: Everything is nonexistent, since the mutual absence of things is established. (4.1.37)
>
> Nyāya response 1: This is wrong, things are established by dint of their intrinsic nature (*svabhāva*). (4.1.38)
>
> Anti-realist argument 2: No, the realist view is untenable, since intrinsic nature is dependently established. (4.1.39)
>
> Nyāya response 2: Your view is untenable as it is beset by self-contradiction. (4.1.40)

The first anti-realist argument is somewhat crude, rehearsing considerations discussed earlier in the context of relational absences (2.2.12). Initially, Vātsyāyana offers several quick responses, some of which hinge on self-contradiction. If *x* is absent with respect to *y*, then *y* at least must bear at least some ontological weight (4.1.37).

The first reply of the sūtras (4.1.38) invokes *svabhāva* as a bedrock consideration. Vātsyāyana interprets the term in various ways, reflecting on the criteria for genuine existence. Under his first interpretation, *svabhāva* means "the specific character of an existing

[13] I reflect on this argument style in Dasti 2018, 147–152. For examples of the reasoning captured in this argument, see *MMK* 13.4–6; 15.2; 20.17; 21.17; 22.22; 24.38.

thing by which it is distinctly understood." To illustrate what he means, he cites both the *Vaiśeṣika-sūtra* and the *Nyāya-sūtra* on fundamental categories and their essential features:

> Universals, starting with *being*, belong to substance, quality, and action. (*VS* 1.2.7)
>
> Substances are the loci of actions. (*VS* 1.1.14)
>
> Earth has all the perceptible qualities up to touch. (*NyS* 3.1.61)

Vātsyāyana notes that these are but a few examples. His central point is that we have enough of a handle on the principles of existence and individuation to discern the basic categories that make up Nyāya's metaphysical system. If all were fundamentally nonexistent, then the grooved paths of disambiguation provided by intrinsic natures would be unavailable.

Under his second interpretation, Vātsyāyana takes *svabhāva* to mean "essence" (*svarūpa*). When we hear the term "cow" (under normal conditions), we comprehend the basic, essential features of a cow. If things were nonexistent, then proper use of language would not result in defined, consistent awareness on the part of hearers.

Under his third interpretation, Vātsyāyana takes the appeal to *svabhāva* to be a rejection of the anti-realist methodology of 4.1.37, which centers on relational absence. Yes, in a superficial way, everything could be described as relationally absent with respect to other things. But understood in relation to *itself*, something is not relationally absent. And the anti-realist makes a fundamental mistake about the use of negations in statements such as "A cow does not exist qua horse." Here negation is just the denial of identity between a cow and a horse, not the denial of a cow as an existing thing.

In response to these refutations, we find the anti-realist view refined and expressed in language that closely resembles Nāgārjuna's (4.1.39). Vātsyāyana's brief gloss focuses on the interdependence that is championed, to great effect, by Nāgārjuna:

> Something that is dependent is contingent on other things. *Long* is contingent on *short*. *Short* is contingent on *long*. Nothing whatever is grounded through its own properties alone. Why? Because it depends upon the efficacy of certain conditions. Therefore, it is false that things are established through their intrinsic nature. (*Commentary* 4.1.39)

The Nyāya response under 4.1.40 attempts to meet Nāgārjuna's challenge, offering three major considerations:

1. Insofar as *long* is contingent on *short*, *short* would have an efficacy that does not vanish into other conditions. Likewise in the opposite direction. The upshot of this is that the "rule of dependence" held by the interlocutor is incorrect. When two things are *truly* dependent upon each other, in the absence of one, the other would be absent. But this does not occur in the case of short things and long things. The absence of a longer stick does not necessitate the absence of a shorter stick.
2. On the view that nothing is grounded by its own nature, two substances of equal size should have their properties in a dependent way. But this is not the case. Whether considered alone or in relation to the other, their sizes remain the same.
3. The real function of conceptual dependence is that it allows us to compare two things and their relative qualities. It does not *generate* their properties as much as allow us to *recognize* their differences by contrast.

Vātsyāyana's commentary here is only the first word in Nyāya's response to Madhyamaka anti-realism. Ensuing commentators will expand upon his replies. But his core point is an affirmation that something's causal/conceptual/linguistic "potency" is grounds for its distinct reality.

We might consider the degree to which this response strikes at the heart of Nāgārjuna's arguments. In the *Vigraha-vyāvartanī*, a work directed primarily against Nyāya, Nāgārjuna worries that his notion of *emptiness* will be interpreted to mean *nonexistence* and therefore something lacking in any potency or capacity at all.[14] He argues that on the contrary, to be "empty," without intrinsic existence, is what allows something to participate in causal networks of various kinds. Emptiness is required for anything to be causally efficacious.[15] Given this, we might wonder if Vātsyāyana is missing the target. A blanket equation of *emptiness* and *absence* would distort Nāgārjuna's thought.

To be charitable to Vātsyāyana, I think that he is doing something more than this. I would suggest that he is challenging Nāgārjuna's criteria for true existence. To be fully real does not mean something has to be independent of any causal or conceptual conditions but rather that it has to possess certain properties and capacities. Vātsyāyana argues that having a specific size or a distinct property such as "being the locus of actions" is enough to ensure that something is a genuine participant in reality. This appears to force Nāgārjuna into a dilemma of his own. If *emptiness* is a label that when applied changes nothing, then it is a platitude without much weight. Nyāya can continue its attempts to identify and follow knowledge sources, locate the structural features of reality, and pursue its philosophical projects. If, on the other hand, *emptiness* has real force, it demands some sort of revisions when applied and would mean something closer to the concept of nonexistence. But then, as a sweeping metaphysical theory, it faces the difficulties outlined above.

Understood in this light, the parallels between Vātsyāyana's response to Nāgārjuna here and those given under 2.1.17–20 are striking. In each case, problems of dependence relations and grounding are put forth by an interlocutor. The dependencies of 2.1.17–20 are epistemic: *pramāṇa*s are said to fall prey to

[14] For Nāgārjuna, to be "empty" is to exist without *svabhāva*. His thesis is that all things are *empty* in this way.
[15] *VV* 1–4, 21–29.

unacceptable outcomes involving regress, circularity, positing, and self-certification and therefore cannot be the epistemic supports Nyāya takes them to be. Here, in this section, the dependencies are ontological; things in general are said to be inextricably dependent upon other things, causally and conceptually, such they cannot stand on their own. There are no stable bases for Nyāya's categorial metaphysics.

With regard to the epistemic arguments of the second chapter, Vātsyāyana makes two points we might recall. First, a skeptic relies on *pramāṇas* just as everyone else does. Knowledge sources cannot be abandoned by Nāgārjuna or anyone who is trying to navigate the world or advocate their position. Second, Vātsyāyana offers what we might call a soft foundationalism in that prima facie veridical cognition is to be taken as true in the absence of legitimate doubt or a defeater.

With regard to the ontological arguments in this section, his strategy is similar. First, if emptiness were, as Nāgārjuna alleges, something consistent with the world of experience, then the concept demands no revisions when applied and can be ignored. Second, to be real simply requires genuine causal capacities and identifiable features. Possession of these is what makes them real whatever their own causal and/or conceptual backstory. This seems to be an analogue to his soft foundationalism with respect to the *pramāṇas*.

Sūtras 4.1.41–43 present the view that all objects can be reduced to a few kinds. Vātsyāyana speaks of these as "views that reduce things to a specific number." Various forms of ancient Sāṃkhya try to identify a certain number of discrete reals, but this interlocutor seems more undefined. This section might reflect ancient debates and verbal jousts over arithmology, the truths represented by specific numbers.[16]

[16] Vidyabhusana (1920, 19n1) suggests that this section of the sūtras is directed toward the doctrine contained in the number-based riddles of Aṣṭāvakra in the *Mahābhārata*, Vanaparva, Chapters 132–134. It is unclear to me how we might establish such a specific target of the section, but those chapters of the *Mahābhārata* do provide helpful examples of the sort of ancient number symbolism that surely precurses the metaphysical reduction-to-numbers discussed by Vātsyāyana under 4.1.41.

The rebuttal voiced in the sūtras is frankly sophistical: if the advocates of number reduction wish to argue for a specific set of reals, then the proof they give has to be something other than those reals, to avoid circular reasoning. But this forces them to admit something additional into their ontology.[17]

In his final remarks under 4.1.42, Vātsyāyana hits at a deeper point:

> If these reductions to specific numbers function by denying the multitude of different objects, which are such because of distinctions among them, then they are simply false, in contradiction with perception, inference, and testimony. Or, if they function by collecting objects through shared properties, and excluding objects through dissimilar properties, they abandon their reduction to a single principle.

In short, these reduction-to-number accounts are overly theory-driven. Their primary reals are determined without proper observation and reflection.

Vātsyāyana concludes this entire section by remarking that the investigation has been undertaken "for the sake of distinguishing genuine knowledge," connecting it to the major goal of inquiry stated under 1.1.1.

4.1.44–54: Results of action (*karma-phala*)

The *Nyāya-sūtra* now returns to the list of knowables, considering the tenth of twelve, the "results of action." In the first chapter, results

[17] A problem with this criticism is that it hinges on an ambiguity that has already been identified by Vātsyāyana in his defense of *pramāṇas* in Chapter 2. One need not step outside of the *pramāṇas*, for example, to defend *pramāṇa* epistemology. A token *pramāṇa* can, for example, support the existence of another token *pramāṇa* without circular reasoning. By the same principle, a proof for a discrete number of reals could itself be a token of one of those types of thing.

are characterized as being "produced by purposeful actions and vices" (1.1.20). In his comments, Vātsyāyana adds:

> That which arises when body, senses, sense objects, and cognition are in place is what we mean by "results": that which comes along with those things. For results are produced by purposeful actions and vices—this includes the body and the rest, too.

While *karma-phala* could mean ordinary results of ordinary actions (e.g., a mug breaking because it was dropped on the floor), the context here is the soteriological question of "karmic" results, which might span multiple lifetimes. This section has three major subsections: reflection on temporal gaps between causes and effects (4.1.44–47), a denial that the effect preexists in the cause (4.1.48–50), and an argument that the locus of moral or religious effects is the self, directly (4.1.51–54).

Sūtra 4.1.44 does not specify the sort of causation in question when it invokes doubt. It simply observes that at times, results occur immediately, and at other times, there are temporal gaps. Vātsyāyana interprets the concern to be the religious effects associated with Vedic ritual. In fact, he blends together results of religious deeds, such as the Agnihotra sacrifice, and a more general sense of karmic consequences associated with ordinary morality.[18] Until sūtras 4.1.51–54, the sūtras seem to concern themselves with cause and effect in a general sense, but Vātsyāyana justifiably reads the karmic notion as the major issue from the onset of this section. He sees the prompting doubt as a concern about the efficacy of Vedic ritual because the results of the practices are said to fructify long

[18] The relationship between religious notions of merit generated by sacrificial rites and the like and a more general moral theory of karma is complicated. The two were not always considered equivalent, especially by the highly orthodox Mīmāṃsā school. Halbfass (1991, 300–311) traces the connections between Mīmāṃsā and Nyāya-Vaiśeṣika on these issues, suggesting that Vātsyāyana's discussion in this section influences the account of the Mīmāṃsaka Kumārila (c. 540–600 CE) in his *Tantravārttika*.

after the rites are completed (4.1.44–47). There are causal gaps. But like his earlier defense of Vedic authority (2.1.58), Vātsyāyana's response is to appeal to ordinary, noncontroversial instances of causation:

> One who desires the fruit of a tree engages in various supporting activities such as watering the roots [which sets in motion a chain of events that eventually terminates in fruit]. . . . In the same way, intentional actions produce an impression [*saṃskāra*] characterized by merit and demerit. At a later time, assisted by other supporting causes, it produces a result. This was already said: "The body is created by a connection with the results of prior acts." (*NyS* 3.2.60)

The interlocutor launches the next subsection by arguing that an effect would exist in a metaphysically ambiguous space (4.1.48). As earlier, the response is that observation makes clear the relationship between causes and effects: effects do not preexist; they are new entities. But there must be continuity between the material cause and the effect. The possibilities of the latter are bounded by the nature of the former (4.1.49–50).[19]

The final subsection addresses the relationship between moral/religious effects and their locus. Under 3.2.68–72, Vātsyāyana has offered anti-Sāṃkhya arguments that the self is the bearer of karmic merit and the like, not an intermediary like *buddhi*. Here he argues that the Nyāya account also makes sense of ritual:

> Felicity (generated by religious merit) is located in the self, as this is directly experienced within oneself. Karma, which is known as "merit" [*dharma*], is located in the self alone, as it is a property of the self. The notion that the result of rites has a different locus from the agent of the rites is untenable. (*Commentary* 4.1.52)

[19] See also 3.2.16 and 4.1.18.

4.1.55–58: Pain and suffering (*duḥka*)

This section is on suffering, the eleventh *prameya* on the list. It answers a question that could have been raised as early as 1.1.9: since suffering—but not pleasure—is listed as one of the primary knowables, "Does this amount to a denial of pleasure, which is experienced by all beings and known internally?" (4.1.55). Here Vātsyāyana agrees that pleasure is a patent fact of life. The sūtras' focus on suffering is mean to facilitate an axiological shift toward meditative insight and away from ordinary sorts of pleasures. It is "an instruction to meditate upon embodied life as suffering" (4.1.58).

Vātsyāyana all but concedes that the sūtras themselves engage in hyperbole when they speak of embodiment and the rest as suffering "only" (*eva*). He remarks that embodied life is not essentially suffering, and neither is pleasure essentially pain (4.1.58). But he offers three ways to reflect on such claims as meditations on the ubiquity of suffering:

1. Suffering is inextricably tied to embodied life and embodied pleasures. While pleasure indeed exists, embodied life is interpenetrated with suffering. Therefore, as we speak of milk mixed with poison as "poisonous" and refuse to drink it, it is fair to speak of life as suffering in general (4.1.55, 58).
2. Craving or intense desire (*paryeṣaṇa*) is itself a kind of mental distress, typically remaining unsatisfied or satisfied only after great duress. Even then, satisfaction is temporary at best, and one is again "afflicted by another desire" (4.1.57).
3. When one becomes habituated to suffering, they become conditioned to think that painful things are, in fact, sources of pleasure (4.1.58).

These reflections underscore the therapeutic bent of early Nyāya philosophy. While its epistemology and metaphysics are meant to be objectively correct, these are carried out in a spirit of personal transformation. Vātsyāyana here uses the word *saṃjñā*, "conception," in a way that is not reducible to other terms seen already for knowledge or understanding. A "conception of embodied life as suffering" is a shift of vision involving reflection and meditation, not something as simple as seeing a red apple as a red apple. While Vātsyāyana would certainly think such a conception is also the *right* one, it involves an irreducibly normative judgment. The somewhat radical focus on suffering in the *Nyāya-sūtra* is, therefore, best understood as a call to rethink ordinary life and goals against the possibility of liberation, the "supreme personal good" (*paramapuruṣārtha*) (4.1.58).[20]

4.1.59–68: Liberation (*apavarga*)

The final section of Chapter 4, Part 1, reflects on the possibility of liberation. It is initiated by a challenge: "Liberation is unreal, since beings are bound to debts, afflictions, and purposive actions" (4.1.59). Sūtras 4.1.59–62 consider the problem of permanent obligations, while 4.1.63–68 consider afflictions and actions together.

The challenge to liberation that instigates the discussion represents not materialism or skepticism but rather the most orthodox of Vedic schools—those devoted to the ritual traditions. It should be understood as an in-house argument amongst Vedic thinkers. The Upaniṣads, as well as the *Bhagavad-gītā* and the philosophical schools of Vedānta that follow them, utterly and unquestionably identify themselves as Vedic and extol the Vedas as sacred revelation. At the same time, they denigrate those devoted to Vedic ritualism as operating on a lower tier of praxis. Ritual action for

[20] See Das 2020 for extensive discussion of Vātsyāyana's use of "labels" (his translation of *saṃjñā*) as a means to enact motivational shifts.

the sake of future pleasure is shortsighted when contrasted with the possibility of liberation. The moral and religious culture of Vedic ritual is merely preparatory, allowing one a firm basis by which to pursue insight into Brahman. A particularly severe example occurs in the *Muṇḍaka Upaniṣad*:

> Deeming sacrifices and gifts as the best, the imbeciles know nothing better. When they have enjoyed their religious merit, atop the firmament, they return again to this abject world. But those in the wilderness, calm and wise, who live a life of penance and faith, as they beg their food—through the Sun's door they go, spotless, to where that immortal Person is, that immutable self. (*Muṇḍaka Upaniṣad* 1.2.10–11)[21]

We might think of the current appeals to debts and obligations as a ritualist pushing back. Within the Vedas, there are statements suggesting that the complex network of individual desires, needs, obligations, and duties that constitute ritual culture perpetuate cosmic balance; they are not something to be extricated from. Vātsyāyana offers a citation (from the *Taittirīya-saṃhitā*) as evidence for this point: "As soon as a Brahmin is born, he is beset by three debts. One pays their debt to the sages by celibate studentship, to the gods through sacrifice, and to the forefathers by producing offspring." Suggesting that such debts are permanently binding, the duty to perform certain sacrifices is said to hold until "old age and death." Here Vātsyāyana quotes a passage from Śabara, the great commentator on the *Mīmāṃsā-sūtra* (*MSŚBh* 2.4.5). The upshot is that the duties of a sacrificer—along with the constellation of commitments such as household life, which are their basis—"do not allow any time for the pursuit of liberation" (4.1.59).

Vātsyāyana's response under 4.1.60–63 is extensive, expanding upon his early remark that Nyāya is an *ādhyātmika* tradition akin

[21] Translated by Olivelle (1998, 441).

to the teachings of the Upaniṣads (1.1.1). We also see a willingness to defend views and texts that are associated with Hinduism in a broad sense that are not found in the Vedas themselves.

Vātsyāyana opens by interpreting the Vedic statement about debts in a secondary sense. In the primary sense of the term, debts are incurred when one borrows goods and must eventually give them back. This is *not* the exact case of being born with obligations to the gods, and so on. Therefore, such claims about debts should be read metaphorically. Our obligations to the gods, and so on, are *like* the debts we incur in life. The metaphor is meant to underscore a Brahmin's need to perform Vedic duties, lest they be subject to blame akin to that of a debtor who fails to repay their debts. Vātsyāyana justifies this reading by pointing out that the phrase "as soon as he is born" must also be taken in a secondary sense, because an infant is incapable of performing any of the duties outlined.

The general principle Vātsyāyana evokes is that the sacred statements of the Vedic sages are to be interpreted in the same nuanced way we interpret ordinary speech, not simply according to an uncontextualized surface meaning. To this end, he also offers an interpretation of the notion that sacrificial duties hold until old age and death. Such duties are binding for "someone longing for results of sacrifice, insofar as their governing motivation for worldly gain has not changed." He accordingly interprets "old age" as meaning "the fourth stage of life, where one adopts wandering mendicancy." This is an appeal to *varṇāśrama-dharma*, class-and-stage-of-life duties, where the fourth and final stage of a Brahmin's life is devoted to asceticism and meditational pursuits.[22]

Although emblematic of classical Hindu culture, the *varṇāśrama* system is not laid out explicitly in the original Vedic corpus. It is elucidated by extra-Vedic works such as the *The Law Code of Manu* and other *Dharmaśāstras* ("Treatises on Dharma"). This is the pertinent background of the interlocutor's remark that "there is a

[22] See *The Law Code of Manu* 6.33–6.86 (Olivelle 2004).

direct injunction within the *brāhmaṇa* texts to maintain the life of a householder. If there was some other stage of life, it would have been enjoined."[23] Again, we might think of the current interlocutor as something of a Vedic purist who is dubious of these other texts and the ways of life they advocate.

It is fascinating that in the context of liberation, Vātsyāyana finds himself defending mainstream Hindu ideas likely articulated by non-Vedic or extra-Vedic movements and traditions before being mainstreamed by the Upaniṣads, the *Dharmaśāstra*s, and the like. He cites several Vedic and Upaniṣadic passages that minimally indicate liberation is a plausible goal of life set against goal-directed ritualism and worldly activity (4.1.60–61). And he further defends extra-Vedic works such as the "Histories" (*Ītihāsa*), "Ancient Chronicles" (*Purāṇa*), and *Dharmaśāstra*s—where the four stages of life are elaborated—as genuine sources of knowledge (*pramāṇa*). "The claim that these are not *pramāṇa*s is to be rejected, since their status as *pramāṇa* is itself proven by an established *pramāṇa* (the *Chāndogya Upaniṣad*)." His supporting citation blends elements from *Chāndogya* 3.4.2 and 7.1.2, which praise histories and ancient chronicles as beneficial and even as "a fifth Veda" (4.1.62). This latter notion serves to frame texts that are not strictly part of the Vedic corpus within the domain of sacred authority.[24] In the end, he appeals to common practice, noting that if secondary texts such as *Dharmaśāstra*s were ignored, societal obligations and practices would collapse, having no foundation.

Sūtras 4.1.63–68 respond to the claim that afflictions (*kleśa*) and activity (*pravṛtti*) are inescapable features of life, such that the quest for liberation is impossible to complete.[25] While the focus is

[23] *Brāhmaṇa*s are the portions of the Veda devoted to reflection upon ritual practice. See *NyS* 2.1.61–67.

[24] The *Mahābhārata*, for example, also speaks of itself as the fifth Veda.

[25] Afflictions are spoken of as "attachment and the rest" in sūtra 4.1.68 and as "attachment, aversion, and misconception" by Vātsyāyana under 4.1.64. This indicates that they are identical to the three major vices (*doṣa*) outlined in 4.1.3.

on afflictions, the two tend to be bound together in this discussion. The initial elements of the response are not very elaborate, other than pointing out a counterexample to the notion that afflictions such as attachment or suffering are inescapable: deep sleep. By explicitly comparing liberation to deep sleep, Vātsyāyana does offer a slight bit of content to his discussion of liberation (4.1.63). And his point that the actions of someone free of vices do not lead to rebirth (4.1.64) adds nuance to the reflections on action and liberation under 1.1.2. He is quick to say that this point does not violate the principle of karmic deserts. One must endure the ripening of one's stored karma in their final birth. Presumably, however, activities to maintain one's existence performed after one is free from vices do not generate karmic merit or demerit. This is expanded upon in his final remarks under 4.1.68:

> Action, which is a causal factor in perpetuating embodiment, will not generate attachment and the rest, because deliberations based on misconception will be destroyed though knowledge of the truth. But the results of [prior] acts, which result in the experience of pleasure and pain, remain.

Sūtras 4.1.65–68 respond to a follow-up by the interlocutor that as afflictions arise "naturally" (*svābhāvikatvāt*), they cannot be removed. They are "beginningless" and therefore cannot be entirely destroyed. The idea is that our entanglement in the cycle of rebirth quite literally has no beginning, and the stream of afflictions are, like atoms and ether, uncreated. By parity of reasoning, it, too, is eternal. A clever response presented in the sūtras is the counterexample of prior absences. The prior absence of a created thing such as my coffee mug is beginningless and natural. It always was. And yet it can cease (4.1.66). Vātsyāyana rejects this, however, since "eternality and non-eternality are properties of positive, real entities," not absences (4.1.67). While it is true that (e.g.) the prior absence of my coffee mug is eternal, the absence is not itself something qualified by being and, hence, specific properties such as eternality or non-eternality.

After rejecting the appeal to prior absences (and another argument about the color of earth atoms), the sūtras provide a conclusive response. Afflictions have identifiable causes. The sūtras identify "deliberation" as one.[26] Vātsyāyana adds others: karma and "one another" in that the vices cause other vices in a cascading way. Ultimately, these causes can be addressed and rectified in accord with the initial sequence put forth in 1.1.2. In particular, misconception must be addressed in order to stop deliberations that engender vice and actions performed under ignorance. Vātsyāyana reiterates that despite an infinite chain of prior causes that precede one's current embodiment, a break is possible. He hastens to add that this does not entail that a positively existing entity that is uncreated is subject to destruction.

Part 2 (4.2.1–51)

The investigation into the twelve major "things to be known," *prameya*, is now over. The rest of this chapter delves into the question of liberating insight or "knowledge of truth," the *tattva-jñāna* spoken of in sūtra 1.1.1 which is said to lead to the highest good.

4.2.1–3: The arising of liberating knowledge

Vātsyāyana's long preamble to this section is triggered by a question: what must the "knowledge of the truth" spoken of under 1.1.1 target to overcome the misconceptions that perpetuate suffering? His answer is that the deep objects of misconception are "the body, senses, *manas*, feeling, and cognition," which we mistakenly

[26] See 3.1.26, which says that desire is caused by deliberation.

identify with the deep self.[27] Reaffirming Nyāya's therapeutic orientation, he summarizes the way these all come together:

> The author of the sūtras distinguishes rebirth, karmic results, and suffering as things that must be understood deeply and says that karma and vices are to be abandoned. Liberation is to be sought. And the means to achieve it is knowledge of the truth. Thus, for someone who is dedicated, repeatedly meditating on the knowables as divided into the four therapeutic categories, proper vision arises, knowledge of the truth, experience of things as they truly are.[28]

We might notice his use of terms for reflection and meditation in this passage. These remarks expand upon the way liberating knowledge starts with the correct metaphysical map but must be developed through reflection. Insight requires more than "correct" cognition; an axiological shift must occur. Unpacking this theme, Vātsyāyana returns to the notion of *saṃjñā* ("conception," "label"), first deployed under 4.1.55–58, that one should conceive of certain things as suffering despite appearances to the contrary. Under 4.2.3, he identifies three conceptions with which we engage objects:

1. Conception of an indicator (*nimitta-saṃjñā*).
2. Conception of a secondary indicator (*anuvyañjana-saṃjñā)*.
3. Conception of a part (*avayava-saṃjñā*).

What the first two have in common is that they are, in the language of sūtra 4.2.3, "mistaken conceptions of the whole," which isolate

[27] Interestingly, he uses the word *ahaṃkāra*, "egoism," to refer to a false sense of self projected onto psychophysical conditions. This is another instance, like *buddhi*, where Nyāya talks about one of Sāṃkhya's mental intermediaries as nothing more than cognition itself.

[28] See 1.1.1 for the fourfold "medical" division of objects and its connection to therapeutic philosophies.

desired objects, framing them through attitudes of appropriation and self-interest. He notes ways in which this occurs in romantic or sexual desire, where the object of desire is seen in an "adorned" or "romanticized" way. We abstract the elements of (e.g.) another's body, its shape, and so on, and engage in a sort of projection coupled with desire.

For the purpose of liberation, Vātsyāyana advises that one instead entertain objects of experience according to a conception of the part. This use of "part" is correlated with "whole" as discussed in sections such as 2.1.32–36, but it has a broader sense of seeing the big picture. As opposed to the way we might abstract or objectify parts of another's body as desirable, this conception sees them for what they are in the big picture: aspects of human physiology, embedded within fairly unappealing biological functions and, like all biological entities, subject to decay. Such a conception is meant to hinder attitudes of possessiveness and clinging.

Let me suggest that we find here a connection between Nyāya's theoretical defense of wholes and its yogic values. The yogic or ethical correlate of holism requires an honest appraisal of things we tend to objectify and appropriate in relation to the "whole" in a broad sense. When taken in relation to the broader world, these things are, in a broad sense, inextricable from suffering and the vicissitudes of life. At the same time, this section also conveys a possible tension between (i) the proto-scientific Vaiśeṣika quest to understand the real world of experience as it is and (ii) the yogic drive for liberation. Both of these are inherited and accepted by Nyāya. The former involves a careful scrutiny of the world, and a defense of its reality. The second, a drive to transcend the world of experience altogether.

To his credit, Vātsyāyana recognizes the way in which a "yogic" deconstruction of ordinary experience seems to play right into the hands of his anti-realist and skeptical opponents. He therefore concludes his discussion by reminding us that "the objects encountered in both the appropriate and inappropriate attitudes are real." A delicate balancing act of defending the real external world while also advocating yogic praxis will dominate the rest of Chapter 4, Part 2.

4.2.4–17: Part and whole

Sūtra 4.2.3 claims that vices are generated by a "misconception about the whole." The following section follows up with a mereological nihilist's attack on the metaphysical status of wholes.[29] We might think of this section as an appendix to the arguments over holism under 2.1.32–36, giving voice to sophisticated responses by the opponent. The first subsection offers a critique of the part/whole relation, concluding that there is no philosophically coherent way to make sense of it (4.2.4–10). This is followed by a Nyāya criticism that such arguments rely on mistaken conceptions of part and whole (4.2.11–12). Finally, there is a defense of Nyāya's view that atoms combine to create the world of macro-objects (4.2.13–17).

The case against wholes amounts to two major arguments:

1. A part could not exist either in the entire whole or in a portion (4.2.7).
2. A whole could not exist within its parts or in something separate from the parts, nor is it identical to its parts (4.2.8–10).

The first argument offers a dilemma to the effect that a part cannot be related to a whole in a satisfactory way. If a part were situated in the entire whole, this would violate the patent difference between

[29] Siderits (2021, 150–158) makes connections between arguments of this broad type and Abhidharma Buddhism, focusing on Vasubandhu in particular. See *ADhKBh*, Chapter 3, "Exposition of the world" (translated in Poussin and Sangpo 2012, 1109–1113), for Vasubandhu's critique of the idea of composite wholes. Other arguments in this part of the *Nyāya-sūtra*—including a comparison between ordinary experience and visual distortions due to cataracts (4.2.13) and an analysis of cloth as nothing more than threads (4.2.26)—also find analogues in Vasubandhu.

their two sizes and prevent the whole from relating to other parts. But the part could not inhere in a portion of the whole, either, since there are no "portions" other than the parts themselves.

The second argument offers a trilemma to the effect that a whole cannot be related to a part in a satisfactory way, either. The whole cannot be situated entirely within an individual part. This is due to the differences of size already mentioned, as well as to the unacceptable consequence that a single substance would inhere in another single substance.[30] But a whole could not be segmentally apportioned among its different parts because, again, there are no "portions" of the whole besides the parts themselves (4.2.8). The whole could not reside in something other than the parts, either. If it did, the whole would have to be eternal, as it could exist without depending upon a material cause—an unacceptable consequence (4.2.9). A whole, therefore, cannot exist in specific parts, or all the parts, or something other than the parts. This trilemma closely matches that found in the chariot metaphor of *The Questions of King Milinda*:

NĀGASENA: If you came in a chariot, Sire, explain to me what it is? Is it the pole that is the chariot?

MILINDA: I did not say that.

NĀGASENA: Is it the axle that is the chariot?

MILINDA: Certainly not.

NĀGASENA: Is it the wheels, or the framework, or the ropes, or the yoke, or the spokes of the wheels, or the goad that are the chariot?

MILINDA: No.

NĀGASENA: Then is it *all* these parts of it that are the chariot?

MILINDA: No, sir.

[30] In Vaiśeṣika metaphysics, a single substance cannot "inhere" within another single substance. Composite substances reside in multiple component substances, while non-composite substances don't reside in other substances at all.

NĀGASENA: But is there anything outside of them that is the chariot?
MILINDA: Again, no.
NĀGASENA: Then, I can discover no chariot. "Chariot" is a mere empty sound. . . . There is no such thing as a chariot! (*QKM* 2.1.1)[31]

Following the sūtras, Vātsyāyana's response is to accuse the interlocutor of a category mistake (4.2.11). The very question of whether *all of a whole* exists in each or some of its parts is based on a misunderstanding of how wholes exist. We might say he inverts the Buddhist argument by alleging that the interlocutor has fallen prey to careless use of language. Terms for distinctions (*bheda-śabda*) do not apply to singular, unified things. The word "all" (*kṛtsna*) only applies to a complete collection of multiple things. And "portion" (*ekadeśa*) refers to an unspecified object that exists within a multiplicity. Therefore, the notion that we can map a whole onto parts in this sort of way is a nonstarter.

Pointing out conceptual confusions in the opposed view can only take us so far, however. The onus is on Nyāya to give a positive account of wholes and how they relate to their parts. Vātsyāyana offers the following:

> How does the whole exist? There is a connection [*prāpti*] between one thing and many things, a relationship between a support [*āśraya*] and that which is supported [*āśrita*]. How does the support/supported relationship work? For something *x*, a support is something *y*, where *x*'s existence cannot obtain were it not located in *y*. An effect substance's existence would not obtain were it not located in cause substances. But the cause substances do not require the effect. (*Commentary* 4.2.12)

[31] Adapted from translation by Rhys Davids (1890, 43–44).

Here, as elsewhere in the *Commentary*, "effect substances" are things such as trees or earthenware crockery, composite effects constructed out of "cause substances," their parts.[32] Without using the term *samavāya*, "inherence," Vātsyāyana does seem to be appealing to the notion, a primitive category of Vaiśeṣika metaphysics:

> Inherence is that by which "this is situated here" is understood with respect to (material) cause and effect. (*VS* 7.2.29)

> A substance is called a cause when there is the inherence of an effect within it. (*VS* 10.12)

Vātsyāyana lists inherence alongside other Vaiśeṣika categories in his alternative summary of the knowables under 1.1.9. Under 4.1.38, he mentions it along other reals that have *svabhāva*.[33]

Returning to the concern about holism and nihilism, Vātsyāyana concludes this subsection by again reminding us that "while misconceptions about the whole must be rejected by someone who desires liberation, the whole itself is not rejected."

Sūtras 4.2.13–17 continue to focus on cause substances, all the way down to atoms. The mereological nihilist attempts a different approach. Arguing by analogy, they compare the experience of macro-objects to a cluster of "hairs" experienced by someone suffering from visual infirmity. Vātsyāyana suggests that the challenger is presupposing the Nyāya argument advanced under 2.1.34, that without wholes, nothing could be experienced. Against that background, the interlocutor now discounts the veridicality of ordinary experience, appealing to examples of perceptual misfire.[34] Appeals to the visual distortions brought upon by cataracts and allied impairments are found in Buddhist literature such as the early

[32] See 3.1.11; 4.2.28.
[33] See also 3.2.41 and 4.1.28.
[34] This anticipates the skeptico-idealist arguments voiced under 4.2.31–32.

Yogācāra text *Laṅkāvatāra-sūtra* as well as the work of philosophers such as Vasubandhu:

> The world of experience is like people with visual impairments who see a cluster of hairs and say to one another, "This is wonderful! Look!" (*Laṅkāvatāra-sūtra* 2.148).

> This world of experience is nothing more than awareness; for even unreal things are manifest to consciousness, as a person with visual impairment sees things like unreal hairs. (*Viṃśatikā* 1)

In the face of such arguments, Vātsyāyana's interpretation of the objection is somewhat unexpected. He does *not* take "seeing a cluster of hairs" to speak of an accumulation of visual floaters or "hairs" without any external correlate, as in the above passages. Rather, he sees the interlocutor as arguing by analogy: one whose vision is diminished cannot see an individual strand of hair, only a cluster of hairs. In the same way, visual perception does not apprehend genuine, coherent macro-objects but rather rough clusters of atoms (4.2.13–14).

In response, Vātsyāyana points out that the analogy is strained. Atoms are by nature imperceptible, unlike strands of hair. Moreover (in line with 2.1.34), unless atoms could become genuine composite wholes at a sufficient level of conglomeration and configuration, experience of anything would be impossible. Further, accepting an aggregation or collection of atoms is not enough to replace genuine macro-objects in one's ontology. This is because aggregation itself relies on the notion of conjunction, a relational quality that holds between two substances. If it did not already hold for observable macro-objects, we would have no way to recognize conjunction.

Sūtras 4.2.16–17 set the table for the next section on the atom (*aṇu*; *paramāṇu*) by portraying it as that beyond which there can be no further material division. It offers a final argument: without a stopping point, there would be an infinite number of substances (parts, sub-parts, etc.), such that a "triad" would cease to be a triad.

The triad is, for Vātsyāyana, the smallest visible substance. Why it must be a "triad" and how such triads are built up from three couplets of atoms are a complicated issue that he leaves alone.[35]

4.2.18–25: The atom

This next set of sūtras naturally follows the preceding set by countenancing arguments against atoms on the part of an opponent that Vātsyāyana calls an *ānupalambhika*, "one who proceeds by non-perception." In a general sense, this could be someone who refuses to accept imperceptibles such as atoms. For Vātsyāyana, however, the interlocutor is akin to a skeptic or nihilist "who holds that nothing is real."

Vātsyāyana defines an atom as "that than which nothing is smaller." The opponent offers the following arguments against it:

1. An atom cannot be impartite, since it can be penetrated by ether (4.2.18).
2. An atom must have parts, since all things that are delimited and tangible have shapes such as "triangular" or "rectangular," which presuppose parts (4.2.23).
3. An atom must have parts, because in the absence of different sides of an atom, it could not form a conjunction with another atom. For example, an atom that is conjoined with other atoms to its front and back, must have separate "sides" to account for the different connections (4.2.24).

In response to the first objection, Vātsyāyana remarks that notions of "inside" and "outside" do not apply to atoms (4.2.20). In response to

[35] See Gangopadhyaya 1980, 21, for a summary account of the triad. See Potter 1977, 73–84 for a concise study of early Nyāya-Vaiśeṣika theories of atomic combinations leading to macro phenomena.

the second, he reiterates the arguments made under 4.2.16 and 4.2.22, that it is a conceptual mistake to think that atoms have parts. They do have a shape, spherical (4.2.23), but that is impartite. In response to the third—and most serious—objection, Vātsyāyana explains why it seems that an atom would have sides, when in fact it does not:

> An atom is tangible; it separates two other tangible atoms by obstructing them, not because it is composed of parts. The obstruction is due to its being tangible. Therefore, the conjunction (between the "central" atom and one of the other two) does not pervade its locus (the atom). It merely appears as if the atom has parts. (*Commentary* 4.2.24)

Vātsyāyana's case hinges on two principles. First, being tangible is why an atom "obstructs" another atom, without its having distinct "sides." Second, contact need not be "locus-pervading." Clearly, in the case of composite substances, it need not be. When I hold a stick, my hand is in contact with the stick. This is enough to make the statement "My body is touching the stick" true. But it would be false to say that my foot is touching the stick. Vātsyāyana holds that this is also true for atoms: for an atom, contact with another atom in front or back need not pervade its entire locus.

In the end, Vātsyāyana counters this third objection by arguing that the alternative to atoms is a vicious regress of material division:

> If such a regress held, then for every object there would be limitless parts and a corresponding inability to apprehend distinctions of size and weight. Further, parts and wholes would have the same magnitude if the atom is further broken up. (*Commentary* 4.2.25)

These arguments hardly put an end to criticisms of Nyāya-Vaiśeṣika atomic theory. Accounts of atomic combination would continue to be articulated and modified by the long line of thinkers who followed him. But Vātsyāyana's appeal to the absurdity of infinite division would remain the bedrock of the Nyāya position.

4.2.26–37: Defense of the external world

This section is the culmination of the *Nyāya-sūtra*'s attempt to reconcile its yogic orientation with its defense of the reality of the world.[36] Other liberation-oriented schools, most notably Buddhist, compare enlightenment to awakening from a dream: the world is little more than a shared illusion that collapses under scrutiny. Scholars have long pointed out parallels between the language of this section and passages from an old text espousing Buddhist "idealism," the *Laṅkāvatāra-sūtra*.[37]

In his introduction to this section, Vātsyāyana frames the interlocutor's argument from an idealist perspective (4.2.26):

1. If there were real objects of cognition, then we would be able to determine their nature simply by reflection on cognition.
2. But we cannot determine the real nature of objects simply by reflection on cognition.
3. Therefore, cognition as of real external objects is false.

The initial sūtra of this section then puts a point on this argument, one that follows naturally from the anti-substantival arguments of the previous sections:

> When we examine things closely through cognition, we do not find true objects, just as we do not find a cloth when we distinguish the threads. (*NyS* 4.2.26)[38]

[36] This section is an expanded and revised version of part 4 of Dasti 2017.
[37] Vidyabhusana 1920, 120n1, 120n2.
[38] Passages in the *Laṅkāvatāra-sūtra* that echo the *NySBh* phrase "when things are distinguished through cognition" followed by a denial of objects' reality include 2.173, 2.196, 10.167, and 10.374.

When we critically examine a cloth, thread by thread, we find that all that exists are the threads, and there is nothing that corresponds to the cognition of a cloth. Cognition of a cloth is simply an error. Similarly, when we critically examine cognition itself, we are unable to locate any object outside of it. Objects are inseparable from cognition itself.

This argument is typically taken to support idealism or anti-realism, though it may also be taken to support skepticism. Both skeptics and idealists minimally share the motivation of refuting realism by illustrating the difficulties of extracting objects of cognition from cognition itself. And insofar as Vātsyāyana's response is to defend what we might call a baseline realism, it pushes back against opponents of both kinds.

At first, Vātsyāyana's response somewhat glibly charges the skeptical challenger with self-refutation. If one holds that "critical examination" occurs at all, one cannot also hold that the objects of cognition are entirely false. Indeed, the goal of "critical examination" is to ensure veridical awareness. As such, it nothing more than the proper functioning of knowledge sources. And since the legitimacy of any thesis within systematic inquiry is settled by knowledge sources, it is absurd to put forth the claim that all things are unreal. That would undermine the status of knowledge sources and support for any claim whatever (4.2.27–30).

It is here that the challenger commits to global anti-realism:

> Your conception of "knowledge sources" and "objects of knowledge" is akin to the conception of dream contents. Or it's like magic, or cities of Gandharvas [castles in the clouds] or a mirage. (*NyS* 4.2.31–32)

Again, we can compare the *Laṅkāvatāra-sūtra*:

> The manifest world is a cluster of hairs, the workings of magic, a dream, a city of Gandharvas . . . it is unreal, simply a vision that people have. (2.155)

Appeal to dreams is a prominent feature of skeptical thought, from Zhuangzi to Descartes. Dreams illustrate the possibility of systematically misleading erroneous cognitive states. In a dreamscape, there is cognition, but the objects of cognition are unreal. It is argued that by analogy, so, too, is the world of stable, independent objects that we discover through the *pramāṇas*. Despite the power of this analogy, Vātsyāyana will, in fact, *employ* the example of dreams to set forth a powerful defense of his epistemology, realism, and the connection of realism with the therapeutic aspects of Nyāya philosophy.

Vātsyāyana begins by asking the challenger to substantiate his view that dream objects are unreal. Unsurprisingly, the response is that such objects disappear upon waking. This concession is enough for Vātsyāyana make several arguments from parasitism, meant to illustrate that without realism of some kind, there is no way to account for the following:

1. the distinction between error and knowledge
2. the causal conditions that allow for varied states of cognition
3. the nature of error
4. the process of replacing ignorance with knowledge

We will consider each in turn.

First, dreaming presupposes the waking state. Specifically, it presupposes that in the waking state, we do have knowledge of objects. It is only against this background that the disappearance of dream objects upon waking is evidence that they are unreal. Thus, the notion of unreality or error—the absence of reality regarding some object or cognitive presentation—must be rooted in real objects and veridical apprehension against which it is determined. The distinction between dreams and waking awareness upon which the objector's analogy rests would itself be undermined by his own conclusion (4.2.33).

Second, dreams take various forms. Sometimes they are fearful, sometimes pleasing, and so on. The interlocutor, who accepts that dreams occur, should give an account of why the contents of dreams vary. The only viable response is that different dreams have different causal conditions. This requires such conditions to be real. *They* cannot be fictitious (4.2.33). Likewise, illusions and visual tricks have distinct causal conditions by which they are produced. A mirage in the distance is caused by heated air near the ground. There are real causal networks by which illusion and the like are generated, and reflecting on such networks helps us understand why error occurs and in what conditions it flourishes (4.2.35).

Third, error states, like dreams, depend on prior veridical cognition. The content of dreams is gleaned from waking experience. I think I see a friend within a dream because I have prior experience of that friend in waking life. Likewise, I can mistakenly "see" a person while visually targeting a post in the distance only if I possess the concept "person." Error is the mistaken ascription of some property to something targeted by cognition (e.g., seeing a post as "person"). But I could never misapply a concept that I do not possess. And as concepts are generated by experience, we need successful cognitive engagement with objects of experience in order to make mistakes. Moreover, to mistakenly take *x* (a post) to be *F* ("person"), there must also be some *x* that is the intentional object of my cognitive state. One cannot mistake a post for a person unless there is, in fact, a post that they are wrong about. Thus, given error's "dual nature" (4.2.37), it targets and combines two separate things (seeing *x* as *F*). While that combination is a mistake, there must be some real thing that I get wrong (*x*), along with the concept I project (*F*) (4.2.34; 4.2.36).

Fourth and finally, when we arise from sleep, waking cognition floods our awareness, and dream contents are recognized as unreal. Buddhist idealists have appealed to the metaphor of "awakening" to express the vantage point whereby the "illusion of the world" is exposed.[39] Vātsyāyana's point here is to agree that waking up *is* required to account for our ability to recognize dreams. But therefore, by analogy, veridical awareness is required not only as a causal and conceptual basis for error but also to account for the fact that false cognition is capable of being corrected and rectified. If there is any question of being improved by cognitive success, there must be knowledge that stands above and ameliorates the vices born of error (4.2.34; 4.2.35). One does not wake up from a dream into another dream, seeing all as false. Access to a real world is the only way to account for the cognitive improvement by which dreams are recognized as false.

I would suggest that in this final aspect of his argument, Vātsyāyana stands with Plato in recognizing that insofar as philosophy has a therapeutic function, to make us better, it requires some type of realism, some kind of friction with reality by which the normative judgments pertaining to noetic health or illness may be settled.

4.2.38–49: Fostering knowledge

This stretch of the sūtras is the final word on "knowledge of the truth" in a deep sense, the liberating insight that brings one to the supreme good. It adds to earlier hints that noetic life for Nyāya does not consist simply in the binary of knowledge/error or even the triad of knowledge/error/doubt but recognizes qualitative depth of understanding.[40] The first subsection defends a notion of yogic praxis as key to liberating knowledge (4.2.38–46). The second articulates the way shared inquiry and truth-centered debate are crucial as well (4.2.47–49).

[39] Like our current interlocutor, Vasubandhu argues that ordinary experience is "just like perceptual awareness within dreams [that occurs without any object]." Yet we do not recognize it, because "the falsity of dream objects is not recognized until one awakens" (*Viṃśatikā* 16–17).

[40] 4.1.55–58; 4.2.3.

Sūtra 4.2.38 begins by identifying "a special kind of *samādhi*" (yogic concentration) as productive of liberating insight:

> The concentration spoken of is a connection between the *manas*—which has withdrawn from the senses and kept focused by effort to restrain it—and the self. This connection is distinguished by an intense desire for knowledge of the truth. (*Commentary* 4.2.38)

There are parallels here with other accounts familiar to Vātsyāyana:

> Direct perception of the self occurs through a special connection between the *manas* and the self. (*VS* 9.13)

> Yoga is the cessation of the fluctuations of the mind. (*YS* 1.2)

Vātsyāyana does not explain in much detail why this sort of meditation and inward concentration produces liberating insight. But it seems to be a state of awareness where one targets the deep self. Much earlier he remarked that it is possible for a yogin to have "direct perceptual experience [of the self]" (1.1.3), and he directly cited *VS* 9.13 as a proof text. The term used for "withdrawn from the senses" (*pratyāhṛta*) in 4.2.38 is cognate with that used for the fifth step of the Eight-Limbed Yoga of the *Yoga-sūtra* called "sensory withdrawal" (*pratyāhāra*) (*YS* 2.29).

> Sensory withdrawal occurs when the senses do not come into contact with their distinct objects and there is a sort of resemblance to the nature of the mind. (*Yoga-sūtra* 2.54)

It seems that in this practice, as one restrains the mind and focuses inward, they are consequently able to effect complete restraint over the pernicious tendency to objectify and appropriate sense objects, as discussed under 4.2.3 and elsewhere. We have already seen that for Nyāya, much of the function of the Sāṃkhya/Yoga "mind" is performed by the self directly. I would argue that for Vātsyāyana, at this stage of concentration, "there is a sort of resemblance to the nature of the *self*." That is, after one has withdrawn entirely from the distractions and demands of sensory experience, consciousness falls back into targeting the self directly. This facilitates the noetic transformation required to achieve liberation, where one forgoes sensory-desire and identifies as much as is possible with the deep self, as opposed to the fluctuating states of the body and the senses. One thus sheds vices, karmic entanglement, and the rest in the order outlined under 1.1.2.

The interlocutors of this section put forth practical doubts about the possibility of such exalted concentration (4.2.39–40; 4.2.43–44). Vātsyāyana's response is to make clear that yogic concentration is the result of long practice, spanning lifetimes of effort (4.2.41–42), and that after liberation, one's peace is no longer threatened, as one is free from the body/*manas* mechanism entirely (4.2.44–45).

The sūtras advise that for the sake of liberation, one should purify themselves by means of the "moral restraints [*yama*] and observances [*niyama*] as well as the psychological prescriptions [*viddhi*] and practices [*upāya*] taught in yoga literature" (4.2.46). Lists of ethical practices to support meditative life were common within classical literature, and famous examples include the Buddha's Noble Eightfold Path and the Eight-Limbed Yoga of the *Yoga-sūtra*.[41] Vātsyāyana's gloss differs from both of these, while overlapping in some ways—especially with the second. "Restraints" (*yama*) are, for him, broad moral obligations for everyone within the Brahmanical culture, regardless of their stage in life, while "observances" (*niyama*) are the specific duties of one's own particular stage (e.g., "householder"). "Prescriptions" (*viddhi*) are directives that include austerity, breath control, sensory withdrawal, meditation, and detachment from externalities, while "practices" (*upāya*) are modes of yogic conduct.

[41] *YS* 2.29–32.

That the individualistic practices of yoga are meant to be performed alongside Nyāya's communal methods of investigation is one of the noteworthy findings of this section. A seeker is to reflect on philosophical teachings and engage in vigorous debate. Vātsyāyana makes plain that these, too, are "for the sake of liberation." He elaborates on the way philosophical reflection and dialectics help one internalize the truth:

> The sūtra mentions "friendly debate with the learned." This provides maturity of understanding, which removes doubts, helps one notice things previously unnoticed, and leads to reflective acceptance of things previously grasped. (*Commentary* 4.2.47)

The friendly, truth-directed nature of this type of debate (*saṃvāda*) encourages one to engage with students, teachers, and others in a spirit of cooperation, not trying to win (4.2.48–49). At best, this suggests the importance of a culture of disconfirmation and a willingness to modify holdings in the light of better-supported views.

4.2.50–51: Protecting knowledge

Sūtras 4.2.47–49 extol friendly debate (*saṃvāda*), which Vātsyāyana takes to be identical with truth-directed debate (*vāda*) which is the tenth subject of Nyāya (1.1.1; 1.2.1). What, then, of the two other types of debate, disputation (*jalpa*), and destructive debate (*vitaṇḍā*)? Do they have a part to play in the quest for truth? Here the sūtras themselves suggest that they do have a limited role, to help protect those who are not mature in knowledge, just as one would protect seedlings from animals by encircling them with thorny branches. Nicholson (2009) shows that we find in the *Nyāya-sūtra* an approach to debate that is moving away—but not entirely divorced—from the agonic, competitive model of earlier treatments (e.g., in the *Caraka-saṃhitā*). These final sūtras of Chapter 4 reflect some of the tensions in this development. Vātsyāyana struggles to defend the sūtras' allowance for disputation and destructive debate in the light of the *pramāṇa*- and *vāda*-centered path of inquiry. He offers two criteria that limit their justified use: they must be directed against sophistical opponents, who "out of attachment to their own view transgress the boundaries of legitimate reasoning" (4.2.50), and they must be done "for the sake of protecting the truth, not for the sake of gaining wealth, honor, or fame." But even as limited in this way, ensuing subcommentators show increasing unease with this practice.[42]

[42] See Keating 2022.

5

Dialectics

Part 1 (5.1.1–43): Dialectical Rejoinders

Chapter 5 of the *Nyāya-sūtra* focuses on topics fifteen and sixteen, dialectical rejoinders and defeat conditions. Its contents are much more skeletal than other sections of the *NySBh*; it is best seen as an appendix to the main text. Even structurally, it functions like an appendix, not a self-standing chapter. We may recall that Vātsyāyana identifies three methodologies of a text like the *Nyāya-sūtra*: to identify major topics, to provide definitions of each topic, and to engage in philosophical investigation (1.1.3). By the end of Chapter 4, the investigation of all sixteen topics is complete. This chapter returns to the issue of definitions by giving an account of each of the dialectical rejoinders and defeat conditions that are summarily mentioned in sūtras 1.2.18–20.

The "rejoinders" (*jāti*s) are responses to an argument meant to controvert it. Introducing them under 1.2.18, Vātsyāyana offers two glosses of the term *jāti* ("birth," "arising") which account for its oppositional and reactive nature:

> A reductio objection that is "born" [*jāyate*] after a reason is put forth is a *jāti*.
> As its content is born from opposition, it is a *jāti*.[1]

[1] Solomon (1976, 144) offers an alternative derivation: as *jāti* commonly means "generality" within Indian philosophical literature, the term is used because of the themes of similarity and dissimilarity that dominate these retorts.

Vātsyāyana's Commentary *on the* Nyāya-sūtra. Matthew R. Dasti, Oxford University Press.
 DOI: 10.1093/oso/9780197625927.003.0005

The name for each of the rejoinders ends with the affix *-sama*. Thus, "the rejoinder based on the addition of a property" is *utkarṣa-sama-jāti* or just *utkarṣasama*. *Sama* has a semantic range that includes balance, equality, and similarity. These rejoinders do not settle an issue or win a case but rather generate equipollence such that another's argument is nullified.

It is likely that within the earliest stratum of literature that discusses *jāti*s, in texts such as the *Caraka-saṃhitā*, they are not considered illicit retorts but stock ways to challenge arguments by counterbalancing them.[2] In the *Nyāya-sūtra* and the *Commentary*, they are seen as appeals to a surface-level similarity or dissimilarity to controvert a reason offered by an opponent. Under *Nyāya-sūtra* 1.2.2, it was also noted that the mode of argument called *disputation* is distinguished from truth-directed debate by allowing use of *jāti*s, equivocation, and defeat conditions. Because of this, the rejoinders are typically seen as sophisms by later Nyāya tradition. Approaching them from this perspective, modern scholars and translators add labels such as "misleading" or "futile" to "rejoinder" when translating the term *jāti*. But as this guide is focused only on Vātsyāyana and the *Nyāya-sūtra*, I prefer a more neutral translation that hints at their borderline status.

The discussion of rejoinders in the *Nyāya-sūtra* not only serves as a primer about rhetorical tricks but is also an early gesture toward identifying what does *not* count as a true entailment. *Jāti*s trade on superficial, irrelevant connections and thus bring the question of relevance to the fore. As Ganeri (2004, 326) remarks, their deficiencies help illustrate that "[an] argument is good if there exists a general relationship between the reason *F* and the property being proved *G*, such that the latter never occurs without the former." Because of this, the discussion of *jāti*s helps set the foundation for Vātsyāyana's insights into the nature of a decisive, probative reason. Prets (2004, 217–218) suggests that the use of *jāti*-style

[2] See Prets 2001.

rejoinders by opponents—most likely Buddhists—put pressure on the use of examples to motivate arguments as found in the *Caraka-saṃhitā* and the *Nyāya-sūtra* and thus facilitated Vātsyāyana's advances:

> It seems that Pakṣilasvāmin [Vātsyāyana] tried to find a way out of the dilemma by clearly distinguishing between the instance to be proved (*sādhya*) and the properties associated with it. This idea enabled him to abstract a relation between the property to be proved (*sādhyadharma*) and the proving property (*sādhanadharma*), which is ascertained in the example irrespective of the instance to be proved, and expressed in the proof by exemplification.

Akin to modern textbooks on fallacies, the *NySBh* describes specific rejoinders and then offers suggestions on appropriate responses. (See Table 16.)

5.1.1–3: Rejoinders 1–2, based on similarity and dissimilarity

Vātsyāyana presents a paradigm argument:

> The self possesses motion,
> since it has qualities that allow for motion,
> like lump of clay, a substance which has qualities that allow for motion.
> The self is like a lump of clay;
> therefore, the self possesses motion.

A lump of clay is a locus of motion when it rolls down the side of a hill or is thrown. It serves as an example of a medium-sized substance that can be moved. Incidentally, this argument is *not* one

Table 16. The twenty-four dialectical rejoinders.

Sūtras	Content
5.1.1	list of rejoinders (*jāti*s)
5.1.2–3	rejoinders based on:
	1. **similarity** (*sādharmyasama*)
	2. **dissimilarity** (*vaidharmyasama*)
5.1.4–6	rejoinders 3–8, based on shared features of a subject and the example:
	3. **addition of a property** (*utkarṣasama*)
	4. **removal of a property** (*apakarṣasama*)
	5. **uncertainty** (*varṇyasama*)
	6. **certainty** (*avarṇyasama*)
	7. **alternation** (*vikalpasama*)
	8. **casting doubt on the example** (*sādhyasama*)
5.1.7–8	rejoinders 9–10, based on the connection between a reason and a conclusion:
	9. **connection** (*prāptisama*)
	10. **disconnection** (*aprāptisama*)
5.1.9–11	rejoinders 11–12, based on problems with the example:
	11. **repeat question** (*prasaṅgasama*)
	12. **opposed example** (*pratidṛṣṭāntasama*)
5.1.12–13	13. **non-arising** (*anutpattisama*)
5.1.14–15	14. **doubt** (*saṃśayasama*)
5.1.16–17	15. **neutralization** (*prakaraṇasama*)
5.1.18–20	16. **being a non-reason (in the three times)** (*ahetusama*)
5.1.21–22	17. **postulation** (*arthāpattisama*)
5.1.23–24	18. **non-distinction** (*aviśeṣasama*)
5.1.25–26	19. **possibility** (*upapattisama*)
5.1.27–31	20. **awareness** (*upalabdhisama*)
	21. **non-awareness** (*anupalabdhisama*)
5.1.32–36	22. **impermanence** (*anityasama*)
	23. **permanence** (*nityasama*)
5.1.37–38	24. **being an effect** (*kāryasama*)

that Nyāya would endorse, since motion is not a property of selves, but this is immaterial to the purpose of illustrating the rejoinders.

> By **similarity** (*sādharmyasama*): The self is inactive since it is like ether (*ākāśa*) in being all-pervasive. Ether is inactive; so, too, is the self.
>
> By **dissimilarity** (*vaidharmyasama*): The self is inactive since it is unlike a lump of clay. A self is spatially unbounded. A lump of clay has a limited size. Unlike clay, the self is inactive.

Here is a more colloquial example of my own:

> Michael would be a good teacher,
> since he is smart and an effective communicator,
> just like Paul (a widely respected teacher).
> Mike is like Paul;
> therefore, he would be a good teacher.

A rejoinder by similarity here would run as follows: No, Michael would not be a good teacher, since he is an artist, and Lou (another artist) is a terrible communicator. A rejoinder by dissimilarity would run: No, Michael would not be a good teacher, since he studies art, unlike Paul, who studies classics.

Vātsyāyana notes that in each of his cases, what is lacking is a "decisive reason" (*viśeṣa-hetu*) that goes beyond mere similarity or dissimilarity. *Viśeṣa-hetu* is an interesting term that comes up multiple times in the *Commentary*, always in the context of a poorly formed argument that is said to be lacking it.[3] The point here is that *neither* of the current debaters is specifying the nature of their prover other than an appeal to superficially similar or dissimilar properties. This should be underscored. In many of the examples he offers, neither debater is on particularly secure footing. In the case of 5.1.2, Vātsyāyana's own

[3] 2.1.20; 2.1.36; 2.1.41.

philosophical views are closer to the rejoinder than the original argument. Nevertheless, all these rejoinders are faulty, as is usually the original argument, since they do not employ the right sort of reason:

> If one attempts to establish a conclusion by mere similarity or dissimilarity, then it would be arbitrary. But arbitrariness does not arise with respect to a decisive property. Something is established as a cow because of similarity with another cow *in the sense of possessing the specific universal cowhood*, not simply properties such as having a dewlap. (*Commentary* 5.1.3)

What is needed is a genuine entailment-generating, "decisive" reason, a nonarbitrary generalization, objective and universal in scope.

5.1.4–6: Rejoinders 3–8, based on shared features of the subject and the example

All of the following rejoinders attempt to controvert an argument by presupposing that the subject of the inference (the self) and the example (a lump of clay) share irrelevant properties or features.

> By **addition of a property** (*utkarṣasama*): If the self is akin to a lump of clay, then it is also tangible. Or if it is not tangible, why, then, think it is active?

> By **removal of a property** (*apakarṣasama*): If the self is akin to a lump of clay, then it is *not* all-pervasive.

For rejoinders by **uncertainty** (*varṇyasama*) and **certainty** (*avarṇyasama*), Vātsyāyana does not appeal to his stock example. He simply explains what they mean. As seen under 1.1.32–39, when an argument is put forth, the subject of the argument (here the self) is something for which conclusion is doubtful (here whether it has qualities that conduce to motion). The very point of the argument is to remove the doubt by concluding that the subject is indeed qualified by the property to be proved. And the example is meant to be a noncontroversial illustration of the connection between the reason and the target property found in the conclusion.

These two rejoinders try to flip the status of the subject and the example, making the example uncertain and/or the subject's status certain. To be sure, it is not illegitimate to dispute a bad example. This rejoinder seems to trade on the principle that the example and the subject are supposed to be relevantly similar. It then fallaciously argues that the example must be in doubt. Likewise in the converse direction. The sophistical nature of the rejoinder by certainty is evident in that it concedes the opposed debater's point but then claims that the whole discussion is unnecessary, since *by similarity with the example*, the conclusion must already be certain. It neutralizes the argument by suggesting it is pointless.

Since Vātsyāyana does not offer examples here, let me illustrate these rejoinders with my "good teacher" argument. By uncertainty: If we aren't sure that Mike will be a good teacher, how sure can we be that Paul is? By certainty: What's the point of this discussion? If we are so sure that Paul is a good teacher, then fine, Mike is too.

> By **alternation** (*vikalpasama*): A lump of clay is heavy, while air (which also possesses activity) is light. Given such a divergence between the two substances, it is possible that a lump of clay's being the locus of motion does not carry over to the self, even though both are substances.

Unlike the rejoinder by dissimilarity, the point of this one is to leverage the fact that some shared properties are often not enough to ensure other shared properties. This casts doubt on the original argument.

By **casting doubt on the example** (*sādhyasama*): Somewhat akin to rejoinder 6, this tries to cast doubt upon the example by showing that it is "like the conclusion" (*sādhyasama*) and thus is dubious.

It is interesting that this rejoinder has the same name as the counterfeit reason offered under 1.2.8, the "unproved." That fallacy is a form of begging the question because it offers a reason whose status is as dubious as the conclusion. Hence the name "similar to the conclusion," *sādhyasama*.[4] This rejoinder is not the same thing, although they have significant overlap. What we find here is a rhetorical trick meant to cast doubt upon the conclusion of another's argument, by alleging that the example must be "similar to the conclusion," hence doubtful.

The response to rejoinders 3–8 is the same: The only shared property between the subject and the example that matters for the sake of an inference is that expressed in the reason. Vātsyāyana does not return to his own example here. To use mine, if someone is smart and a good communicator and this is both a property of a well-attested example and of the subject of the proof, only this matters. The rest are incidental features.

5.1.7–8: Rejoinders 9–10, based on the connection between a reason and a conclusion

These two rejoinders are focused on the connection (*prāpti*) between the reason and the target property found in the conclusion. They combine false dilemma and equivocation. If a reason and target property are truly *connected*, they are tethered in such a way that they are functionally identical. If they are disconnected, on the other hand, then they are too far apart for the reason to establish the conclusion.

[4] The word *sādhya* is literally "that which is to be proven," the target fact that is meant to be established in a proof. I am translating it somewhat loosely as "conclusion."

The reason cannot be effective in either case. As Vātsyāyana does not return to his example, I will again employ my own.

> By **connection** (*prāptisama*): If being smart and a good communicator is tantamount to being a good teacher, it is illicit to use one to prove the other, since their status would be the same.

> By **disconnection** (*aprāptisama*): If being smart and a good communicator is unconnected to being a good teacher, then it cannot serve as a reason for it.

That this rejoinder involves a false dilemma is patent. That it also involves equivocation can be seen in that it takes the somewhat fluid term *prāpti* in a very strong sense to be equivalent to identity and *aprāpti* to mean a lack of *any* relationship. Sūtra 5.1.8 notes that many things that are held to be causally effective function through contact (*prāpti*) (without collapsing into identity). And others, such as occult processes, do so without contact (*aprāpti*).

5.1.9–11: Rejoinders 11–12, based on problems with the example

Both of these rejoinders seek to neutralize an argument by focusing on the example. The first, by repeat question, demands justification for the example, something that in principle could be reiterated for any further example given. The second, by opposed example, cites a counter-example that is meant to counterbalance that given in the original argument.

> By **repeat question** (*prasaṅgasama*): Why should I take a lump of clay to be something that has qualities allowing for action?

> By **opposed example** (*pratidṛṣṭāntasama*): Ether has qualities conducive to action, and yet it does not move.

The illustration of opposed example is somewhat convoluted. Vātsyāyana explains that ether is connected to wind, which has the disposition to cause movement in things such as trees. Yet ether does not move. To use my example, it would say "But *Emily* is a bad teacher!" without clearly tying it to a probative reason.

A rejoinder by repeat question fails because a well-attested example need not be further justified. Rejoinder by opposed example fails because a counterexample unconnected to a decisive reason is ineffective.

5.1.12–13: Rejoinder 13, based on non-arising

To explain this rejoinder, Vātsyāyana returns to the issue of sound and impermanence.

> Initial argument: Sound is impermanent, since it follows from effort, like a jar.[5]
>
> Rejoinder by **non-arising** (*anutpattisama*): Sound does not exist before it is produced, so it can have no relationship with the effort said to bring it about.

While the sophistry of this rejoinder is obvious, it arguably has parallels with some of the relational paradoxes put forth to great effect by Nāgārjuna.[6] The sūtras respond by agreeing that something exists with its properties only after it has been produced. States such as *being a product* are attributed to something once it exists. We might add that the effort that precedes (e.g.) verbalized sounds

[5] Gangopadhyaya's (1982, 385–408) translation that sound "is followed by effort" confuses the point. What sound and a pot are held to have in common is that they both *follow from effort*.

[6] See Hayes 1994 for a critical appraisal of Nāgārjuna's arguments as employing equivocations of the sort illustrated here.

operates on its triggers, like the air being expelled from the lungs through the larynx.

5.1.14–15: Rejoinder 14, based on doubt

We may recall that doubt, as defined under 1.1.23, is a wavering cognition whose object is compatible with multiple, incompatible qualifiers. This rejoinder tries to generate doubt about the status of sound.

> By **doubt** (*saṃśayasama*): Sound shares a property with a universal and with a jar in that both of these things are perceptible by the senses.

According to Nyāya, some universals are directly perceived. The current *jāti* trades on the fact that being perceptible to the senses is a property shared by permanent and impermanent things. The sūtras' response not only addresses the rejoinder but considers the limits of reasonable doubt. When there is doubt about a rule due to some similarity between cases, identifying relevant distinguishing features should settle it. In the case at hand, sound's arising after effort distinguishes it from universals, which are eternal and not produced. To continue doubting in this case would be obtuse; such doubt could be endless. In any case, similarity as such is not enough to motivate doubt. Though a six-foot-tall post and a person may be similar in terms of height, this does not confuse us when we see a person walking in the distance.

5.1.16–17: Rejoinder 15, based on neutralization

This rejoinder has the same name as the counterfeit reason discussed under 1.2.7. The term *prakaraṇa* means "topic," and in the context of 1.2.7, the fallacy of *prakaraṇasama* is offering a reason that fails to adequately address the issue at hand. Here, in contrast, *prakaraṇasama* refers to a situation where two opposed arguments target the same topic. What it shares with the fallacy is that the issue at hand remains unsettled, due to the second argument "neutralizing" the first.

> Initial argument: Sound is impermanent, since it follows from effort, like a jar.
>
> Rejoinder by **neutralization** (*prakaraṇasama*): Sound is permanent, since it is audible, like *soundhood.*

Again, this rejoinder appeals to Nyāya's view that many universals can be directly apprehended. Soundhood is a feature of every instance of sound. Insofar as it is a universal, soundhood is eternal. And if it is apprehended through hearing, it would be a case of the co-location of "being heard" and "being eternal." As pointed out by Matilal (1998, 69–70), the oddity of this example is that soundhood's being audible is a unique case, unlike the countless examples of created things that are impermanent, which support the inductive generalization "Whatever is created is impermanent."

The sūtras do not offer a clear way to respond to this rejoinder, but they do say that it does not refute the original argument as much as it generates uncertainty about the bigger issue. The uncertainty will remain until further, conclusive information is discovered that will help overcome the impasse.

5.1.18–20: Rejoinder 16, based on being a non-reason (in the three times)

The problem of the three times has already surfaced in skeptical arguments entertained under 2.1.8–11. Its inclusion here (and in other ancient debate manuals) suggests that it is a stock trick to counter any attempted proof that may have been adapted by various debaters for their purposes. No specific example is presented, but

Vātsyāyana explains that **being a non-reason (in the three times)** (*ahetusama*) employs the following dialectic: Reason *R* cannot exist *before* the property *P* it is meant to prove, because something non-existent cannot be proven. Nor could it exist *after*, because *P* then would occur first, needing nothing to establish it. Nor could they be *simultaneous*, because there would be no way to distinguish which is meant to prove the other.

The response suggested is akin to that offered under 2.1.12–15. We already have a handle on cause-effect relationships that span temporal distances. And we may speak of causes as related to that "which will be produced" by them even when the latter is not yet existent. Furthermore, the *jāti* proffered here is self-refuting since, according to its own reasoning, it could not properly connect to *that which it is meant to refute* in any of the three times.

5.1.21–22: Rejoinder 17, based on postulation

As explained under 2.2.4, postulation (*arthāpatti*) is something that allows one to understand the unspoken entailments of a statement. The rejoinder based on **postulation** (*arthāpattisama*) occurs when a debater, by appeal to postulation, reads an unintended and unwarranted entailment into an opponent's statement.

Sūtra 5.1.22 says that this mode of reasoning is a nonstarter, since it could be used *against* the debater employing the *jāti* themselves. Vātsyāyana makes a deeper diagnosis of the problem. It tries to use *arthāpatti* based on superficial similarity as opposed to a genuine entailment relation. As such it is a faulty inference that "deviates":

> An exclusive (non-deviant) *arthāpatti* does not function through mere reversal. The statement "A stone, which is solid, falls to the ground" does not entail "Water, which is liquid, does not fall to the ground."

Given that Vātsyāyana claims earlier that *arthāpatti* is a legitimate *pramāna*, reducible to inference, and that it reliably hits its target (2.2.4), I take him to be speaking loosely when referring to deviant instances of postulation, which would really be "counterfeit postulation." The instances here are imitators put forth as legitimate instances by debaters.

5.1.23–24: Rejoinder 18, based on non-distinction

> Initial argument: Sound is impermanent, since it follows from effort, like a jar.
>
> Rejoinder by **non-distinction** (*aviśeṣasama*): If a property shared between the subject of the inference and the example (here "follows from effort") is enough to support inference, there is the absurdity that anything could prove anything else, since the property *being* is shared by everything.

The response to this rejoinder is that a prover property entails something else because it is consistently co-located with it. But there are no *specific* properties co-located with being itself that allow for inferences from being to *those specific properties* as opposed to others.

Interestingly, Vātsyāyana seems to refer to a Buddhist argument for universal impermanence, invoking an objector who argues that there is a correlation between "existence" and "impermanence." Vātsyāyana rejects this argument because it violates the requirements of a well-formed proof. By framing the *proposition* to be proven as "All things are impermanent" and the *reason* "because they exist" the objector has put themselves in a position where any corroborative example would be an instance of circular reasoning—taking something you are currently arguing about to be an illustration of the truth of your case. But to omit an *illustration* would leave the argument improperly formed and it would fail to be probative.

5.1.25–26: Rejoinder 19, based on possibility

The rejoinder by **possibility** (*upapattisama*) is functionally akin to 15, by neutralization. In the current rejoinder, one suggests that a counterargument is *possible*, while by neutralization, one makes a complete counterargument. Colloquially, one finds people responding to an argument for something by saying, "You might believe that, but other people have other ideas." This neither refutes the original argument directly nor specifies exactly what counterargument is being appealed to.

The major problem with the rejoinder is that it concedes the initial argument while suggesting that some counterargument might be equally plausible. We might think of it as the inverse of *tu quoque*. Instead of admitting a fault, while also imputing it to the other side, one allows the opposed argument to stand while suggesting that one's own is also possible.

5.1.27–31: Rejoinders 20–21, based on awareness and non-awareness

> Initial argument: Sound is impermanent, since it follows from effort, like a jar.

> Rejoinder by **awareness** (*upalabdhisama*): We are aware of sounds that are not produced by effort. Therefore, your argument cannot stand.

Vātsyāyana's diagnosis of *upalabdhisama* recognizes it as akin to denying the antecedent: to say that sound arises after effort does not mean that it arises *only* after effort. It could have other causes.

To put it otherwise, it mistakes a merely sufficient condition for the production of sound for a necessary condition (5.1.28).

Initial claim: A sound does not exist before it is uttered.

Rejoinder by **non-awareness** (*anupalabdhisama*): Non-awareness often occurs because of obstacles to apprehension, like our inability to see underground water. Therefore, this argument fails.

The response to this rejoinder follows closely the dialectic found in 2.2.18–21. If such obstacles are not established by knowledge sources, their mere possibility is irrelevant. The objector's retort that the non-apprehension of the non-apprehension of obstacles allows us to continue to accept such unseen and unknown obstacles as blocking the "manifestation" of sound when it is not present are, in effect, cases of the fallacy *appeal to ignorance*.

5.1.32–36: Rejoinders 22–23, based on impermanence and permanence

Initial argument: Sound is impermanent since it is similar to a jar.

Rejoinder by **impermanence** (*anityasama*): Since everything is like a jar in some respect, then everything is impermanent.

Vātsyāyana connects this *jāti* with number 18, by non-distinction. Both function by appealing to the broadest kind of similarity, *being* itself, to counter any putative argument. Vātsyāyana reiterates that legitimate inference relies on something more fundamental than mere similarity or dissimilarity, namely, a genuine entailment relation.

Initial claim: Sound is impermanent.

Rejoinder by **permanence** (*nityasama*): If impermanence is a permanent feature of sound, then sound is permanent.

Vātsyāyana diagnoses this rejoinder as based on a confusion. To say that impermanence is a feature of sound is not equivalent to claiming it is a positive property that inheres within a single entity. We may say that it commits equivocation on the word "sound" in that the first mention of sound refers to sound as a type or class, and the second refers to any particular instance of sound. The rejoinder works only by ignoring this distinction.

5.1.37–38: Rejoinder 24, based on being an effect

Initial argument: Sound is impermanent, since it follows from effort.

Rejoinder by **being an effect** (*kāryasama*): that something is an effect might mean it is not produced but rather "manifested" by the causal process that precedes it. Akin to the response to rejoinder 21, Vātsyāyana notes that the "manifestation" view requires us to posit obstructions to something's being manifest. However, there must be positive grounds to allege such obstructions.

Being an effect is a very specific rejoinder with narrow scope. But it plays a role in arguments forged by Vātsyāyana's successors. A major Nyāya argument for God is that things like the earth are effects and therefore require an agential cause. In a rebuttal, the Buddhist Dharmakīrti expressly denies that he is committing *kāryasama* when he counters that effects like the earth are very different from effects like pots such that the argument cannot stand. The Naiyāyika Vācaspati Miśra insists that he is committing *kāryasama*, nonetheless (*NyVT* 5.1.37).[7]

[7] See Guha, Dasti, and Phillips 2021, 82–83.

5.1.39–43: A failed "six-step debate"

Vātsyāyana's discussion of *jāti*s often places the blame for a stalemate on the shoulders of the original arguer, whose failure to provide a decisive reason makes room for the interlocutor's use of dialectical rejoinders. The six-step debate of this section illustrates how such a stalemate occurs. Vātsyāyana diagnoses the major problem as occurring in the third step. In response to an original argument (step 1), an interlocutor commits the *jāti* of being an effect (step 2). But instead of clarifying and pointing out why the *jāti* fails to be applicable, the original arguer simply claims that the reasoning of step 2 is also inconclusive (step 3). The argument then collapses into a counteraccusation of inconclusive argumentation (step 4), and counteraccusations by each side that the other has fallen pretty to the defeat condition of sharing the fault (see Chapter 5, Part 2) (steps 5 and 6).[8]

Part 2 (5.2.1–24): Defeat Conditions

Defeat conditions (*nigraha-sthāna*) are grounds for disqualification in competitive debate. Someone found to commit one of these mistakes immediately loses. *Nyāya-sūtra* 1.2.19 summarizes them as cases of misunderstanding or failures to understand. Now, in these last sūtras, they are unpacked into twenty-two separate grounds for forfeiture. These conditions have not received the same amount of scholarly attention as other sections of the *Nyāya-sūtra*.[9] While they are mostly irrelevant to truth-directed debate, the final two are relevant because they involve epistemological or logical problems.[10]

[8] Prets 2003 is helpful on this passage, making a comparison to a successful six-step argument in the Buddhist debate manual *Upaya-hṛdaya*.

[9] Matilal 1998, 81–87, is a summary study. See Todeschini 2010 for an interpretation of the defeat conditions as violations of Gricean maxims. Kang 2004 reflects on defeat conditions as rules in a time-bound "game" of debate.

[10] *NySBh* 1.2.1.

5.2.1–6: Conditions 1–5, based on mistakes with respect to one's own proposition or reason

The proposition is the first part of a formal proof, which expresses the thesis one is attempting to prove, for example, "Sound is impermanent." The reason or prover is the second part, a property of the subject that entails the target fact. *Being produced* is a reason that entails *impermanence*. Thus, "Sound is impermanent, since it is produced."

1. **Loss of the proposition** (*pratijñā-hāni*): Admitting the counterarguer's conclusion. In effect, this is to admit defeat without realizing it.
2. **Changing the proposition** (*pratijña-antara*): Introducing a different proposition under pressure. This is akin to a topic switch.
3. **Contradicting the proposition** (*pratijñā-virodha*): Offering a reason that contradicts, as opposed to supporting, one's position.
4. **Abandoning the proposition** (*pratijñā-sannyāsa*): Disavowing one's proposition under the force of counterargument. Unlike condition 1, which is an implicit admission, this is to explicitly give up one's proposition.
5. **Changing the reason** (*hetv-antara*): Introducing a different reason under pressure. This is akin to a topic switch.

5.2.7–10: Conditions 6–9, based on mistakes with respect to linguistic meaning

6. **Irrelevant speech** (*artha-antara*): Indulging in irrelevant digressions that have no bearing on the argument.

7. **Meaningless speech** (*nirarthaka*): Uttering meaningless sounds, seemingly for the sake of stalling or as a distraction.
8. **Incomprehensible speech** (*avijñātārtha*): Speaking in a way that is incomprehensible or obfuscating. Unlike condition 7, one makes a statement, not mere gibberish. But the statement is ambiguous or obscure. It is noteworthy that this sūtra mentions that the "assembly" (*pariṣad*) will review a statement three times before pronouncing it incomprehensible—a rare reference to the social setting of a debate.
9. **Incoherent speech** (*apārthika*): Uttering words or phrases that are not syntactically connected. Unlike condition 7, which involves meaningless sounds, this condition involves coherent words that are disconnected from each other, not forming a meaningful sentence.

5.2.11–13: Conditions 10–12, based on failures to properly formulate an argument

10. **Improper sequence** (*aprāptakāla*): Mis-ordering the parts of a proof, for example, placing the *illustration* before the *reason*.
11. **Omission** (*nyūna*): Omitting one of the parts.
12. **Unnecessary addition** (*adhika*): Adding extra reasons or illustrations to a single proof. Vātsyāyana adds that this is only a point of defeat if it is agreed upon in advance.

5.2.14–15: Condition 13, based on repetition

13. **Repetition** (*punarukta*): Unhelpful reiteration of statements, whether by direct repetition or rephrasing the same point in multiple ways.

5.2.16–19: Conditions 14–17, based on failures to properly respond to inquiries or points raised

14. **Failure to reiterate** (*ananubhāṣana*): Inability to repeat an interlocutor's statement that has been stated three times and understood by the debate assembly. This complements condition 8.
15. **Failure to understand** (*ajñāna*): Failure to understand an opponent's point. Vātsyāyana comments that the requirement that the point has been made three times and understood by the assembly also applies here.
16. **Failure of intellect** (*apratibhā*): Inability to formulate a response to an opponent's argument. Unlike condition 15, which is an inability to understand the interlocutor's position, this condition is a failure to come up with any sort of answer.
17. **Evasion** (*vikṣepa*): Attempting to leave mid-debate on the pretext of other responsibilities.

5.2.20–22: Conditions 18–20, based on attempts to identify faults by the other party

18. **Sharing the fault** (*matānujñā*): Admitting a flaw in one's argument but claiming it holds for the other's position as well. This is identical to the fallacy *tu quoque*.
19. **Overlooking a fault** (*paryanuyojya-upekṣaṇa*): Missing an opportunity to identify a defeat condition the opponent has committed. Vātsyāyana remarks that this is a condition that the debate assembly invokes, since neither debater would admit to a defeat condition in the course of alleging this against the other.
20. **Censuring what is not a fault** (*niranuyojya-anuyoga*): Mistakenly alleging that the other debater has fallen into a defeat condition.

5.2.23–24: Conditions 21–22, based on philosophical errors in the defense of one's position

These final two conditions are the most philosophically relevant and are applicable even in truth-directed debate.

21. **Conceding something against one's settled theses** (*apasiddhānta*): A "settled thesis" is a deep principle or well-reasoned view within a school of thought (1.1.26–29). If, in the course of argument, one contradicts one of these deep holdings of one's own school, it is grounds for defeat. Vātsyāyana's example of Sāṃkhya returns to problems with the *satkāryavāda* theory of causation that was discussed under 3.2.15–17.
22. **Employing "counterfeit reasons"** (*hetv-ābhāsa*): Sūtra 5.2.24 mentions that counterfeit reasons have already been discussed (under 1.2.4–9). They are reasons that fail to be decisive in proving a point, loosely akin to fallacies within contemporary informal logic.

APPENDIX A

Thematic Reading Plans and Recommended Scholarship

These thematic reading plans are designed primarily for the philosophical reader or instructor. I would suggest that a reader start with the primary readings, then consult associated sections in this guide, and then finally engage with the relevant scholarship to expand their understanding.

Primary readings are listed according to sūtra numbers, along with corresponding sections of the translations in Dasti and Phillips 2017, Gangopadhyaya 1982, and Jha 1919. With Jha in particular, it is important that readers focus only on the sections labeled "Bhāṣya" (the *Commentary* itself) and not the *Vārttika* subcommentary. Do not be confused (or intimidated!) by the much larger page ranges for Jha's translation, as the *Vārttika* makes up roughly 75 percent of his text. Recommended scholarly sources are meant to help students develop literacy with respect to Nyāya and Indian philosophy more generally. Some studies that are germane to finer-grained issues within the *Commentary* are mentioned in the footnotes of the main body of the guide.

Introduction to the *Nyāya-sūtra* and the *Commentary*

These selections promote a baseline understanding the *Nyāya-sūtra* and the *Commentary* as philosophical literature.

Primary readings: *NySBh* 1.1.1–2

- Dasti and Phillips 2017, 156–160
- Gangopadhyaya 1982, 1–11
- Jha 1919, 1–89

Recommended scholarship

Bronkhorst 2018 is a helpful introduction to sūtra literature as a genre. Ganeri 2011, 103–107, offers a typology of commentarial literature within classical India. Tubb and Boose 2007, 1–5, explain the major functions of a classical Sanskrit commentary. Dasti 2017 is an article-length account of Vātsyāyana's philosophy, centering on the theme of cognition as a guide to action. Matilal 1977 is a concise introduction to Nyāya-Vaiśeṣika literature, with Chapter 2 focusing on early Nyāya. Potter 1977, Part 1, is a wide-ranging study of early Nyāya-Vaiśeṣika philosophy. Perrett 2016 is a thematic introduction to classical Indian philosophy, situating Nyāya within the context of interschool debates in epistemology, metaphysics, and value theory.

Epistemology 1: Knowledge Sources

These selections present the major *pramāṇa*s according to Nyāya.

Primary readings: *NySBh* 1.1.3–8

- Dasti and Phillips 2017, Chapter 1
- Gangopadhyaya 1982, 12–20
- Jha 1919, 100–209

Recommended scholarship

Matilal 1986 is a classic study of Nyāya epistemology by a pioneering philosopher/Sanskritist. Chakrabarti 1992 examines Nyāya's account of testimony, with emphasis on its irreducible status as a sui generis mode of knowing. Phillips 2012 examines Nyāya's *pramāṇa* theory as a comprehensive epistemology in conversation with issues and debates in modern analytic philosophy. Dasti and Keating 2016 is a select, annotated bibliography of scholarship on *pramāṇa*s for Nyāya and other major Indian schools of thought.

Epistemology II: Doubt, Skepticism, and Cognitive Review

The selections from Chapter 1 of the *Nyāya-sūtra* cover Nyāya's approach to doubt, suppositional reasoning, and certainty, which collectively articulate its approach to the resolution of disputed views. The final, longer passage under

Chapter 2 responds to a skeptical attack that forces Nyāya to articulate how knowledge and the knowledge sources are justified.

Primary readings: *NySBh* 1.1.23; 1.1.40–41; 2.1.8–20

- Dasti and Phillips 2017, Chapter 2
- Gangopadhyaya 1982, 32–35, 47–51, 77–89
- Jha 1919, 299–302, 445–461, 606–658

Recommended scholarship

Mohanty 1965 is a classic study of Nyāya's theory of doubt. Guha 2012 is an article-length investigation of *tarka* as a faculty for cognitive review. Phillips 2012, Chapter 2, explores Nyāya's epistemology as consisting of two tiers, the second involved in certification and review. Westerhoff 2010 is an annotated translation of Nāgārjuna's *Vigraha-vyāvartanī,* the work most associated with the skeptical interlocutor of 2.1.17–20.

Logic and Debate

The first two selections from *Nyāya-sūtra* Chapter 1 are the heart of this section, focused on the structure of an argument and on counterfeit reasons. The third selection from Chapter 1 discusses a broader range of fallacies, including equivocation. The materials from Chapter 5 center on dialectical rejoinders that, while relevant, might prove tedious for some students. Looking at Chapter 5 of this guide should help one decide if—and what portions—they would like to read more closely.

Primary readings: *NySBh* 1.1.32–39; 1.2.1–9; 1.2.10–20; 5.1.1–43

- Dasti and Phillips 2017, Chapter 9; see 150–154 for equivocation
- Gangopadhyaya 1982, 39–47, 52–61, 62–69, 375–408
- Jha 1919, 355–445, 471–565, 566–584, 1429–1725

Recommended scholarship

Matilal 1998, Chapter 1, is a thematic introduction to classical Indian logic, with emphasis on Nyāya and Buddhist epistemology. Solomon 1976, Chapters 5–6, and

Matilal 1998, Chapter 3, are useful studies of equivocation, misleading rejoinders, and defeat conditions in Nyāya and other leading classical schools. Gokhale 1992, Chapters 1–2, targets fallacies in the *NySBh* as well as the sources that precede it. Gillon 2022 is an article-length, synoptic study of logic in classical India.

Metaphysics I: External World Realism

This selection responds to an interlocutor that compares the world of experience to a dream or illusion. It would not be unreasonable to place this section within the category of responses to skepticism. But the interlocutor also echoes the arguments found in Buddhist variants of idealism, and this section is in general taken to be a defense of external world realism.

Primary readings: *NySBh* 4.2.26–37

- Dasti and Phillips 2017, Chapter 3
- Gangopadhyaya 1982, 359–367
- Jha 1919, 1628–1647

Recommended scholarship

Feldman 2005 examines Buddhist arguments from illusion in conversation with the Nyāya arguments found here. Dasti 2012 interprets Nyāya epistemology as an epistemological disjunctivism, based on the parasitism of error on veridical awareness. Vaidya 2013 engages with Dasti 2012 and considers other possible interpretations of the Nyāya's defense of the external world. Matilal 1986, Chapter 6, examines the account of perceptual illusion held by each of the major Indian schools, including Nyāya, along with corresponding views about the content and intentionality of veridical experience.

Metaphysics II: Arguments for the Self

Two selections present the main arguments for the self in Nyāya, focusing on diachronic and synchronic unity, respectively. Accounts of the self in relation to embodiment, the *manas*, preexistence, karmic merit, and so on, are found throughout *Nyāya-sūtra* Chapter 3. Specific readings in relation to these issues can be found in the corresponding portions of this guide.

Primary readings: *NySBh* 1.1.10; 3.1.1–6

- Dasti and Phillips 2017, Chapter 4
- Gangopadhyaya 1982, 21–23, 169–175
- Jha 1919, 216–219, 1068–1127

Recommended scholarship

Chakrabarti 1982 is a study of sūtra 1.1.10, informed by analytic philosophy. Chakrabarti 1999 is a careful study and philosophical defense of Nyāya's notion of self. Chakrabarti 1992 (reprinted in Chakrabarti 2020) is a pioneering examination of the argument from cross-modal synthesis under 3.1.1. Ganeri 2001a is a sophisticated examination of cross-modal synthesis and the self, arguing for a more restricted account of Nyāya's conclusion than Chakrabarti 1992. Siderits 2021, Chapter 2, is a helpful summary of Buddhist arguments against the self with which Nyāya contends.

Metaphysics III: Substances and Holism

The first two selections, under 1.1.9 and 4.1.31, illustrate Vātsyāyana's appeal to the Vaiśeṣika scheme of categories as the basic nature of reality. The final two passages are defenses of holism against forms of mereological nihilism.

Primary readings: *NySBh* 1.1.9; 4.1.38; 2.1.33–36; 4.2.4–17

- Dasti and Phillips 2017, Chapter 5
- Gangopadhyaya 1982, 20–21, 305–307, 344–354
- Jha 1919, 210–212, 1515–1517, 707–773, 1586–1607

Recommended scholarship

Halbfass 1992 is an erudite exploration of Vaiśeṣika's ontology of categories. Mishra 2006 catalogs Nyāya-Vaiśeṣika accounts of matter and material composition. Gangopadhyaya 1980 focuses on atomism but also engages with questions of holism and material composition. Mishra 2008, Chapters 1–3, studies the notion of causation in the *Vaiśeṣika-sūtra*, *Nyāya-sūtra*, and Vātsyāyana's *Commentary*.

Philosophy of Religion

The first selection is about God, while the final three are about yogic praxis. Anyone interested in Vātsyāyana's approach to sacred testimony is directed to the guide on 1.1.7–8, 2.1.57–68, and 4.1.59–63.

Primary reading: *NySBh* 4.1.19–21; 1.1.2; 4.2.1–3; 4.2.38–46

- Dasti and Phillips 2017, 118–119, Chapter 8
- Gangopadhyaya 1982, 289–292, 8–11, 339–344, 368–371
- Jha 1919, 1456–1461, 83–89, 1577–1585, 1647–1655

Recommended scholarship

Bulcke 1968 is a concise study of God's place in early Nyāya-Vaiśeṣika. Ram-Prasad 2001 investigates the relation between knowledge and transcendence in leading Indian schools, focusing on Nyāya. Phillips 2009 is a thematic examination of yoga, karma, and rebirth, which engages with Nyāya as a yogic tradition.

Philosophy of Language

The first selection is about the meaning of common nouns, the second is about secondary meaning (in the context of the fallacy of equivocation), and the third is about the general relationship between a term and its referent.

Primary reading: *NySBh* 2.2.58–69; 1.2.10–17; 2.1.52–56

- Dasti and Phillips 2017, Chapter 7
- Gangopadhyaya 1982, 162–168, 62–67, 116–119
- Jha 1919, 1009–1066, 566–578, 832–846

Recommended scholarship

Raja 1963 is a classic study of Indian philosophy of language that is a good starting place for anyone interested in the major issues and thinkers. Matilal 1990 is a philosophical excavation of major themes in philosophy of language in India. Deshpande 2020 is an article-length study of theories of linguistic meaning with emphasis on the classical grammarians.

APPENDIX B

Vātsyāyana's Philosophical Commitments Summarized

Epistemology

Knowledge is a cognitive episode that targets some feature of reality, presenting it with a qualifier it genuinely has (1.1.1; 4.2.37).

Knowledge is produced by the functioning of knowledge sources (*pramāṇas*). These are four irreducible types of cognitive process: perception, inference, comparison, and testimony. These sources can generate knowledge without the need for introspection or confirmation, on reliabilist grounds (1.1.1; 1.1.3–8).

One is entitled on pragmatic grounds to trust apparently true cognitive presentations in the absence of legitimate doubt. If such doubt arises and one deems it worthy of investigation, second-order reflection and certification of disputed cognition are triggered (1.1.23; 1.1.40–41; 2.1.19–20).

Skeptical regress arguments are countered by this notion of our entitlement to default trust in cognitive presentations, and that *pramāṇas* can confirm other *pramāṇas* on a token-token basis (2.1.8–20).

Skeptical appeals to illusion or dreams are countered by the view that error/falsehood is parasitical upon knowledge/truth (4.2.26–37).

Metaphysics

The major Vaiśeṣika categories: substance, quality, action, inherence, universal, and individuator effectively capture the inventory of reality (1.1.9; 4.1.38).

The material basis of the world is atoms, which combine to create macro-objects (4.1.18–25).

Composite macro-objects are real and distinct even as they depend upon their material causes (2.1.33–36; 4.2.4–17).

The external world is real and much of it exists independently of cognition (1.1.4; 4.2.26–37).

Individual selves are irreducible, fundamental features of reality and are eternal (1.1.10; 3.1.3–26).

Value Theory and Philosophy of Religion

Human beings pursue satisfaction and try to avoid suffering. Proper understanding of reality makes success in this project possible (1.1.1–2). The goals of life are varied, encompassing the specific aspirations of individuals (1.1.24), but summarized as the "four goals of life" of classical Hinduism (2.1.20). Spiritual felicity, "liberation," is the most worthy goal to which humans may aspire (1.1.1–2; 1.1.22; 4.1.59–62).

The way to liberation includes proper understanding of the self and its relationship to the world, as well as an axiological shift away from fleeting pleasures(1.1.2; 4.2.1–3; 4.2.48–49). In terms of praxis, it requires the cultivation of morally healthy patterns of living as well as yogic meditation (1.1.2; 4.2.46–47).

Vedic texts, along with allied Brahmanical works, are sources of sacred testimony that provide information about unseen realities (1.1.8; 2.1.57–68; 4.1.59–62).

Karmic merit is a property that directly inheres in individual selves. It is generated by people's moral/religious acts and influences future embodiment as well as the range of experiences they will have (1.1.20; 3.1.27; 3.2.60–72). While scripture teaches what sorts of practices lead to fulfillment in a future life, the existence of karma itself is supported by a teleological argument (3.2.60) as well as by an appeal to the principle of sufficient reason (3.2.67).

God is a unique self, who stands above and administers the law of karmic consequences, influencing events in accordance with individuals' moral deserts (4.1.21).

APPENDIX C

Immediate Inference, Postulation, and Contraposition

On Vātsyāyana's Logical "Error"

Vātsyāyana clearly recognizes the limitations of analogical, case-based reasoning in Chapters 1 and 5. He sees that inferential knowledge requires an objective, universal inference-warranting relation between a reason and a target fact. Under 1.1.36–37, he claims that this relation may be expressed in two forms, involving *similarity* and *dissimilarity*. His example:

1a. If something has the property of being produced, then it is non-eternal.
1b. If something has the property of not being produced, then it is eternal.

When discussing postulation (*arthāpatti*), a form of inference, he says:

> Postulation is something that follows [*āpatti*] from implication [*arthāt*]. "Something that follows" means a consequence that obtains. Postulation, then, is the understanding that is a consequence of some other thing that is conveyed. Upon hearing "(2a) When there are no rainclouds, there is no rain," one understands "(2b) When there are rainclouds, there is rain." (*Commentary* 2.2.1)

In Vātsyāyana's treatment, postulation seems akin to a capacity for immediate inference, a faculty by which one can translate an entailment relationship into its equivalent. This is confirmed later under 5.2.15, which discusses the defeat condition *repetition*. Repetition is not only saying the same words repeatedly but also saying phrases that have the same meaning:

> Having said "sound is non-eternal, since it has the property of being produced," one goes on to say something else, the meaning of which was already conveyed: "that which has the property of not being produced is eternal." This should be understood to be an instance of repetition as well. (*Commentary* 5.2.15)

With each of these pairs of statements, we may note:

1. They are held to be equivalent.
2. That they are equivalent is recognized by something akin to an immediate inference.
3. Postulation is the mode of inference that is employed.

The first point is, of course, the most troubling. According to the logic of conditionals, "If something is produced, then it is non-eternal" *should* entail "If something is eternal, then it is not produced." Noticing this, Matilal (1977, 81) remarks offhandedly that Vātsyāyana "mis-states the contrapositive of the inferential relation."[1] While Vātsyāyana is an important transitional figure, it is true that he is firmly situated on the "pre-Dignāga" side of the soft division of Indian logical thought into its early starts versus its maturity. Matilal seems to require little more explanation than this.

In a nuanced and sensitive study, Gillon (2010, 177–181) probes further. His diagnosis is that Vātsyāyana conflates obversion and contraposition; he does agree with Matilal that "Vātsyāyana has made an error." Trying to understand the basis of this error, Gillon suggests that it stems from Vātsyāyana's adoption of causal reasoning as the prototype for inference in general. In classical India, causes are typically captured by the following reasoning: "When *a* is present, *b* is present; when *a* is absent, *b* is absent." This allows one to identify *a* as the cause of *b*.

Gillon's diagnosis makes good sense. In response to the interlocutor of 2.2.4, who points out that rainclouds may be present without any rain falling, Vātsyāyana clarifies that what we get from postulation here is a general rule:

> An effect occurs contingent upon the existence of the cause. That is, the arising of an effect will not deviate from the presence of its cause. This is the knowledge produced by postulation. (*Commentary* on 2.2.4)

Vātsyāyana was likely influenced by the *Vaiśeṣika-sūtra*'s account of causes:

> In the absence of the cause, there is the absence of an effect. (*VS* 1.2.1; cited directly by Vātsyāyana under *NyS* 1.2.9 and 2.2.53)

> It is not the case that in the absence of the effect, there is the absence of a cause. (*VS* 1.2.2)

The relationship between cause and effect is not, for the *Vaiśeṣika-sūtra*, best captured by an "if cause, then effect" conditional, where causes are sufficient for a target effect. Rather, causes are typically thought of as members

[1] Gokhale (1992, 19–20) concurs with this assessment.

of a collection of necessary conditions, each being individually insufficient.[2] A lump of clay is the material cause of a pot. It can exist without the pot, but the pot cannot exist without it. And more than the clay itself is required to generate a pot.

Vātsyāyana himself directly appeals to causal reasoning when identifying the visual faculty as the cause of visual perception.

> If a capacity does not occur in the absence of *x* but does occur in *x*'s presence, we understand that the capacity belongs to *x*. (*Commentary* 3.1.2)

Under 5.1.28, he also remarks that identifying a rule-bound cause-and-effect relationship would determine a cause that is necessary, not sufficient for a specific outcome.

Gillon is likely correct that this causal principle is a reason for Vātsyāyana's use of obversion, not contraposition, when he converts an entailment relation into an equivalent. Only with Vasubandhu and then Dignāga does Indian logic become formalized and the contrapositive identified as a truth-preserving transformation of a conditional. Still, I think there is more to this story than logical naivete or adoption of causal reasoning as a model for inference in general. Three further clues in the *Commentary* speak to this issue.

First, Vātsyāyana does apply the rule modus tollens—the close cousin to contraposition—multiple times.[3] Indeed, modus tollens is the backbone of *tarka*, suppositional reasoning, which allows one to reject a position because of unacceptable entailments that it generates. He also identifies and rejects a form of reasoning that matches *denying the antecedent* under 5.1.27–28. These do not guarantee that Vātsyāyana understood the logical equivalence between a conditional and its contrapositive. But he did explicitly recognize that if *a* entails *b*, denying *b* forces one to deny *a*, and further, denying *a* does not force one to deny *b*.

Second, Vātsyāyana acknowledges that careless attempts at postulation can generate faulty, misleading translations:

> A non-deviant *arthāpatti* does not function through mere reversal. The statement (3a) "A stone, which is solid, falls to the ground" does not entail (3b) "Water, which is liquid, does not fall to the ground." (*Commentary* 5.1.22)

Here he rejects the equivalence between "A solid falls to the ground" and its obverse, "A non-solid does not fall to the ground." This suggests that under 1.1.36–37 and 2.2.4, Vātsyāyana is *not* offering rules of equivalence that apply broadly to any case of "reversal." But why does he think that the transformation of 3a to 3b fail, while the others we have viewed succeed?

[2] Indeed, ensuing tradition often speaks of a cause (*kāraṇa*), as a member of a cluster of necessary conditions (*kāraṇa-sāmaghri*), which combine to generate an effect.

[3] 1.1.1; 1.1.40; 2.2.1; 3.1.5; 3.1.7; 5.1.30.

This brings us to the third and most important clue. Vātsyāyana's approach to entailment relations sees them as what we might call prima facie justified yet defeasible heuristics. In this context, the two statements regarded as equivalent remain so, as long as possible undermining conditions are identified and addressed. This is his *explicit* approach. Starting with 2b, the raincloud/rain entailment discovered through postulation, Vātsyāyana concedes that there are legitimate counterexamples before he even introduces the anti-postulation interlocutor of 2.2.3. Under 2.2.1, in the context of absence as a source of knowledge, he remarks:

> When there are rainclouds above, but no rain falling, one infers that the rain is being obstructed by wind. (*Commentary* 2.2.1)

Meteorologically, his account is dubious, but the principle it illustrates is crucial. Vātsyāyana accepts the general rule that the presence of rainclouds overhead is a legitimate reason to infer that it will rain. In fact, this very inference is the example of legitimate cause-to-effect inference that he offers under 1.1.5. But under 2.2.1, he makes clear that the truth of this general rule does not guarantee the absence of extraneous obstructions, factors that may impinge upon specific causes such that the effect does not arise. He tells us that the translations generated by postulation do not inform us about contingent obstructions to a rule that might arise in any particular instance.

We can say that for Vātsyāyana, statement 2b is a heuristic that serves us well in normal cases. At a picnic, when dark clouds form overhead, we pack up and find shelter, although we know that in rare cases, there may be circumstantial violations of the basic rule. We know that under *standard conditions*, the rule holds. And with respect to actually navigating the world—his core concern, and the very motivation for epistemological refinement—this rule helps us avoid rain more effectively than the "If there is rain, then there are rainclouds" contrapositive.

This approach to equivalent transformations also applies to inferential rules about purely theoretical topics. Returning to the pair 1a and 1b, the first proposition is widely held by thinkers of Vātsyāyana's epoch. The second is also widely held. The two are not, however, strictly speaking, equivalent without amendment—*as Vātsyāyana acknowledges explicitly.* Under 2.2.15 and 4.1.66, he points out that an absence caused by destruction (e.g., the absence of a coffee mug that I drop and smash) is both eternal and produced, an apparent counterexample to rule 1b. He therefore adds the qualifier that "eternal" in rule 1b strictly refers to *positive* entities, the sorts of things with which he is concerned in his reasoning. An absence caused by destruction is an exceptional case that does not undermine the basic principle. Positive things such as atoms exist unproduced, as do selves. They are therefore eternal, while material composites are both produced and non-eternal.

Let us consider an example more familiar to our world. On the first day of a new job, someone in an office is told "Keep the switch down, and the lights remain off." Through postulation, they consequently understand "When the switch is up, the lights turn on." This is an exact analogue of Vātsyāyana's case. And the reasoning is fine as a rule, because special instances of power outage or problems with the local electrical system are exceptional and bracketed as irrelevant to the pragmatic value of the information.

Putting this all together, we may say that for Vātsyāyana, inference is an action-guiding knowledge source that often relies on heuristics that presuppose that we are operating in normal conditions. From a purely formal perspective, his rules to translate "similarity-based" and "dissimilarity-based" entailment relations do not preserve logical validity. And yet they produce *knowledge*, so long as normal conditions hold and undermining factors are either absent or identified and bracketed. By being sensitive to indicators that we are not in normal conditions, individuals can revise and adjust as new information presents itself. Inference is a source of knowledge in both small and big things; the rules of entailment that inference relies on are generated by induction from experience (1.1.5). These rules may be scrutinized, modified, and/or certified in the face of new information (2.1.37–38).

In a fascinating paper on what is dubbed "Fugu" after the poisonous delicacy that must be eaten with care, Sorenson (2016, 141) argues that "we can gain knowledge by invalid reasoning" and that "A leaky argument may hold water after a few holes are plugged (139)." More substantively:

> Inductive knowledge is always a matter of having *enough* evidence. Since we are sacrificing rather than optimizing, empirical knowledge survives the revelation of a minor error. (Sorenson 2016, 140)

Vātsyāyana's project is not to formalize rules of entailment as much as to identify inference-warranting relations that hold as general, amendable rules. This, I would suggest, is as much a source of his "error" as is his application of causal reasoning.

Works Cited

Alston, William. 1993. *The Reliability of Sense Perception*. Cornell University Press.

Alston, William. 1995. "How to Think about Reliability." *Philosophical Topics* 23: 1–29.

Aristotle. 1995. *The Complete Works of Aristotle*, Vol. 2. Edited by Jonathan Barnes. Princeton University Press.

Balcerowicz, Piotr. 2010. "What Exists for the Vaiśeṣika?" In *Logic and Belief in Indian Philosophy*, edited by Piotr Balcerowicz, 241–348. Motilal Banarsidass.

Balcerowicz, Piotr. 2012. "When Yoga Is Not Yoga: The Nyāya-Vaiśeṣika Tradition and the *Artha-śāstra*." In *World View and Theory in Indian Philosophy*, edited by Piotr Balcerowicz, 173–245. Warsaw Indological Studies 5. Manohar.

Bhattacharya, Kamaleswar. 1974 "A Note on the Term Yoga in Nyāyabhāṣya and Nyāyavārttika on 1.1.29." *Indologica Taurinensia* 2: 39–44.

Bhattacharya, Kamaleswar. 1977. "On the Relationship between the *Vigraha-vyāvartanī* and the *Nyāyasūtra*-s." *Journal of Indo-European Studies* 5: 265–273.

Bodhi, Bhikku. 2000. *The Connected Discourses of the Buddha*. Wisdom Publications.

Bronkhorst, Johannes. 1985. "Nāgārjuna and the Naiyāyikas." *Journal of Indian Philosophy* 13: 107–132.

Bronkhorst, Johannes. 1993. "On the Method of Interpreting Sanskrit Texts." *Asiatische Studien/Études Asiatiques* 47.3: 501–511.

Bronkhorst, Johannes. 2018. "Sūtras" In *Brill's Encyclopedia of Hinduism Online*, edited by Knut A. Jacobsen, Helene Basu, Angelika Malinar, and Vasudha Narayanan. http://dx.doi.org/10.1163/2212-5019_BEH_COM_2020110.

Bryant, Edwin F. 2014. "Agency in Sāṃkhya and Yoga: The Unchangeability of the Eternal." In *Free Will, Agency, and Selfhood in Indian Philosophy*, edited by Matthew R. Dasti and Edwin F. Bryant, 16–40. Oxford University Press.

Bulcke, C. 1968. *The Theism of Nyāya-Vaiśeṣika: Its Origin and Early Development*. Motilal Banarsidass.

Burge, Tyler. 1993. "Content Preservation." *Philosophical Review* 102: 457–488.

Cardona, George. 1972. "Pāṇini's Kārakas: Agency, Animation, and Identity." *Journal of Indian Philosophy* 2: 231–306.

Cardona, George. 1991. "A Path Still Taken: Some Early Indian Arguments Concerning Time." *Journal of the American Oriental Society* 111: 445–464.

Cardona, George. 2014. "Pāṇinian Grammarians on Agency and Independence." In *Free Will, Agency, and Selfhood in Indian Philosophy*, edited by Matthew R. Dasti and Edwin F. Bryant, 85–111. Oxford University Press.

Chakrabarti, Arindam. 1982. "The Nyāya Proofs for the Existence of the Soul." *Journal of Indian Philosophy* 10: 211–237.

Chakrabarti, Arindam. 1983. "Is Liberation (Mokṣa) Pleasant?" *Philosophy East and West* 33: 167–182.

Chakrabarti, Arindam. 1992. "I Touch What I Saw." *Philosophy and Phenomenological Research* 52.1: 103–116.

Chakrabarti, Arindam. 2020. *Realisms Interlinked: Objects, Subjects, and Other Subjects*. Bloomsbury.

Chakrabarti, Kisor Kumar. 1999. *Classical Indian Philosophy of Mind: The Nyāya Dualist Tradition*. SUNY Press.

Chattopadhyaya, Debiprasad, and Mrinal Kanti Gangopadhyaya. 1990. *Cārvāka/Lokāyata: An Anthology of Source Materials and Some Recent Studies*. Indian Council of Philosophical Research.

Chemparathy, George. 1965. "The Testimony of the Yuktidīpikā Concerning the Īśvara Doctrine of the Pāśupātas and Vaiśeṣikas." *Wiener Zeitschrift für die Kunde Süd-und Ostasiens* 9: 119–146.

Chemparathy, George. 1968. "The Īśvara Doctrine of Praśastapāda." *Vishveshvaranand Indological Journal* 6: 65–87.

Chemparathy, George. 1987. "Nature and Role of Āpta in the Nyāya-Vaiśeṣika Thought." In *Kusumāñjali: New Interpretation of Indian Art and Culture, Sh. C. Sivaramamurti Commemoration Volume*, Vol. 1, edited by *M. S. Nagaraja Rao*, 39–47. Agam Kala Prakashan.

Conee, E., and R. Feldman. 1998. "The Generality Problem for Reliabilism." *Philosophical Studies* 89: 1–29.

Das, Nilanjan. 2020. "Vātsyāyana's Guide to Liberation." *Journal of Indian Philosophy* 48: 791–825.

Dasgupta, Surendranath. 1922 [1988]. *A History of Indian Philosophy*. Vol. 1. Motilal Banarsidass.

Dasti, Matthew R. 2011. "Indian Rational Theology: Proof, Justification, and Epistemic Liberality in Nyāya's Proof for God." *Asian Philosophy* 21.1: 1–21.

Dasti, Matthew R. 2012. "Parasitism and Disjunctivism in Nyāya Epistemology." *Philosophy East and West* 62.1: 1–15.

Dasti, Matthew R. 2013. "Systematizing Nyāya." *Philosophy East and West* 63.4: 617–637.

Dasti, Matthew R. 2014. "Nyāya's Self as Agent and Knower." In *Free Will, Agency, and Selfhood in Indian Philosophy*, edited by Matthew R. Dasti and Edwin F. Bryant, 112–136. Oxford University Press.

Dasti, Matthew R. 2017. "Vātsyāyana: Cognition as Guide to Action." In *The Oxford Handbook of Indian Philosophy*, edited by Jonardon Ganeri, 209–230. Oxford University Press.

Dasti, Matthew R. 2018. "Skepticism in Classical Indian Philosophy." In *Skepticism: From Antiquity to the Present*, edited by Diego E. Machucha and Baron Reed, 145–161. Bloomsbury.

Dasti, Matthew R. 2020. "Early Nyāya on the Meaning of Common Nouns." In *The Bloomsbury Research Handbook of Indian Philosophy of Language*, edited by Alessandro Graheli, 155–164. Bloomsbury Academic.

Dasti, Matthew R., and Malcolm Keating. 2016. "Epistemology (Pramāṇas)." In *Oxford Bibliographies Online: Hinduism*. https://www.oxfordbibliographies.com/view/document/obo-9780195399318/obo-9780195399318-0169.xml.

Dasti, Matthew, and Stephen Phillips. 2010. "Pramāṇa Are Factive: A Response to Jonardon Ganeri." *Philosophy East and West* 60.4: 535–540.

Dasti, Matthew, and Stephen Phillips. 2017. *The Nyāya-sūtra: Selections with Early Commentaries*. Hackett.

Deshpande, Madhav. 2020. "Language and Testimony in Classical Indian Philosophy." In *The Stanford Encyclopedia of Philosophy* (Summer 2020 Edition), edited by Edward N. Zalta. <https://plato.stanford.edu/archives/sum2020/entries/language-india/.

Donniger, Wendy. 1981. *The Rig Veda: An Anthology*. Penguin.

Edelglass, William, and Jay L. Garfield. 2009. *Buddhist Philosophy: Essential Readings*. Oxford University Press.

Enoch, David, and Joshua Schester. 2008. "How Are Basic Belief-Forming Methods Justified?" *Philosophy and Phenomenological Research* 76.3: 547–579.

Feldman, Joel. 2005. "Vasubandhu's Illusion Argument and the Parasitism of Illusion upon Veridical Experience." *Philosophy East and West* 55.4: 529–554.

Franco, Eli, and Karin Preisandanz. 1995. "Bhavadāsa's Interpretation of Mīmāṃsāsūtra 1.1.4 and the Date of the Nyāyabhāṣya." *Berliner Indologische Studien* 8: 81–86.

Freschi, Elisa, and Alessandro Graheli. 2005. "Bhāṭṭamīmāṃsā and Nyāya on Veda and Tradition." In *Boundaries, Dynamics and Construction of Traditions in South Asia*, edited by Federico Squarcini, 287–323. Firenze University Press.

Ganeri, Jonardon. 2001a. "Cross-Modality and the Self." *Philosophy and Phenomenological Research* 61.3: 639–657.

Ganeri, Jonardon. 2001b. *Indian Logic: A Reader*. Curzon.

Ganeri, Jonardon. 2003. "Indian Logic as a Theory of Case-Based Reasoning." *Journal of Indian Philosophy* 31: 33–45.

Ganeri, Jonardon. 2004. "Indian Logic." In *Greek, Indian and Arabic Logic*, edited by Dov M. Gabbay and John Woods, 309–395. Elsevier.

Ganeri, Jonardon. 2011. *The Lost Age of Reason: Philosophy in Early Modern India 1450–* Tubb *1700*. Oxford University Press.

Ganeri, Jonardon, ed. 2017. *The Oxford Handbook of Indian Philosophy*. Oxford University Press.

Gangopadhyaya, Mrinalkanti. 1980. *Indian Atomism: History and Sources*. K. P. Bagchi.

Gangopadhyaya, Mrinalkanti. 1982. *Nyāya-sūtra with Vātsyāyana's Commentary*. Indian Studies.

Gillon, Brendan S. 2010. "Obversion and Contraposition in the *Nyāyabhāṣya*." In *Logic in Earliest Classical India*, edited by Brendan S. Gillon, 167–182. Motilal Banarsidass.

Gillon, Brendan S. 2022. "Logic in Classical Indian Philosophy." In *The Stanford Encyclopedia of Philosophy* (Summer 2022 Edition), edited by Edward N. Zalta, https://plato.stanford.edu/archives/sum2022/entries/logic-india/.

Gokhale, Pradeep P. 1992. *Inference and Fallacies Discussed in Ancient Indian Logic*. Sri Satguru.

Gokhale, Pradeep P. 2015. *Lokāyata/Cārvāka: A Philosophical Inquiry*. Oxford University Press.

Gonda, Jan. 1975. *Vedic Literature (Saṃhitās and Brāhmaṇas): A History of Indian Literature*, Vol. 1. Otto Harrassowitz.

Guha, Nirmalya. 2012. "Tarka as Cognitive Validator." *Journal of Indian Philosophy* 40.1: 47–66.

Guha, Nimalya, Matthew Dasti, and Stephen Phillips. 2021. *God and the World's Arrangement: Readings from Vedānta and Nyāya Philosophy of Religion*. Hackett.

Halbfass, Wilhelm. 1988. *India and Europe: An Essay in Philosophical Understanding*. SUNY Press.

Halbfass, Wilhelm. 1991 *Tradition and Reflection: Explorations in Indian Thought*. SUNY Press.

Halbfass, Wilhelm. 1992. *On Being and What There Is: Classical Vaiśeṣika and the History of Indian Ontology*. SUNY Press.

Halbfass, Wilhelm. 1997. "Happiness: A Nyāya-Vaiśeṣika Perspective." In *Relativism, Suffering and Beyond: Essays in Memory of Bimal K. Matilal*, edited by J. N. Mohanty and P. Bilmoria, 150–163. Oxford University Press.

Hattori, Masaaki. 1968. *Dignāga, On Perception: Being the* Pratyakṣapariccheda *of Dignāga's* Pramāṇasamuccaya *from the Sanskrit Fragments and Tibetan Versions*. Harvard University Press.

Hayes, Richard P. 1994. "Nāgārjuna's Appeal." *Journal of Indian Philosophy* 22: 299–378.

Jha, Ganganatha. 1919. *The Nyāyasūtras of Gautama with the Bhāṣya of Vātsyāyana and the Vārttika of Uddyotakara*. 4 vols. Motilal Banarsidass.

Joshi, Rasik Vihari. 1965. "Treatment of Fallacy in Indian Logic." In *Felicitation Volume Presented to Mahamahopadhyaya Dr. V.V. Mirashi*, edited by Ajay Mitra Shastri, G. T. Deshpande, and V. W. Karambelkar, 45–73. Vidarbha Samshodhan Mandal.

Joshi, S. D. 1981. "The Text of the Nyāyabhāṣya on the Nyāyasūtra 1.1.5." *Mysore Orientalist* 14: 21–27.

Kang, S. Y. 2004. "Some 'Points of Defeat' in Early Indian Logical Traditions Considered in the Context of Public Debate as a Game with a Time Factor." In *Proceedings of the 2nd Tokyo Conference on Argumentation*, edited by Takeshi Suzuki, Yoshiro Yano, and Takayuki Kato, 99–104. Japan Debate Association.

Kang, S. Y. 2009. "What Does -*Sama* Mean? On the Uniform Ending of the Names of the -*jāti*-s in the *Nyāyasūtra*." *Journal of Indian Philosophy* 37: 75–96.

Keating, Malcolm, ed. 2020. *Controversial Reasoning in Indian Philosophy: Major Texts and Arguments on Ārthāpatti*. Bloomsbury.

Keating, Malcolm. 2022. "Debating with Fists and Fallacies." *International Journal for Hindu Studies* 26: 63–87.

Krishna, Daya. 1991. *Indian Philosophy: A Counter Perspective*. Oxford University Press.

Lackey, Jennifer. 1999. "Testimonial Knowledge and Transmission." *Philosophical Quarterly* 49: 471–490.

Locke, John. 1975. *An Essay Concerning Human Understanding*. Edited by Peter H. Nidditch. Oxford University Press.

Matilal, B. K. 1977. *Nyāya-Vaiśeṣika*. Otto Harrassowitz.

Matilal, B. K. 1986. *Perception: An Essay on Classical Indian Theories of Knowledge*. Oxford University Press.

Matilal, B. K. 1990. *The Word and the World: India's Contribution to the Study of Language*. Oxford University Press.

Matilal, B. K. 1998. *The Character of Logic in India*. Edited by Jonardon Ganeri and Heeraman Tiwari. SUNY Press.

Matilal, B. K., and Arindam Chakrabarti. 1994. *Knowing from Words*. Synthese Library 230. Kluwer Academic.

Mishra, Arun Ranjan. 2008. *Nyāya Concept of Cause and Effect Relation*. Pratibha Prakashan.

Mishra, Umesh. 2006. *Nyāya-Vaiśeṣika: Conception of Matter in Indian Philosophy*. Bharatiya Kala Prakashan.

Mohanty, J. N. 1965. "The Nyāya Theory of Doubt." *Visva Bharati Journal of Philosophy* 3: 15–35.

Mohanty, J. N. 1994. "Is There an Irreducible Mode of Word-Generated Knowledge?" In *Knowing from Words*, edited by B. K. Matilal and Arindam Chakrabarti, 29–49. Kluwer Academic.

Muroya, Yasutaka. 2006. "Some Observations on the Manuscript Transmission of the Nyāyabhāṣya." *Journal of Indological Studies* 18: 23–62.

Nicholson, Hugh. 2009. "The Shift from Agonistic to Non-Agonistic Debate in Early Nyāya." *Journal of Indian Philosophy* 38: 75–95.

Oberhammer, Gerhard R. F. 1964. "Pakṣilasvāmin's Introduction to His Nyāyabhāṣya." *Asian Studies* (Philippines) 2.3: 302–322.

Oberhammer, Gerhard R. F. 1967–1968. "Notes on the Tantrayukti-s." *Adyar Library Bulletin* 22: 600–616.

Olivelle, Patrick. 1998. *The Early Upaniṣads: Annotated Text and Translation.* Oxford University Press.

Olivelle, Patrick, trans. 2004. *The Law Code of Manu.* Oxford University Press.

Perrett, Roy W. 2016. *An Introduction to Indian Philosophy.* Cambridge University Press.

Perry, Bruce M. 1995. "An Introduction to the Nyāyacaturgranthikā: With English Translations." PhD diss., University of Pennsylvania. UMI (AAT9532256).

Perry, Bruce M. 1997. "Early Nyāya and Hindu Orthodoxy: Ānvīkṣikī and Adhikāra." In *Beyond Orientalism: The Work of Wilhelm Halbfass and Its Impact on Indian and Cross-Cultural Studies*, edited by Eli Franco and Karin Preisendanz, 449–470. Rodopi.

Phillips, Stephen H. 2005. "Self as Locus/Substratum (*Adhikaraṇa*) of Psychological Continuities and Discontinuities." *APA Newsletter for Asian and Asian-American Philosophers and Philosophies* 5.1: 4–8.

Phillips, Stephen H. 2009. *Yoga, Karma, and Rebirth: A Brief History and Philosophy.* Columbia University Press.

Phillips, Stephen H. 2012. *Epistemology in Classical India: The Knowledge Sources of the Nyāya School.* Routledge.

Phillips, Stephen H. 2017. "A Defeasibility Theory of Knowledge in Gaṅgeśa." In *The Oxford Handbook of Indian Philosophy*, edited by Jonardon Ganeri, 541–558. Oxford University Press.

Potter, Karl H. 1977. *Encyclopedia of Indian Philosophies*, Vol. 2: *Nyāya-Vaiśeṣika.* Motilal Banarsidass.

Poussin, Louis de La Vallée, and Gelong Lodrö Sangpo. 2012. *Abhidharmakośa-Bhāṣya of Vasubandhu*, Vol 2. Motilal Banarsidass.

Prasad, Jwala. 1930. "Discussion of the Buddhist Doctrines of Momentariness and Subjective Idealism in the Nyāya-sūtras." *Journal of the Royal Asiatic Society of Great Britain and Ireland* 1: 31–39.

Preisendanz, Karin. 2000. "Debate and Independent Reasoning vs. Tradition: On the Precarious Position of Early Nyāya" In *Harānandalararī: Volume in Honour of Professor Minoru Hara on His Seventieth Birthday*, edited by R. Tsuchida and A. Wezler, 221–251. Dr. Inge Wezler Verlag für Orientalistische Fachpublikationen.

Preisendanz, Karin. 2005. "The Production of Philosophical Literature in South Asia during the Pre-colonial Period (15th to 18th Centuries): The Case of the Nyāyasūtra Commentarial Tradition." *Journal of Indian Philosophy* 33: 55–94.

Preisendanz, Karin. 2018. "Text Segmentation, Chapter Naming and the Transmission of Embedded Texts in South Asia, with Special Reference to the Medical and Philosophical Traditions as Exemplified by the Carakasaṃhitā and the Nyāyasūtra." In *Pieces and Parts in Scientific Texts*, edited by Florence Bretelle-Establet and Stéphane Schmitt, 159–220. Springer.

Prets, Ernst. 2001. "Futile and False Rejoinders, Sophistical Arguments and Early Indian Logic." *Journal of Indian Philosophy* 29: 545–558.

Prets, Ernst. 2003. "Parley, Reason and Rejoinder." *Journal of Indian Philosophy* 31: 271–283.

Prets, Ernst. 2004. "Example and Exemplification in Early Nyāya and Vaiśeṣika." In *The Role of the Example (Dṛṣṭānta) in Classical Indian Logic*, edited by Shōryū Katsura, 197–224. Arbeitskreis für Tibetische und Buddhistische Studien.

Prets, Ernst. 2012. "A Review of the Early Nyāya Fragments." In *World View and Theory in Indian Philosophy*, edited by Piotr Balcerowicz, 155–171. Warsaw Indological Studies 5. Manohar.

Raja, K. K. 1963. *Indian Theories of Meaning*. Adyar Library and Research Centre.

Ram, Sadhu. 1958. "References to Sāṃkhya in the Nyāya-bhāṣya." *Adyar Library Bulletin* 22: 8–24.

Ram-Prasad, Chakravarthi. 2001. *Knowledge and Liberation in Classical Indian Thought*. Palgrave Macmillan.

Randle, H. N. 1930. *Indian Logic in the Early Schools*. Oxford University Press.

Rhys Davids, T. W. 1890. *The Questions of King Milinda*. Oxford University Press. Motilal Banarsidass, 1965.

Russell, Bertrand, 1910–1911. "Knowledge by Acquaintance and Knowledge by Description." *Proceedings of the Aristotelian Society* 11: 108–128.

Ryle, Gilbert. 1954. *Dilemmas*. Cambridge University Press.

Scharf, Peter M. 1996. "The Denotation of Generic Terms in Ancient Indian Philosophy: Grammar, Nyāya, and Mīmāṃsā." *Transactions of the American Philosophical Society* 86. 3: 1–336.

Schuster, Nancy. 1972. "Inference in the Vaiśeṣikasūtras." *Journal of Indian Philosophy* 1: 341–395.

Sen, P. K., ed. 2003. *Nyāyasūtras with Nyāyarahasya of Rāmabhadra Sārvabhauma and Ānvīkṣikītattvavivaraṇa of Jānakīnātha Cūḍāmaṇi*. Vol. 1. Asiatic Society.

Siderits, Mark. 2015. *Personal Identity and Buddhist Philosophy: Empty Persons*. 2nd ed. Ashgate.

Siderits, Mark. 2021. *Buddhism as Philosophy: An Introduction*. 2nd ed. Hackett.

Siderits, Mark, and Shoryu Katsura. 2013. *Nāgārjuna's Middle Way: Mūlamadhyamakakārikā*. Wisdom Publications.

Solomon, Esther. 1976. *Indian Dialectics*. Vol. 1: *Methods of Philosophical Discussion*. B.J. Institute of Learning and Research.

Sorabji, Richard. 2006. *Self: Ancient and Modern Insights about Individuality, Life, and Death*. University of Chicago Press.

Sorenson, Roy. 2016. "Fugu for Logicians." *Philosophy and Phenomenological Research* 92: 131–144.

Sosa, Ernest. 1980. "The Raft and the Pyramid." *Midwest Studies in Philosophy* 5: 3–25.

Taber, John. 1992. "What Did Kumārila Bhaṭṭa Mean by Svataḥ Prāmāṇya?" *Journal of the American Oriental Society* 112.3–4: 204–221.

Thakur, Anantalal. 1963. "Vātsyāyana and the Vaiśeṣika System." *Vishveshvaranand Indological Journal* 1: 78–86.

Thakur, Anantalal. 1974. "The Mahābhārata and the Nyāyaśāstra." *Proceedings of the All-India Oriental Conference* 27: 403–408.

Thakur, Anantalal. 1996a. *Nyāya-vārttika-tātparya-pariśuddhi*. Nyāyacaturgranthikā, vol. 4. Indian Council of Philosophical Research.

Thakur, Anantalal. 1996b. *Nyāya-vārttika-tātparya-ṭīkā*. Nyāyacaturgranthikā, vol. 3. Indian Council of Philosophical Research.

Todeschini, Alberto. 2010. "Twenty-Two Ways to Lose a Debate: A Gricean Look at the *Nyāya-sūtra's* Points of Defeat." *Journal of Indian Philosophy* 38: 49–74.

Tubb, Gary A., and Emery R. Boose. 2007. *Scholastic Sanskrit: A Handbook for Students*. American Institute for Buddhist Studies.

Tucci, Giuseppe. 1929. *Pre-Diṅnāga Buddhist Texts on Logic from Chinese Sources*. Gaekwad's Oriental Series 49. Oriental Institute.

Tuske, Jeorg. 2008. "Teaching by Example: An Interpretation of the Role of Upamāna in Early Nyāya Philosophy." *Asian Philosophy* 18: 1–15.

Vaidya, Anand J. 2013. "Nyāya Perceptual Theory: Disjunctivism or Anti-Individualism." *Philosophy East and West* 63.4: 562–578.

Vidyabhusana, Satis Chandra. 1919. *The Nyāya Sūtras of Gotama*. Reprint. Munsiram Manoharlal.

Vidyabhusana, Satis Chandra. 1920. *A History of Indian Logic*. Reprint. Motilal Banarsidass.

Westerhoff, Jan. 2009. *Nāgārjuna's Madhyamaka: A Philosophical Introduction*. Oxford University Press.

Westerhoff, Jan. 2010. *Nāgārjuna's Vigrahavyāvartanī: The Dispeller of Disputes*. Oxford University Press.

Westerhoff, Jan. 2018. *The Golden Age of Indian Buddhist Philosophy*. Oxford University Press.

Wezler, A. 1984. "On the Quadruple Division of the Yogaśāstra, the Chaturvyūhatva of the Cikitsāśāstra, and the Four Noble Truths of the Buddha." *Indological Taurinensia* 12: 289–337.

Index

For the benefit of digital users, indexed terms that span two pages (e.g., 52–53) may, on occasion, appear on only one of those pages.

Tables are indicated by *t* following the page number

cognition (*cont.*)
as distinct from bodily properties, 181–83
as ephemeral, 180–81
as indicator of self, 28–29, 129–37
inferential cognition *see* inference
metaphysically, as a property of self, 170–79
as part of the content of memory, 143–44
perceptual cognition *see* perception
as possible indicator of God, 201–2
in relation to Buddhist arguments against an external world, 231–35
see also *pratisaṃdhāna*
coherentism, 51, 71–72
common nouns, 117–25
comparison, 14, 23, 44–45, 46–47, 52–53, 73, 91–92
counterfeit reasons (*hetv-ābhāsa*), 18–19, 56–59, 67, 80, 85–86, 114, 247, 250–51, 261

Dasgupta, S., 26–27
debate, xvi, 5, 10–11, 20–22, 42, 51, 54–56, 59n.68, 63–64, 65, 238–39, 258–61
destructive, 7–8, 54–56, 238–39
disputation, 7–8, 54–56, 238–39, 241
early manuals on, xv–xvi, xx–xxi, 20–22, 46, 62, 105n.41, 251–52, 257n.8
six step version of, 257
truth-directed, 7–8, 42, 54–56, 62, 238–39, 241, 257, 261
denying the antecedent, 254–55, 274
desire, 10, 16, 28–30, 55, 77, 96–97, 130, 144, 146, 161*t*, 177, 178–79, 191, 215, 222–23, 227, 236
dharma
as Buddhist term for momentary property-particulars, 128–29
as duty/religiosity, 8, 24, 102, 109–10, 161*t*, 218
as a synonym for karmic merit, 77–78, 185, 191–92, 200–1, 214
Dharmakīrti, 256
Dharmaśāstra, 218–19
dialectical rejoinders (*jāti*), 46n.49, 54–55, 61–62, 65, 108n.44, 112n.49, 240–57
Dignāga, xxi–xxii, 14n.11, 16–17, 22, 45, 49, 78, 133–34
disjunctivism, xvii, 18–19, 105–6
doubt, 10–11, 19, 38–41, 45–46, 53–54, 58, 63–64, 71–72, 75, 118, 134–35, 150, 160n.36, 185, 204, 211, 235, 238, 245–46, 247, 250
dualism, 32, 33, 137n.11, 139–41, 162–64, 172, 176–77, 189–90

empiricism, 17–18, 28, 82, 205
equivocation, 54–55, 60–61, 62, 65, 241, 247–48, 249n.6, 256
ether, 32, 39, 108, 114, 115, 148–49, 150, 156–57, 159, 160, 173–74, 202–3, 220–21, 229, 244, 249

false dilemma, 71, 247–48
figurative meaning, 60–61, 118, 120, 140–41, 197, 218
foundationalism, 3n.4, 70–71, 211

Ganeri, J., 48, 49, 127, 136–37, 241–42
Gillon, B., 273–74
goals of life (*puruṣārtha*), 2–3, 73, 152–53, 179, 185–87, 215–16
Gonda, J, 95
Grammarians, 16–17, 67–68, 89, 117–25
Gupta empire, xix–xx